M000111247

This Is My Song

a memoir

PATTI PAGE

with Skip Press

Published by:
Kathdan Books
A division of
C.A.F. Records
484 Lang Road
Bath, NH 09740

Printed in the United States of America.

Dedicated to my husband Jerry,
and to all who are dear to me.

ACKNOWLEGEMENTS

I love to read. When traveling or just at home for relaxation, I am in the middle of another good book. When it was suggested about ten years ago that I should write a book I thought, "not me, what would I say?"

I've had a nice career but have been private about my personal life, what could I write that would be of interest? At that time, my manager Michael Glynn introduced me to Skip Press, a very talented writer who, like me, came from a small town in the South. But I didn't feel ready to take on such a big project. While doing three days of press interviews for a recent tour in Canada, I pondered all the great questions I was being asked about my career and thought maybe now is the time to put it all together in a book.

It has taken nearly two years of reminiscing and story telling and surprisingly it has been a fun and rewarding journey for me, thanks to the many people who have helped along the way.

To Skip Press, who didn't lose interest after ten years, for his creativity, and for understanding and conveying my point of view.

To my manager, Michael Glynn, who planted the seed more than ten years ago and whose pleasant persistence kept this project on track.

Also, thanks to my friend and fellow Oklahoman Vince Gill, for his Foreword to this book.

To Amy Collins MacGregor at The Cadence Group and Greg Snider at Blu Sky Media Group, for their expertise and guidance. And to my editors, Vanessa Mickan-Gramazio and Tracy Quinn McLennan for their talent and patience.

To Beth Filiciotto, my assistant and Claudia Buckley, my former assistant, who in turn provided daily support.

And of course, to my loving husband Jerry for his wit, wisdom and unpredictability.

CONTENTS

This Is My Song

a memoir

PATTI PAGE

with Skip Press

FOREWORD 🌿 by Vince Gill

For me, the only thing sweeter than singing with Patti Page was getting to know her. After recording our duet of "Home Sweet Oklahoma," I found Patti and her husband Jerry to be kind, sweet, beautiful people. I'd only met them briefly when Patti appeared with me onstage in Escondido, California to sing her massive hit, "Tennessee Waltz." I was supposed to do a duet with her on that song, but I couldn't. I was too choked up and in tears.

Music is its own transcendent language, someone's creative, emotional, heartfelt thing that crosses all kinds of barriers. I've always felt that music is where true democracy has a chance, where people gather for the common good. Music offers completion; it's a beautiful thing.

"Tennessee Waltz" is like that, a great ballad, one of the state songs of Tennessee and the #1 song of all time for a female singer. Almost sixty years after it was recorded, it's still amazing. More personally to me, it was one of the reasons I wanted to learn to play music. And that was what made me cry, because my Mom taught me to dance to that record.

I love waltzes. My first big hit, "When I Call Your Name," was a waltz, and so were "Pocketful of Gold" and "No Future in the Past." In today's crazy world, a waltz is a sweet thing.

People need sweetness, and that's Patti. Like me, she's from Oklahoma, a part of the country where folks know what hard times and living off the land is like. It's a real common sense, salt of the Earth kind of area where there's a very grounded nature to people. My Mom was a farmhand who drove a tractor and did all the things her dad needed her to do to help out. At the age of eighty-three, as I write this, she still has a great work ethic, and is tougher than nails, an amazing woman.

Sweet as she is, Patti's tough, too. She's able to play to sold-out crowds after six decades in show business. Sixty years! And the sound of her voice! It's big and it's rich, even today. A lot of folks, when the years start to add on, have a tendency to lose some of those things that made them so great, like not being able to push enough air, but Patti doesn't have that problem. Her voice has remained as beautiful today as it was in the 1950s, when she was the biggest star on records and TV and in the middle of selling 100 million records.

Then there's the matter of class. When Patti Page exploded with "Tennessee Waltz," it was the first pop hit to cross-over and also go #1 on both the country and rhythm & blues charts. On her TV shows (I've seen clips thanks to YouTube), she was always as classy as the song, dressed to the nines. The late great Patsy Cline patterned her own outfits after Patti, and I have to think Patsy's dresses and high heels influenced my friend Dolly Parton, who is always dressed elegantly. That's important, maintaining respectfulness through the generations in how you present yourself to the public. At those times when I go to the Grand Ole Opry in a suit and tie, it never goes unnoticed by older stars. Somebody will always come by me and say "That's the way country music stars are supposed to look." Well, Patti's always looked that way onstage.

She's lived a quiet personal life, but Patti's always gone out of her way for her fans. She's a consummate professional in the studio and in concert, and even though her career reads like something out of a storybook, she's as down to Earth as they come. I'd be a big fat liar if I said I knew all of the biography and discography of Patti Page, but the fun thing is, as we got to know each other, I started catching on, and boy was I impressed. Just about everybody has heard her sing "Doggie in the Window" and I have personal favorites, like "Mockingbird Hill" and "Mister and Mississippi," but that doesn't even scratch the surface. When someone's had 111 hits like Patti, it's an unbelievable encyclopedia of accomplishment.

There aren't many singers like Patti any more. Maybe there never will be; there's just so much competition for airplay. They're only going to play twenty current songs on pop radio and twenty current songs on country radio. Every now and then, some song's going to come along and transcend everything, but most of the time something is a hit in its own world and that's it. Patti was well loved in all formats because she was unique. You tell me, who's ever going to do a single that sells 10 million units again, like "Tennessee Waltz"?

There are a handful of people with a voice that comes through the speakers and engages you in an amazingly believable and touching way, something that truly speaks to your soul. That's Patti Page. Listen to her music and read her story here in this book. Whenever you do, you're going to feel better, I promise. To me, she represents what the music business and life is supposed to be all about. God love her! I know I do.

Vince Gill
Nashville, Tennessee

It Takes Fifty Years to Get to Carnegie Hall

May 31, 1997. I was scared and excited standing in the wings about to walk onto the most famous stage in New York City: Carnegie Hall. The greatest singers of our time had graced this stage. In many ways, it was the ultimate test for a performer. The hall rang with the sounds of applause. I took a deep breath. Fifty years in show business, and now here I was.

Frankly, I felt a lot like Clara Ann Fowler in those moments before I went on that stage. That's the name my mom and dad gave me when I was born. Patti Page was appearing in concert at Carnegie Hall, celebrating a long show business career, but Clara Ann was battling butterflies.

That's because at heart I was—and still am—that country girl from Oklahoma, thrilled to be able to sing for people and entertain them. People paying me for something I absolutely love to do? That's like whipped cream on top of hot cherry pie. And I appreciate every opportunity.

I was born with three great advantages: My family was very poor, very large, and very religious. By being poor, I learned value, and so I've always thought it important to try to give my audience the very best show I can. I was the second youngest in a family of eleven; even when I had the biggest hit song in the country, my people back in Oklahoma never let it go to my head. And my faith has gotten me through many hard times. It has always been important to me, and I feel that the sincerity I learned singing in church has found its way into my recordings and performances.

When I was a girl, I hated the poverty, resented the lack of privacy that came with living in a tiny house with so many brothers and sisters, and thought my parents were way too strict. Now, as a mother and a grandmother, I see life from a long and full perspective. It's funny how you can look so far back and yet so much of your life seems like it happened the day before yesterday.

A flood of memories, good and bad, washed over me as I stood backstage about to go on at Carnegie Hall. I thought of the fans, friends, and family who were in the audience, some of whom had traveled across the country to see me perform. I couldn't let anyone down.

I would give the audience everything I had. That is my whole approach to singing—that's what it has always been about with me.

Still, I sometimes get a nagging thought: *Your voice could go at any time, you know. Better make the best of it while you can.* That night, I was excited to get out and sing to the loyal fans who had stood by me for decades, but there was a little fear in me, too. Because I knew some of the audience—the critics, for instance—would be coming along to answer the question, "Does she still have it?"

The show would be great, I decided. It had to be.

And then, it was showtime. Time to leave the comfort and security backstage and step onstage. After their opening overture, the orchestra took a bow to thunderous applause, and the stage went dark. Then, on a massive screen, a scene from one of my old TV shows showed me singing "Tennessee Waltz."

I entered stage left under a soft spotlight. I couldn't start singing, though, because the crowd got to its feet to lift my spirits up with a wonderful surprise—a standing ovation.

And you know what? Clara Ann's butterflies flew away to rest in some old memory tree and Patti Page stood there proudly on that stage, feeling grateful for her career and family and fans and blessed by God. I knew everything would turn out all right.

"Who is that person on the screen?" I sang as more scenes from my TV show played silently on the screen behind me. "It is someone I am sure that I have seen. Though it's been so very long, and I could be very wrong, to believe that the face I see is the person who used to be me. Time can play tricks on me, I know. I have trouble now remembering the show...."

Those were the lyrics, but I didn't really have trouble remembering those shows. They were vivid and clear in my mind. I turned with a flourish and sang to those images, so happy to still be singing, feeling no remorse at all about days gone by. The orchestra sounded superb! My heart was soaring. Isn't it a wonderful thing what music can do? It accents our lives, making it seem at times as though God is orchestrating our every step.

As I soaked up the glow of the spotlight, I thought about an old showbiz joke. A violin maestro is making his way down New York's Seventh Avenue when a man on the street asks for directions: "How do you get to Carnegie Hall?" Rushing to rehearsal, the maestro shouts over his shoulder without breaking stride, "Practice, practice, practice!"

I chuckled inside. What no one told me was that it would take fifty years!

Until now, I've kept quiet about my private life. I've always found my audiences to be more than sympathetic, but as a performer I felt I was there to give people a chance to forget about their worries and feel a little better about life, not burden them with my own troubles.

But the fact is, I've overcome a lot of personal and professional challenges in my life. Many times, I thought life was pretty comfortable, that I'd somehow stepped into a fairy tale, but then something would happen to spoil the storybook ending. Remember that old saying about it being lonely at the top? Everyone has his or her ups and downs, but when the music industry pegs you as the #1 songbird in America, the perch gets pretty precarious.

I never sought fame and fortune. I just wanted to sing. What I didn't know that night as I stood on the stage at Carnegie Hall was that my proudest achievements, both at home and onstage, were in fact still ahead of me. Fifty years was a long career, but I had no plans of stopping. I still had a lot of living to do.

And you know what the wild thing is? The years truly have gone by quickly—so quickly that I have learned the importance of savoring every moment along the way. It hasn't always been smooth sailing, but then anything worth doing rarely comes easy.

Let me tell you all about my ups and my downs. I promise you, it's really quite a story... even if I did live it myself.

ONE   How Clara Ann Fowler Became Patti Page

Looking back, I see that all the wonderful things that happened in my life to give me a career as an entertainer would not have happened if I had been an only child or one of those rich kids on the right side of the tracks or if my parents had let me do as I pleased.

No one would have suspected that the girl who was born on November 8, 1927 as Clara Ann Fowler, the tenth of eleven children in a poor family in Claremore, Oklahoma, would become a famous singer. Claremore is about thirty miles northeast of Tulsa, near the Arkansas border and not too far south of the Kansas border. My mother and all of her brothers and sisters were from Claremore, which was a small town with a population around 4,000 people when I was born. Its claim to fame was being the home of world-famous Will Rogers. Maybe I was God's "answer" to Will in that we both became known as audience pleasers.

My dad, Benjamin A. Fowler, was thirty-nine at the time of my birth, and my mother, Marguerite Malvina Fowler, was thirty-seven. My oldest sister, Hazel, was born in 1908, followed by Daniel Benjamin (1910), Trudie Jane (1913), Louise (1914), Mack (1917), Charles Edward (1918), Rema Ruth (1920), Ruby

Nell (1922), and Virginia Bell (1925). Two years after me, Margaret Ellen (1929) was born. With a family spread out over the years like that, I had siblings living on their own by the time I was born, but we still had a pretty crowded house. Even when I was in high school, after I'd become Patti Page singing on radio station KTUL in Tulsa, I was sleeping at night with two other sisters on a full-size bed. I suppose I learned to get along well with people because of my family situation. I had to get along; there literally wasn't room for much fighting.

My father was a railroad man. He'd started out as a laborer, one of the men who rode the clickety-clack pump carts up and down the rails, fixing any tracks that were out of alignment. Dad and my two older brothers worked for the railroads all their lives as trainmen or switchmen or whatever jobs they could. My father was always so proud when people would ride over his tracks without noticing them. "That's one of my jobs," he'd say about the smoothness of the ride. I learned pride in my craft from my father.

The railroad had a huge influence in my family and even gave me my family nickname. At our house, everyone called me "Katy," which came from my father working on the Katy Railroad—the Missouri, Kansas and Texas, or MKT. When Peggy and I were old enough, we would run across the tracks every afternoon as Dad got home, at 4:30 or 5:00, to meet him. Naturally, he'd pick up baby Peggy first and give her a kiss. I couldn't talk that well when I was little, but I would blurt out, "Do me kakat!" meaning "Do me like that!" And then I'd be in my Dad's arms right there on the Katy railroad tracks. To him, I was Katy. My mother would call me Honey or Katy. Everyone outside the family knew me as "Clarann," my two given names run together. They were never separate, never Clara Ann.

The town where I went to elementary school was even smaller than Claremore. I attended elementary school in Avant, Oklahoma through the sixth grade and appeared in a talent show there, which I guess you could say was my first public performance.

In fields near Avant, my mother and older sisters picked cotton while I played barefoot, and there was little of note about my early years, which was simple country living. Our family was largely self-sufficient, and we girls learned a lot from our mother, though she was too busy to give any of us much singular attention. She grew her own garden, ran the house, ran the family, got the groceries, and did the cooking. She used to make quilts for all of our bedding and even made towels with hand-stitched embroidery that we dried dishes with. I wonder sometimes how many young women learn to sew today. I'm glad I don't know the answer because it would probably disappoint me. Every morning my mother was up at five, making breakfast and packing lunches for my father to take to work and my brothers and sisters to take to school. Then she did the family wash and cleaned the house. At eight, she went to the fields to pick cotton. In addition, she had our cow, chickens, and pigs to look after. She even canned vegetables for the winter from her own garden.

We all learned to work hard. The older girls helped prepare the meals, so they grew up knowing all the good recipes. As one of the younger ones, I never learned to cook. I was great at cleaning up the table, though! We all had our own special little jobs and my mother would change them up every week so that we wouldn't get too bored. She left me a couple of her cookbooks when she passed, but most of her meals were prepared from her personal knowledge as it was with most of her generation. When I think of what I learned from her example, I suppose it could best be summed up as self-sufficiency—a quality that has helped me all my life.

When Peggy came along and took my place as the baby of the family, I didn't like losing my position as the blameless special one.. I took many opportunities as we grew to blame Peggy for things I did because I knew she'd get away with it. That doesn't mean I wasn't found out. And when I was, my mother enforced her strict discipline. If my sisters and I did anything bad, she would say, "At 4:00 this afternoon, you're going to get a whipping." So in school or out, we would be angels all day long, trying to make Mother forget she said that. And no matter what we did, at 4:00 she would go out and get a tiny little tree branch off a tree, her "switch" to spank us on our legs. One by one we'd go up, and one by one we'd stand back crying, "Mom, don't do that—don't hurt her!" And she would say, "If you want to get a whipping you keep on talking because you're going to be here right along with her."

My mother was willing to do that every day if she thought it was called for. Whether it was right or wrong from today's perspective, it was her psychology and, as a result, we were angels a lot more than we were trouble. She had to wait until 4:00 to use the switch because she didn't have the time before then. My father would come home from work around 4:30, so by the time he finished walking home she would be finishing with her switching.

Mom had to watch every penny, particularly with an impulsive child like myself. In those days, small town grocery stores had charge accounts. You bought groceries and said, "Charge it." Then the clerk noted it in a ledger, and the bill was paid on payday, whenever that might be. If a kid figured this scheme out, and they were cute enough, it wasn't unusual to have certain unplanned items appear on the bill. Mom was quilting one night after supper when she said, "I have a question to ask you girls. Who charged 25¢ on the grocery bill last week?" And almost before she finished her question, I exclaimed, "Wasn't me, wasn't me, wasn't me!" as I dove under the quilting frames to hide.

It wasn't just that I had a sweet tooth. I knew that the candy I charged—and in those days you could buy a lot of candy for 25¢—would buy me some friends in school. I could pass it out in our classroom and become a big person to my fellow students. I won't say how I paid for that little bit of larceny, but a quarter of a dollar meant a lot to us. For example, our family never went to a movie. I never saw a movie in a theater until I was eleven years old. We had a radio, but my mother was the only one allowed to turn it on and find the stations. Why? We needed to save on electricity. It was a radio for everybody, and Mom ruled it. Later, when I had my first room of my own, one of the first things I did was buy my own radio and listen to whatever I wanted to hear. At home, however, we didn't hear that many shows. I mostly remember the *Chicago Barn Dance*,

The Grand Ole Opry, and *The Eddie Cantor Show*, which is where I heard Dinah Shore for the first time.

I had a bath on Saturday night "whether I needed it or not" and after breakfast on Sunday morning, my mother insisted we kids would be bundled off to church—no excuses. We attended the Church of Christ. My father didn't start going to church until just before I left home at age eighteen. It was probably because he was getting older and thinking about dying I can only suppose, but it made my mother happy. I rebelled as a child against the strictness and discipline that my parents considered part of a religious upbringing, but I'm glad they made me go to church. I enjoyed singing with the congregation and my sisters. It was nice to see boys in their Sunday best and to have them see me. Later in life, I realized how much my religious upbringing did to make me what I became. The strictness and discipline I learned had a direct influence on my personal life and career—but more on that later.

The Church of Christ was a regular Christian church, like the Methodist or Baptist churches, and there was a lot of singing of hymns. The big difference was that there was no musical accompaniment. I always thought it was interesting that I grew up attending a church where there were no musical instruments played during the service. None of the churches we attended had a choir. The hymn was started with a little pitch pipe blown by the singing leader. We sang from hymnals like most other Christian churches. There was an emphasis on not being showy and fitting in with the congregation, which might be why, even when I was becoming well known as a singer on the radio in high school, no one ever asked me to sing a solo at church.

Over the course of my career, people have sometimes suggested that my full and resonant voice came about from trying to be heard at the dinner table among all those older kids, but that wasn't true. I simply always loved singing. In fact, the first professional singing I did was as a part of a trio with my sisters Rema and Ruby when I was in the seventh grade. I had talked them into doing it with me, but in my family it was always believed that Ruby was the singer because she had such a sweet, clear voice. And if we'd had a manager, Ruby would have been it—she somehow got our parents' permission for us to sing on a local radio station in Muskogee. For four months, we were regulars on a show with a fantastic guitar player, doing the Pop songs of the day.

I was a good student and always got As in school, but the only thing that made me stand out in any way was that when all the family would get together, someone would inevitably point to me and say, "Sing something, Clarann!" And I'd get up and do "I Want to Clap My Hands," which had its roots in gospel. Other than that, I don't remember much in the way of my being outgoing or anything special. Certainly, there was nothing about me that would make anyone think I'd have a big singing career. I never had an ambition for anything like that.

That was my life before we moved to Garden City, a small suburb in the poor section of Tulsa, in 1941 when I was fourteen. When we moved into our Frisco section house in Garden City my sisters and I kept singing but not on the radio. Our house was by the railroad tracks, and our backyard was where the porch was located, overlooking the Texaco oil refinery. It wasn't such a great area but we made lovely friends there. Life and housing were designed around making friends then because people had grown up helping each other through hard times like the Great Depression. The porch of our house was one of those cozy screened-in types that Midwesterners and Southern people love, and there was a big bench swing, too. When we first moved in, word got around quickly about the new people in town who had five girls. Since my sisters and I loved to sing, we'd just sit out on the porch or in the swing and sing our hearts out doing mostly Pop songs we learned from song sheets in *Song Hits* magazine. The boys would come to listen, and the girls, too. It was just people enjoying the music, but nothing big because the town was no more than 100 or so people.

It didn't take my father long to see how the boys were looking at us when we were singing, and he threatened once to electrify the wire fence. Mostly he would listen in, but sometimes he'd play the guitar and accompany us. Mom played the organ, but we didn't have one in the house. She always encouraged music.

The one thing Dad would *not* let his girls do was sit out in the yard and sunbathe. The train tracks were back there. He didn't want any "lewd men" on the passing freight trains looking at his girls.

Most railroad company section houses were five rooms total. We had a kitchen, a living room, a dining room, and two bedrooms. There were seven of us children at home when we moved to Garden City—two boys and five girls. The boys slept in the living room, five girls slept in one bed in one bedroom, and my mother and father slept in the other bedroom. I would have been happy to keep the singing trio going, but after we moved, Ruby joined the Marines. I couldn't blame her—she was five years older than me and no doubt ready to get a bed of her own, even if it was only a bunk! After Ruby joined the Marines, Rema got a job at Amerada Petroleum and moved into her own apartment in downtown Tulsa. What a relief it was to finally sleep just three girls in one bed!

Such close living conditions were probably why we had the cleanest house in town. My mother was, in fact, the cleanest lady of all time. She put us through spring cleaning, summer cleaning, fall cleaning, and winter cleaning. She'd take the bedding outside and whip it on the clothesline, pounding with the broom to get all the dust out of everything. With all those kids, it was the only way she could stay on top of everything and keep it clean.

We had no toilet in the house—you did your duty in an outhouse, and your "out" got pretty cold in the middle of winter. If you've never used a privy, let's just say that it's not the tidiest experience. Instead of toilet paper, we made handy use of the pages of the Sears catalog, which we rarely could afford to order from. We didn't have a bathtub until my last two years of high school. Instead, we had our baths in a washtub. Then Mom, ever the busy woman, installed a bathtub by herself just so that we could have the semblance of the pleasures experienced by people with indoor plumbing. We would boil water on the stove, then pour the hot water in the tub. The tub had a drain that she dug herself. The Texaco fields were right across the railroad tracks past our backyard, so thanks to Mom's drain, the bathroom waste water would drain right into those fields.

Speaking of fields, there was very little put on our table that my mother didn't grow. She grew all the vegetables. There was a mom and pop store in the little town of Garden City where we bought staples like flour and sugar and milk, but with only $50 a month coming in from my Dad, we always cut corners. For meat, my parents would chip in with other locals to buy and kill a cow. We had no freezing capabilities and no refrigerator; in those days, fridges required blocks of ice. We didn't have a car, so there was no way to haul a block from the local icehouse even if we could afford a refrigerator. My father could drive but he didn't have enough money to buy a car except for one old car that gave out when I was really young, a Model T or something. All through high school, my family didn't have a car. When we weren't walking or on the railroad, we rode the bus. Still, there were places where you could keep meat, like a butcher's warehouse. One of my parents, usually my mother, would go down and say their name and the folks behind the counter would say how much was left of their cow portion.

We girls almost never bought any clothes. My mother made all of our dresses. The only thing I was rich in was shoes; one pair for school and another for church on Sunday.

At least we had the railroad. One of my favorite things was going to visit our family members living in Wichita, Kansas. I don't know what it was about Wichita, but eventually I had three sisters living there and thought of it as my second home. They all lived on that same rail route that my dad worked for. All the trainmen knew my dad and would take care of us all the way to Wichita, a five-hour trip. We rode in the only car that held passengers, a little red caboose. My sisters would meet us at the train. I first began to get an idea of what life was like in the rest of the country on train trips.

One summer we kids went and stayed a week with our sister, Trudie, who had children our age. I remember coming back from that trip to Wichita and asking my brother Charles about black and white people.

"Why is it in Kansas you can ride with everybody?" I inquired. "What's different about living here than there?"

"Well, that's just how it is, Katy," he replied.

He didn't bother to explain it was because we lived below the Mason-Dixon Line, or maybe he didn't know. I just wanted to know why. When we got home I asked my mother, who was originally from Mississippi, and my father, who was from Arkansas. I don't remember either of them explaining segregation to me at all.

My folks were usually quiet about anything they couldn't answer easily, so I just dropped the subject. Ours was always a close family and I didn't want to rock the boat. Despite the obvious poverty we knew, I remember my years at home as a lovely time. When my older sisters and brothers came to visit it was like company coming and we looked forward to it very much because it was the joy of having all our family together again. Because they lived so far away in Kansas, they might only get to visit once in the summer and maybe at Christmas.

As I look back on my life, it seems obvious that singing was to be my destiny because lucky little "accidents" kept happening in that direction. One day at the beginning of the ninth grade, my class was in the upstairs balcony of the auditorium at Daniel Webster High School in Tulsa, Oklahoma. There were people from radio station KTUL coming over to entertain us at our Friday assembly, but the talent was late arriving. The station's program director got there and explained to our principal why the assembly was being delayed. The principal suggested that maybe there was someone in the audience, perhaps among the new students who had come over from junior high, who would like to perform while we waited.

This prompted my homeroom teacher, who had moved over with us from the eighth grade, to stand up and announce, "We've got a little girl up here that can sing!"

My sister, Virginia, was in the eleventh grade, and when she heard the principal suggest someone "who had come over from junior high" she knew who he was talking about. When my homeroom teacher volunteered me, I could see Virginia slink down in her seat. I knew just what she was thinking because she told me later: *Oh no, not my sister!* She was shy and terribly embarrassed by another Fowler getting up in front of the entire school assembly.

I knew how she felt as I am shy, too. I have been all my life, as odd as that might sound given my profession.

I went up on the auditorium stage where they had a piano player, Bruce Riddle, who did all of their talent shows. Bruce told me to just start singing and he would play. I didn't know a key or anything. I sang "Frankie and Johnny" and he followed along. The audience seemed to appreciate it, and my performance filled up the time until the scheduled talent arrived.

What I didn't know that day was that my performance would shape my future in ways I could never have imagined.

I loved school, but surprising as it might sound, I never joined any music classes. I was a member of the glee club but that was just boys and girls singing together. I never really learned music with all the different keys, major and minor. I just sight read and that's what I've done my whole career. It's just a natural process that came to me, although in retrospect I wish I had studied music.

Art was something that, excuse the pun, I was drawn to. I planned to be a commercial artist and dreamed of getting a job in some fancy advertising agency, of becoming a sleek career girl and moving to the right side of the tracks. But as much as I love art—and I still like to paint—it was only a means to an end. My dream, my basic need, was independence. If it took money to be free, I'd get money. And I'd get it myself.

As soon as I could, I was eager to go to work, make my own money, and find my own place. It wasn't that I didn't love my family members. I just wanted a little more space between us, and maybe a bubble bath that I could easily refill from the faucet once in a while.

If I'd had a steady boyfriend in high school, maybe I would have been thinking I'd get married and move out, but that didn't work out for me. I got lucky for a little while when I fell in love with the quarterback for our football team. His name was Jack Honaker, and he was a beauty! The last I heard of him, he got married to a lady in Tulsa and still lived there. Jack and I were only together for a short time. I use the word "together" loosely since I never actually went out with him because my mother wouldn't let me. I could go to the football games and watch him, but that was it. I suppose it was just as well—even if we had been allowed to go out, there wasn't really much of any place for underage teens to go.

All of these things conspired to push me into going to work.

The Dean of Girls at our high school tried to help all the girls who didn't come from money to get jobs. Teachers in the 1940s actually cared about their students becoming useful members of society. We were taught to be responsible, to go and help our family and work and bring some money in. So the Dean helped me get my first summer job delivering telegrams for Western Union. I worked in one of the oil company buildings in downtown Tulsa. There were so many oil companies in that area that they had their big executive offices in one building, and there were a huge number of offices that received telegrams.

Telegrams were almost as plentiful as e-mail is today, and they were cheaper than long distance phone calls. After I became a recording artist, there was a newspaper story that I got fired for doing musical improvisations on a singing telegram, but that never happened. I did do a few singing telegrams in that building, when it was a birthday or an anniversary, but you never sang, "The stock is going up 10¢" or anything like that.

I also worked at one of the 5¢ and 10¢ stores during the Christmas holidays when they hired extra help, but the summer job that I was thrilled about was when I got a chance to interview at KTUL as an artist. I was excited because I thought I was launching my longed-for art career while still in high school. Not quite. I went to work in what they called the traffic department in their production area on the twenty-second floor. "Traffic" referred to a written log into which was noted every commercial that was aired and every song that was played. This department was also responsible for any artwork that was needed for promotions. So there I was, working on posters in the traffic department, typing logs, and even running the switchboard sometimes. Back then it was one of those big electric switching boards where cords with plugs like guitar jacks were stuck into the proper hole to route incoming and outgoing calls. I believe I was working on a poster when the station's program director walked in one day and said,

"Excuse me, aren't you that girl that sang at the assembly at Daniel Webster High?"

"Before the radio station thing? Sure, that was me. Clara Ann Fowler."

He smiled and nodded thoughtfully. "Miss Fowler, have you ever thought of being a singer? As a career, I mean."

"Oh no," I said firmly. "I want to be an artist and do paintings. That's why I'm working in the art department here."

The program director chuckled a little. "Well," he said, "singing is an art, you know."

"I didn't know that." Honestly, I didn't. I was only fourteen years old and not very sophisticated.

His faced turned serious and he said, "Tell you what. We have a staff musician who is always here. We have two in fact, two piano players. Glenn Hardman is the main one and he's pretty good. Matter of fact, he's married to Alice O'Connell who sings with Horace Heidt's Orchestra. She's Helen O'Connell's sister."

I knew the names, and I was impressed. "Well, thanks for telling me."

He chuckled again. "I'm telling you because I think you should think about being a singer. Matter of fact, I want you to go into the studio here with one of our piano players and record some songs. We'll pay you while you're doing it."

Now I smiled. "Well, why not," I said. "Just tell me where to go and I'll do it."

And that's how I went into the studio at KTUL and put down some tracks on an acetate disk, the recording medium in use at the time, to show them how I could sing. I had nothing else in mind. I wasn't aspiring to get a job singing. After all, I was making $25 a week in their traffic/art department, and my dad had made $50 a month working on the railroad for a long time. I forgot about the tracks after I cut them. I didn't think much of the recording until a few weeks later when someone from the station called and wanted to know if I would come down and audition for a new weekly variety show they were starting. And they wanted to call me Ann Fowler instead of Clara Ann Fowler.

How could I turn that down? It was a show with a number of different artists who were with the station, both Country and Pop, and they paid me $12.50 per show. I figured they liked me pretty well because they asked if I could do another one with Al Clauser and His Oklahomans. They wanted to call me Ann Foster on that one, and let everybody think they had a huge staff of singers, and I agreed. I didn't know any better. I did that for a while and then one day when I was at the station, I was told that the girl who was doing the show *Meet Patti Page* sponsored by the Page Milk Company was leaving and asked if I would be interested in being her replacement.

I said sure, and I didn't mind being called Patti Page either!

I don't know much about what happened to the original singer who used the name, but on occasion over several years I used to hear "You had black hair the last time I saw you." They obviously were referring to the original KTUL Patti Page. Oddly enough, I never ran across her, but I did hear that she moved to the East Coast. One time in Detroit I saw a small newspaper ad that said she was working there at a club and billed as "The Original Patti Page." After I gained a little success, she capitalized on it. I didn't think much of it until she wrote me a couple of years later while I was playing in Boston and claimed that she was the original, so she was going to sue me to enforce her claim to "being Patti Page." I had my name changed legally, and she never followed up on her lawsuit.

It took a long time for family and friends to think of me as Patti. Friends kept calling me Clarann. Later, when I was performing in concerts, I found I suddenly seemed to have a *lot* of friends—turned out quite a few folks had got the idea that saying they were "a friend of Clarann" was a good way to get into a show for free. My family didn't call me Patti for years because they never called me Clarann to begin with—I was Katy.

You would think that being a singer with three different names on one of the two local radio stations might have made me more popular at school, but no such luck. Nobody thought of me as the big local singing star or anything because I was always very bashful. When anybody made a big thing of my being on the radio, I would get embarrassed. I still do!

Thinking back to those days, it was such a different world. There weren't many individual recording artists, mostly bands. And truthfully, radio was not that big. Nor was there a national route to becoming a music star like today's *American Idol*. Every young person wanted to be a movie star, but that was almost impossible. Even when my show *Meet Patti Page* became the highest-rated show in Tulsa, I just wanted to fit in with my friends.

Still, you have to wonder about destiny because I did manage to gain the attention of a very big star at the time, none other than the great comedian Bob Hope. Before I even got a job on the radio station, I learned that Hope was having a statewide singing contest in Oklahoma in connection with the other Tulsa radio station, KVOO, the NBC station. He was scheduled to appear at Avey's Coliseum, the big arena in town, on a Friday night, and the winner got to sing a number during his show. I had no idea there would be several thousand people in that auditorium watching us. I was told that anywhere from seventy-five to 240 singers entered the contest, and the field was narrowed to nine people, including me. The finalists each made an acetate recording that Hope supposedly listened to, and I got picked. When I won the contest, KVOO called me "Miss Cinderella" and the newspapers did the same.

I kept the $100 winner's check for a long time. It was drawn on the Bank of America out of Hollywood, California. I couldn't believe it. Before long, I began getting letters from Bob Hope's accountant to go ahead and cash it. I wrote back and said I just wanted to keep Bob Hope's signature. I was a fan! Finally, the accountant wrote to say they'd make a copy of it and send it to me, and that's what they did, so I finally cashed the check and let them get their books straight. I have the copy of that check stored away.

I can't swear to you that Bob personally picked me as the winner, but later, when I became successful, he would make a big thing of stating, "I discovered this young lady, you know. They say Jack Rael did, but I did." I heard him say it many times over the years.

Technically, singing with Bob was my first major exposure to a national show business figure, but he didn't exactly take me on the road with him as his new discovery. The fellow who did that was Jack Rael, and the story of how Jack became my manager for fifty years was, again, another little bit of luck.

TWO

The Rael Road to Chicago

Αll through high school, when I wasn't in school or church or on the bus, I was singing. At age sixteen, I was on *Meet Patti Page* every day at 4:15 p.m., and I was also known as Ann Foster on *Melody and Stars*, a weekly variety program. Another show I did was with singer Warren Larroux called *Five Guys and a Gal*. I sang Country music on a Saturday radio show with Leon McAuliffe, a Tulsan who was famous for playing the steel guitar with Country swing legend Bob Wills. For anyone who ever heard Wills chirp, "Play it, Leon!" on those great old songs, that's who he was talking to. On Saturday nights, I sang with a Country and Western band, Al Clauser and His Oklahomans, at dances that lasted until 11:00 at night. No matter how late I stayed up, I had to get up the next morning and go to church, and Mom would make me sit up front with her. There was no sitting in the back where I could fall asleep like a normal teenager!

It's amazing how different life was then. There was no such thing as "celebrity" in Tulsa and certainly nothing like celebrity stalkers. I still have a clipping from an article the local paper did about "Patti Page and Her Pages" in October 1944. It included all sorts of personal details—that I was a sixteen-year-old high school senior, the daughter of Mr. and Mrs. B.A. Fowler—and, incredibly, it even listed our home address, 705 2. 36th Place. Can you imagine a newspaper article about a singer today listing her home address?

I'd managed to keep the same schedule for a couple of years, getting out of school slightly early so that I could catch a bus to the station downtown in time to go over the songs for the afternoon and then go on the air. Since I was making money, at night I could afford to take a cab home—it was too far to walk to our house in the dark from the main road.

Despite all the singing and my busy schedule, I hadn't forgotten my art. I'd kept at it and ended up winning a scholarship to Tulsa University. The award only covered the cost of the course, but I was determined to make the money for the rest of my tuition and other expenses and become the commercial artist my family thought I could become. I'd had offers to do more work as a singer. One offer came from a fellow named Dick Abbot who heard me on the radio and called to ask me to sing for one night at the Hotel Tulsa in the club called After Five. I sang with him for two months but felt I couldn't take him up on an offer to leave with the band after their engagement at the hotel ended. To keep extra income coming in for college, in addition to singing at the station, I got a job singing with a band at another place downtown called the Bengalair Supper Club.

I graduated Daniel Webster in May of 1945. A Vesper Service at the high school auditorium included a sermon and an a capella choir singing "The Lord Bless and Keep You," among other selections. This was a public high school at the end of World War II with so many loved ones fighting for freedom around the world and God and country seemed inseparable. If such a service happened at one today, someone would probably file a lawsuit for separation of church and state. Thankfully, my family hadn't lost anyone in the war, and with the conflict almost over, life as a high school graduate looked very promising.

And that's what my life was like one October afternoon when a fellow named Jack Rael checked into the Bliss Hotel in Tulsa and lay down exhausted in his room. There were no televisions in hotel rooms in those days, but there were coin-operated radios that cost a quarter to listen. Maybe luck was with me once again because, as I would later learn, Jack Rael normally would have felt that spending 25¢ to hear the radio was exorbitant. That day, the previous occupant of the room had not used up his quarter's worth, so when Jack turned on the radio, he heard me singing on KTUL. He was instantly puzzled because he couldn't recognize the voice and, as a traveling musician, he thought he knew all the major singers of the day. Jack told me later he thought he was listening to a professional recording and not a young girl singing live.

At that time, my show started at 3:30 each afternoon, and was only a fifteen-minute show, so Jack heard me some time between 3:30 and 3:45. To satisfy his curiosity, he called downstairs to ask them what radio station he was hearing and what number it was on the radio dial. The desk clerk told him KTUL, 1430. Jack called KTUL and, thinking it was a network show, asked where the show originated from. The person who answered the phone told him it was their very own Patti Page singing right there in the studio, and Jack said he couldn't believe it. He wanted to talk to me to verify it and was told he'd have to wait until Patti Page was off the air. So he waited and called back.

I answered the phone and heard him explain that he was the tenor saxophonist and the road manager for the Jimmy Joy Orchestra. They were coming into Tulsa for a one-nighter at the Casa Loma, a big ballroom outside of town. Jack was traveling around the country with the band.

"Miss Page, I'd like to invite you out to the ballroom tonight to see the band," he said. "I think you're a very special talent and I'd like to talk to you about that."

I didn't take long to reply. "I can't do that." To me, he sounded like a New York sharpie, and there were a lot of stories going around then about young women being abducted and taken to foreign lands to be sex slaves. I was afraid.

"So, you can't come out to the ballroom?" he asked again.

"Of course not!" I snapped. "I'm working another job at a little supper club downtown called the Bengalair."

I said that just on the chance he was legitimate because I thought it might impress him. The Bengalair served dinner and had violin music. I was singing with a nice little sextet that had a string section and a saxophone player. I worked there every night from 6:00 p.m. to 9:00 p.m. My show at KTUL was over at quarter of four, so I'd just stay at the radio station and wait. I suppose I could have mentioned that to this strange man on the phone, but why take a chance?

"Well then, I'll come to the club to see you," he said.

"Oh...okay," I said. Could it be? Was he telling the truth? I thanked him for the call and hung up and immediately called my sisters, Rema and Ruby. Ruby had finished her time in the Marines and was married to a Marine named Al Celeste. I told my sisters that if they would come to the club and sit over in the corner and watch out for me, I would buy them dinner. They agreed. After all, they didn't want some stranger grabbing their sister by the hair on her head and dragging her out of the club!

So Jack Rael showed up, listened closely, and seemed to like what he was hearing.

When I was ready to go home he introduced himself to me and said, "You're still invited to come to the concert tonight or the dance."

"No, we can't," I said. By now, my family was standing there with me. "My sisters are here to take me home."

That didn't seem to put him off. "Well, if you ever get a chance to take something off the air, we're gonna be in Dallas, Texas for the next six weeks. You could send the recording to me there, and we could discuss this further."

I had no idea of discussing it further because I wasn't sure what he might have in mind besides just singing with the band. I'd been busy all day! I was tired, and I didn't really know how to dance. I politely declined, but I did take down the information about where to reach him in Dallas.

I later learned that Jack wasn't as anxious to meet up with me again as I thought. In those days, big band singers like Helen O'Connell were as glamorous as the music they sang and what Jack was seeing that night was "a chubby teenager." I was wearing an old sweater and skirt and saddle shoes. I wasn't exactly a model of sophistication even by Tulsa standards. Jack was simply trying to gracefully get out of his initial enthusiasm by offering to listen to a demo I would send him in Dallas. Because I didn't know what he was *really* thinking, I surprised him. I got the guys in the KTUL control room to put something on acetate. I don't recall if I did it right away, but I didn't take too long. One reason was that I had a personal shakeup that made me weigh my plans for the future. I was going with one of the radio announcers at the station and I thought we were going steady until I found out he gave another girl his fraternity pin. That broke my heart, and I told him "I'm leavin' this town for good!"

I sent Jack Rael something from the radio show hoping he could provide me with a ticket out of town and that he did. He told me once that when he heard my voice again he forgot how I looked.

He heard something unique. He called a short time after hearing the recording and asked if I could come to Dallas to try out with the band. My heart leaped at the opportunity. I borrowed money from one of my older sisters who was working more than I was and bought a $69.95 suit from the best store in town. The outfit was, in retrospect, God-awful. The bright pinstripes on it were horizontal, making me look even heavier! Naturally, I also wore my glasses, which I've worn all my life except when performing. I flew down to Dallas and I must have looked a sight when they picked me up.

I stayed with their current girl singer, who was leaving the group—or so the boys told me. I got the impression they hadn't told her why I was there, which probably explains why she was cordial to me.

The afternoon I arrived we had a rehearsal, and I sang the lead singer parts to whatever songs they had. I'm not sure now what the songs were except I do remember "Ma, He's Making Eyes at Me" being one of them.

Later on, when I'd been hired, Jack told me that when I sang, the musicians had heard things in the arrangements that they had never heard before. To this day, I don't know what it was they heard.

I stayed in Dallas that night and sang a couple of songs with the band at the venue, Pappy's Showland, and the next day I got on a plane and flew back to Tulsa. They said they would let me know. Sure enough, a few days later, Jack called me and said they would like me to join the band in Chicago around December 9. I would be working with them at the Martinique Ballroom on the South Side. It was a six-week run, not just some two-week thing.

When I explained the offer to my parents, I knew my mother wasn't too happy. She never said I could go, really, but it wasn't long before I heard from Mrs. Hobby, her friend down the street, who told me, "I hear you're going to Chicago." That's how I knew my mother was going to let me go, and I wouldn't be attending art school.

I didn't go directly to Chicago. First, I had to meet the orchestra in Corpus Christi and sing for one night.

That's how I left home and the $125 a week I was making, for a job with a band I barely knew at $75 a week. All things considered, it just seemed glamorous because I could get national exposure via the radio broadcasts originating live from the Martinique in Chicago. I didn't know what was coming up after the six weeks in Chicago, but I was so enchanted by the big city, I spent $85 on a gold compact, maybe to feel important, and found myself without money for rent or food. It was my first Christmas away from home, which was kind of sad, but it was fun being with the band. I was still getting used to having my own bed and didn't mind that I had to share a bath with saxophone player, Joe Reisman, and his wife, Jeanne, who became a friend. I had my room on one side and them on another with a bathroom in between. It was certainly better than the bathroom at home! Joe went on to become a fantastic arranger. He did a lot of my first recordings and later became the head of Artists and Repertoire for RCA Records.

During our engagement in Chicago, a lot of agents came out to the ballroom wanting to talk with me but, to my surprise, Jack told me not to talk to any of them.

"I'm your manager," he told me one night. "Have them come and talk to me."

That was news to me. We'd never discussed such a thing. But as a single woman far from home, the idea of having a manager felt a bit comforting. One day in early January of 1947, Jack took me into the Sherman Hotel in the business district of Chicago. Jack had a musician friend who was a lawyer. He drew up a contract for Jack and me to sign, which we did. And while we finished out our stay at the Martinique, the agents kept coming in and wanting to meet me, having heard me on the radio. Every time they talked to me, I just let it go right by me like noise. After all, Jack had promised me that no matter what happened, he would be my manager and we had signed a contract.

When Jimmy Joy found out about the arrangement, he was very upset. Jimmy was under the impression that he had discovered me because I was singing with his band, but Jack told Jimmy he didn't have any rights.

"He didn't take it upon himself to sign you to a contract," Jack told me later. "I did."

Despite the tension between Jack and Jimmy, we continued with the band to Omaha, Nebraska. The band had been hired to back up the headliner, Connie Boswell. In those days, movie houses had a theatrical stage in front of the screen and singers and bands played there. It was the rage in those days for singers and the band to precede the feature film. I did an opening song with the band and I was happy with the response I got from the crowd, but after the first show Jimmy Joy came to me and said, "You don't have to sing anymore."

"Oh, really?" I asked, wondering what was wrong.

"Yeah," he continued, "the set has to be shortened."

Once I talked it over with Jack, I figured it out. Connie Boswell didn't want me singing on the same show—she felt threatened. I don't blame her. I wouldn't have wanted another girl singer to open the show. Frankly, it was ridiculous. The band could have had their boy singer open, or he and I could have done a duet.

Since they told me I didn't have to sing anymore, for the rest of the engagement I just went to the theater and played cards, listened to the music, or listened to Connie sing. She was a lovely lady, so there were no hard feelings. I know when I became successful I wouldn't have hired a girl singer with my band.

The job in Omaha lasted only a week, and suddenly, I was done with the band. Jack and I went back to Chicago, and he started pounding the streets of the Windy City to find me work. So much for my $75 a week!

I had little choice but to start borrowing from Jack. He'd been in the Army and he had some savings from his military service. One thing I learned about Jack—he was good at saving his money. It was easy; he just didn't spend any! Before long, I started getting little jobs that sort of sustained me. I got a room at the Montrose Beach Hotel, which was right next door to a very famous entertainment lounge called Helsing's Vodvil Lounge. Helsing's was where singer Frankie Laine was discovered, along with the comedian George Gobel and quite a few others. I didn't stay at the hotel because of its proximity to the club—I liked it because it was cheap. I actually did end up getting booked to sing at Helsing's and worked there off and on for that whole year.

One night I thought I'd blown it, though, because Jack threatened to send me back home to Oklahoma. After work, I would stay out late with a singing group called The Honey Dreamers whose members lived in the same building as me. We would hang out at Helsing's or maybe go bowling. There were five of them, male and female, and they were a lot of fun. I didn't think I was doing anything wrong. I wasn't being wild—I would just stay out all night and bowl. I wasn't doing anything else, which is sort of sad when I look back on it. However, I was doing Don McNeill's *The Breakfast Club* on the radio in the morning and I'd get up and take the El, or elevated railway, into downtown Chicago to do the show.

I felt fine, but Jack didn't think my voice sounded very fresh or exciting. And so he threatened to send me back to Tulsa. He even called one of my sisters to come get me. I guess his purpose was to scare me to death, which he did. I never stayed out much after that.

With my social habits under control, Jack set about getting me a record deal. I knew it wasn't an easy task, but I was thrilled to have him peddling me to different record companies. There weren't many then: Capitol, Columbia, Decca, Mercury, and RCA Victor were the top ones. Singers didn't receive advances for records unless they were very famous, and few albums were done. Most of the business was about singles.

I'm not sure what Jack presented the record companies with to persuade them—probably a recording he'd had made of one of the shows at the Martinique. I was over the moon when I got the news that I had a recording contract from Jimmy Hilliard at Mercury. The company was based in Chicago and its business revolved around balladeer Frankie Laine. I was singing on WBBM, the CBS station in Chicago, and as I recall, the assistant news director at the station helped arrange the deal.

Mercury wasted no time in getting their first female artist, Patti Page, into the studio to begin recording. On July 23rd, 1947, backed by the Eddie Getz Quintet, she recorded the single "Every So Often" with "What Every Woman Knows" on the B side. This became Patti Page's first single, released on August 15, 1947.

At the recording session on July 23rd she laid down a further two tracks: an A side, "Can't Help Loving That Man of Mine," and a B side, "I Got Some Forgetting to Do." This second single was released on September 1.

In total, she would release five 78 RPM singles for Mercury in 1947. Between recording

34

sessions, she played local dates in Chicago while being on the Breakfast Club regularly and doing an ABC Radio show on Saturdays called *Wake up and Smile.*

Mercury had me in the studio whenever they could because, the way it looked, no one would be recording for the whole of 1948 due to the Petrillo Ban, the name of a musician's strike set to begin at midnight, December 31, 1947. Everything the record companies were going to release in the coming year had to be recorded before 1948 arrived.

Jack and I grew concerned after my next three singles came out. I hadn't put down a track that turned into even a moderate hit. Later, after the success of "Tennessee Waltz," a Country song that crossed over into a Pop hit, I used to kid Mercury that if they'd had me record Country when they first signed me, I would've been a superstar. But the fact is, Country was not big then. At Mercury, the attitude was just "Oh, Country," and singers were looked down upon if they sang it.

After my initial excitement about getting a recording contract, I now began to wonder about my future. To borrow from one of the songs of the day, I was going through "the bluest kind of blues." Was this where it would end? Would I end up back in Tulsa, having seen all my dreams die in the big city?

THREE Singing with Myself

ith the Petrillo Ban looming, I was on the lookout for something
special for my next single. If I couldn't record for a year, I wanted
to make it count. Jack found a song at Universal Studios in
Chicago. Eddie Hubbard, a disc jockey in Chicago, had written and recorded a
song called "12 O'Clock Flight." When it came out, nobody played it. Instead,
they played the B side, a song called "Confess." Mercury was saving the song
for Vic Damone, but Jack talked them into letting me do it.

So there we were in the studio on December 31, 1947 recording "Confess."
The arrangement called for an "echo," which meant when I sang "Confess"
in the chorus, you were supposed to hear "Confess, Confess" sung in the
background. We couldn't afford a backup singer. So what to do? I said to Jack
and the Mercury A & R man, Jerry Wexler, "Why can't I answer myself on this
song?" I suggested that I record my own "answer" voice. Patti Page singing with
Patti Page. Why not?

With the recording equipment at the time—which had only one "pot," or
volume control—you could lose a lot of audio "presence" trying to do such a
thing. Basically, it would sound weak. The A & R man wasn't sure it would

work. I didn't want to argue with him. Besides, we had no time to waste arguing as it was getting close to midnight. So, when he went out to the men's room, I recorded the "Confess, Confess" part myself.

The members of my backup group, the Eddie Getz Quintet, liked the idea, and so did our engineer, Bill Putnam, who somehow figured out the technical details.

The catch was, with the witching hour nearly upon us, if I didn't sing it just right, I would ruin the whole track, and we wouldn't have time to fix it.

"It'll be either a big success or a giant flop," I told the guys that night. I knew we were taking a chance, but sometimes you have to do that to get ahead.

Little did we know when we were recording it that we were making history. Jack and I had just wanted to add a little something special. We had no idea that "Confess" was anything innovative at all. But that night, I was the first singer to ever double her own voice.

It's odd to remember that we had only one track to record on back then. Making "Confess" was only possible because the engineer was so talented. Naturally, I couldn't replicate the effect when I played live. Instead, I'd have a saxophone echoing the "Confess, Confess" part. Thankfully, there weren't too many people who came to see me perform that expected to see me sing two voices at once! To this day, I'll demonstrate the technique onstage by singing the melody of "Tumbling Tumbleweed" with two pre-recorded voices of my own. It works out well, but you always cross your fingers when you're working with something like that.

These days it seems that some stars don't even need to be able to sing. It amazes me what can be done with electronics now, even onstage. Engineers with software like ProTools can fix pitch and everything else as the performer "sings" to an audience. It's bizarre. When I've heard some of the "singers" who couldn't sing yet have won Grammys, it's just unbelievable to me.

Singing the different voices on "Confess" changed my own recording; after that, I almost always did all the voices on my records. The funny thing is, it hardly added anything to our recording time.

Ever since those early recording days, I have often been asked where my style came from. God only knows, honestly. My mother only let us kids listen to the radio maybe half an hour a week and that was when she wanted to listen to the *The Eddie Cantor Show* or *The Grand Ole Opry* or maybe *The Chicago Barn Dance*. Those are the three shows that I remember. I didn't feel influenced by anyone I heard on the radio, though. Dinah Shore was on *The Eddie Cantor Show*, but I don't think I sound anything like her. I certainly never emulated Minnie "How-dee!" Pearl on *The Grand Ole Opry* or any other of the Country singers I heard. I just learned songs and sang them.

"Confess" became Patti Page's first moderate hit when it was released in June 1948, but perhaps the greatest boost it gave to her fledgling career was that it made her a familiar name with disc jockeys. The fact that the hit song was produced using an innovative recording technique and was performed by "Patti Page and Patti Page" was something to talk about on the air. That year, in a nationwide poll of disc jockeys, Page was voted Most Promising Female Vocalist. Newspaper columnist Studs Terkel accurately predicted in his "Hot Plate" column that she was "a cinch to become one of the best ballad singers." All the attention brought her offers to work in theaters around the country, including the prominent nightclub Chez Paree in Chicago.

Even so, the single was eclipsed by established stars Doris Day and Buddy Clark, who had a hit record called "Love Somebody" with "Confess" on the B side.

Undaunted, Patti Page quickly built on her initial success. In 1949, she released "So In Love," from the Broadway hit musical Kiss Me Kate, and the single sold well. "All My Love," based on the famous classical piece Bolero, was an even greater success. It went to #1, was on the charts almost six months, and sold 700,000 copies.

For many listeners, part of Page's great charm as a singer was that all the voices on her records were her own. The recording technique she pioneered was rapidly adopted by other singers. Later, Les Paul used a similar method, with a guitar, and this led to a perception amongst some people that it was he who invented "over-dubbing." In truth, a little girl from Tulsa, Oklahoma, and her engineer got there first.

It looked like I could make it in the big world, after all.

Jack and I realized that it was time for me to leave Chicago for the center of the show business universe: New York City. There were more places to play on the East Coast, and most radio originated from New York, as well. Jack thought that I had done everything I could in Chicago on radio. In addition, television was just starting up in New York, and we felt that TV would eventually dominate the entertainment business.

My arrival in New York in January 1948 was magical. A day or two after we arrived, the city was hit by the biggest snowstorm they'd ever had. It was cold, but Chicago winters were a lot colder, so I was happy to have moved. In New York, people just seemed more alive to me—maybe it was because they weren't always battling the wind like in Chicago or maybe it had something to do with how people lived in much closer quarters in New York.

We checked into a hotel called the Shelton. My older sister, Virginia, came along to travel with me because, once again, Jack thought I was staying out too late at night and I needed some stability.

Rosemary Clooney, who would become my best friend, moved to New York about the same time. By chance, a woman named Jackie Rose, who had been a friend of Rosemary's for a long time and was also her secretary, was on the same train Jack and I took from Chicago, and I got to know Jackie on that train. Later I got to know Rosemary, too. Rosie and I were both working so much we rarely got a chance to see each other, but her sister, Betty, had an apartment at the Vendome, a famous apartment building, and Rosie would stay with her sister and I'd go over there sometimes for a bite to eat. We always had a great time. I went to cooking school with Jackie, and we had to make an appetizer or an entrée for our assignments. We would take turns having a dinner for everyone with the food we made at school.

I was constantly busy, and new areas of my career were opening up in New York. I appeared in Carnegie Hall for the first time but not as a singer. I was invited to be a guest judge on a show called *Quizdown* on TV station KQV. More exciting, however, was appearing on NBC's first commercial show, *The Kraft Music Hall* in January of 1948. I got $100 for my appearance, which was great considering that most guests got $25. Later, I did another show with drummer Gene Krupa and some other stars and got paid $125. I was hooked on television.

I also played a lot of dates around Milwaukee, Wisconsin—no doubt because it was Jack Rael's hometown. I liked Milwaukee well enough; Jack knew everyone there and got me on shows like Al Buettner's *Music Till Past Midnight* on WTMJ. I was working a little club in Racine, not far from Milwaukee, when I met a student from the University of Wisconsin named Jack Skiba. He came in to see the show, hung around afterward, and we started talking. I was so gullible in those days, very impressed that he was a college student. I think we were both infatuated—me with his being a college student and he with my being in show business. We only knew each other a few months before we married in May 1948.

To my chagrin, Jack dropped out of college, preferring to spend time with me on the road. I appreciated his company, but the way he quit college was a little surreptitious, maybe even underhanded. Since he was a very good student and came from a well-to-do family, I thought we'd be all right. He followed me to New York and we lived in an apartment uptown on 125th Street, right next to Harlem. The apartment wasn't that expensive, but it troubled me that my husband didn't go to work immediately like he told me he would.

He did go out every day wearing a suit and a tie. I even ironed his shirts. Then he'd come back at the right time of day like a good working man, but nothing was being accomplished. In the beginning Jack did look for work, then his attempts got to be further and further apart. He found a temporary job, but I don't even remember what he did. I seem to recall he was a salesman because he was a nice-looking man, but he never brought in much money.

Meanwhile, he tried to get involved in my business, which didn't make my manager Jack very happy. My husband would at times argue with my manager about career decisions. Finally, my manager told me my husband was not allowed anywhere I was working! I knew that was the beginning of the end. The friction escalated and finally my husband went home to Wisconsin. I was going to Milwaukee soon to work the Riverside Theater, but in truth we were in a separation.

When I arrived in Milwaukee, my husband came up to the hotel where I was staying. My sister, Virginia, was no longer traveling with me. She had fallen in love in New York and married a fellow named Joe Cristiantiallo. So, there I was, all alone, when my "better half" came up to the hotel. He seemed to be under the impression that he could just pick up where we left off. We'd been married less than a year and he'd met hardly anyone from my family. I suppose that should have told me something. Now we had been apart only a couple of months, but I'd completely lost interest. I just didn't want to be married anymore.

"This isn't going to work," I told Jack. I crossed my arms and looked out the window.

He was both deflated and angry. "You're my *wife,*" he insisted. "It *will* work."

That was all he had to offer. I looked back at him and shook my head. "No," I said. "I'm not your wife anymore."

There wasn't much more to it. He left, and I proceeded to contact a lawyer who was Jack Rael's brother-in-law. I got a divorce in Wisconsin, a no-fault judgment.

Sometimes a woman will change her mind if a man will make an effort, but Jack Skiba just let it go. I suppose I don't have to tell you that my short first marriage soured me on dating for a long time. I don't think I was being unreasonable by expecting my husband to hold up his end of the bargain.

Hit songs were sometimes a hit for someone else many years earlier. For example, the legendary Al Jolson had a hit with "Are You Lonesome Tonight?" long before it was a smash for Elvis Presley. Similarly, in 1934, a fellow named Leo Reisman had a hit with the song "With My Eyes Wide Open, I'm Dreaming," which was about to become a hit for me, too. It was written for the movie *Shoot the Works* by Mack Gordon and Harry Revel. (In one of those little coincidences in life, Mack Gordon would later become Jack Rael's father-in-law.)

I first heard "Eyes Wide Open" sung with four-part harmony by a quartet fronted by Jazz musician Don Elliot at a resort in upstate New York, where I was playing and Don's group was backing me up. I would sit and listen to them. They did such neat songs, they were a pleasure to hear! I loved the song and told Jack I should record it, although I meant to do only one voice on it. Jack liked the idea but the more we talked about it, we realized it just lent itself to four voices, so why shouldn't I do all four?

Back in New York, we presented the idea to Mitch Miller, who was now the Artist & Repertoire man in charge of recording for Mercury. Mitch wasn't smiling when he heard what I wanted to do.

"I don't like the four parts," he said, stroking the beard that became so famous later on his TV show.

"What's not to like?" Jack asked. "You should hear it done that way, it's great."

"I know the song," Mitch replied. "Won't work."

"I won't have any trouble doing all four parts, Mitch." I watched his reaction, which wasn't encouraging. "I've done this kind of thing a few times."

Mitch gazed off into space and bounced a pencil off his desk. "Okay," he said finally. "Tell you what. Record about eight bars of it and bring it to me—with an arrangement."

My manager looked perplexed. So was I, but I just chuckled and stepped out of Mitch's office.

We worked on it in the basement of a club where we were playing in Milwaukee, and when we got back to the East Coast, Jack dutifully went out and found an arranger to chart out eight bars of the song. He wrote the parts for me, and I had to learn them. And there I was—unable to read music! I had to learn the parts for those eight bars almost like four individual songs.

In January of 1949 we went out to a studio in New Jersey where Bill Putnam was the engineer. It could be that there weren't any studios available in New York or, more likely, we saved money at the place across the river since Mercury wasn't paying for this experiment and we were. At first, Bill didn't think the recording could be done. We had him record me singing the first part on acetate. That recording was fed back to me while I sung the second part, which was then recorded on a separate acetate. The idea was that we would keep doing this until we finally had four acetates that we would play all together.

Recording the first two wasn't so bad, but when I put the third voice in, it sounded terrible. The process was quite an education. You see, I was used to three-part harmonies, which are simple. If you're doing a three-part harmony, it sounds good as soon as you put the second harmony on, and the third one just fits in. When it's four parts, it's a different thing altogether because in the third part you sing notes that you wouldn't ordinarily and the full sound doesn't come together until you add the fourth voice. If you make a mistake on the third voice, you might not hear it until you try to add the fourth. The whole thing didn't sound natural until I added the fourth part.

We lost some "bottom" doing it that way, so we made the rhythm section louder. When we finally mixed it all down onto one acetate, it blended perfectly. Even the engineer was happy.

When we played it for Mitch he got a big smile on his face. Suddenly, he understood what I'd heard in my head. We were booked into the Bob Fine studio in New York immediately. Bob was a very well-known engineer who recorded most everything for Mercury's classical label; I felt comfortable working with such an excellent technician. (He was a marvel. A couple of years later, when I was in his studio recording on tape a song called "And So to Sleep Again," doing four voices, somehow in the cutting it came out as "And so to leap again…." I remember it as if it were yesterday. Bob looked all over the studio for the piece of tape containing that "s," and he found it and was able to fix it! How he did, I still don't know.)

For "Eyes Wide Open," we laid down the tracks in only six hours. The record business and music engineering had changed quite a bit since I'd recorded "Confess." There were plenty of channels to put down the various voices by the time I recorded "Eyes Wide Open.," and by that time Les Paul and Mary Ford were putting out some of their innovative records, with him overdubbing his guitar and her doing all kinds of other parts. The style had become popular.

Later, Mitch took credit for the four voices idea. That didn't bother me. What did bother me was that I lost track of my recording of those eight bars. I wish I'd kept it; it was the oddest audition I was ever asked to do.

"With My Eyes Wide Open, I'm Dreaming" was Patti Page's first million-selling hit. It would take her career to a whole new level, and for a long period after this, each single she released would sell at least 300,000 copies, an unprecedented level at the time.

It was not only the advancements in recording technology since "Confess" that enabled the ambitious recording of a four-part harmony by one singer. It would never have been possible without Page's extraordinary vocal range, which spans bass, alto, soprano, tenor, and low F.

Having a hit with "Eyes Wide Open" helped me get over the failure of my marriage.

I was working constantly, and not long after Jack Skiba and I broke up, I got a job singing with a band that I would have thought way out of my league only a couple of years before. The leader was a musical legend that just happened to be related to my ever-clever manager, and I was about to get an unexpected education about show business people.

FOUR | Big Shows
and Road Hazards

Jack Rael learned that his famous relative, Benny Goodman, was planning a
special two-week engagement with his septet at the Clique in Philadelphia.
Benny was looking for a girl singer who had somewhat of a name but not
too big a following, and I fit the criteria. Like Jack, Benny wasn't crazy about
spending a lot of money, and Patti Page was in his price range.

I auditioned and Benny, who I believe was Jack's second cousin, hired me.
The musicians were fabulous! There was Wardell Gray on saxophone, Teddy
Wilson on piano, and Mary Lou Williams would come in from New York and
alternate with Teddy. Benny had discovered the brilliant clarinet player Stan
Hasselgard in Sweden, who was also in the group. I suppose I should have been
intimidated by the great musicians—especially the great Benny Goodman—
but I was just too naïve to be awed.

Benny didn't have the warmest personality—everything was all business.
We played seven days a week; there was no such thing as a day off. With
a schedule like that, the guys liked to let off steam after hours, and so did
I. I didn't date many musicians at that time. After Jack Skiba, I was a little
man-shy, but when I found out the guys were having a party the second

weekend, I told Jack Rael I wanted to go.

"No, you don't want to go," he said nonchalantly.

If Jack was trying to keep me away from the musical wolves, I wasn't sure I wanted to be saved.

"No, really, Jack," I protested. "I'd like to go."

He took a sip of coffee. "No, really, trust me. You don't want to go to that party."

"It's just a get-together in someone's room. What could it hurt? And why can't I go?"

Someone else might have taken a hint by then, but like I said, I was pretty naïve.

"You really want to go, then?"

"Well, I sure as heck don't want to go back and sit in my hotel room!"

So up we went to the room, which turned out to be a suite, and there was a funny smell in the hallway outside. Jack opened the door and escorted me in, and the air was filled with smoke. The musicians were all sitting around the bed, sprawled on the floor, and passing around this one little cigarette.

Was everyone out of smokes at once? I thought.

I turned to Jack, perplexed. "You know, I have a brand-new pack of cigarettes in my purse. Don't you think I should offer them one?"

"Cool it," he said, smiling at a musician who had begun laughing at me. "Just forget it."

He then explained what was what, and when I reacted in horror, he got me out of there, away from my introduction to marijuana. Later, when I had my own TV show in New York, Benny Goodman made an appearance on a bill with Julius La Rosa and Sammy Davis Jr., but I never brought up that smoking party in a Philadelphia hotel.

Someone once told me, "The awful thing about wanting something very badly is, you get it." Well, I wanted independence. I got it. I had to learn how cold and lonely independence can be. In those early days of my career touring on the road, with my only home a succession of impersonal hotel rooms in strange cities and towns, independence was a lonely business indeed. I was free of parental control, but I was also free of parental care and concern and the kind of everyday love you get only from your own family.

But there were some things a country girl from Tulsa had to learn the hard way. One lesson, in November of 1949, changed my life on the road forever. It made me think twice about getting a lot of publicity and started my looking more deeply into human nature. I was playing at a theater in Toronto, Canada, and staying at the King Edward Hotel. I didn't travel with a band or a secretary at the time. It was just myself and Jack, in our own separate rooms. That day, I didn't have a sound check until 2:00 in the afternoon and didn't have to perform until that night, so I was sleeping late. About 11:00 in the morning, I got a call that there were some flowers downstairs that a messenger would like to deliver to my room. I said okay. How nice, I thought, to wake up to fresh flowers. I looked in my purse for some money to give the guy a tip. There was a knock on the door, and when I opened it there was a man holding flowers, but in his other hand he had what looked like a gun pointed at me. I froze.

"Get back in the room," he said, stepping forward. "Be quiet and you won't get hurt!"

I was scared, so I did what he said.

"Sit down on the bed!" he barked, and I did.

I began acting very calm. I was not calm inside, but he didn't know that.

"What are you going to do?" I asked flatly.

He blinked when he heard my tone, but then he said, "I'm going to help myself to your body."

I could feel myself shaking as he got some duct tape out of a little case I noticed he was carrying. The flowers were sprawled on the floor nearby.

"Put your hands together!" he snapped.

I did it, but as he taped them together I began asking questions like an inquisitive schoolgirl.

"What kind of tape is that?"

"Shut up and you won't get hurt."

"I just wanted to know. Don't you want to tell me?"

He didn't answer so I kept talking. "What else do you have in that case?" He hadn't tried to undress me yet. I wondered if I'd gotten to him a little.

"You want to see too much!" he exclaimed, and with that he grabbed a pillow and yanked the case off and started to put it over my head.

I screamed my head off, and my voice carries pretty well, so he took one final look at me and ran out the door. Luckily for me, just at that moment, there were some painters coming up the stairs and my room was right next to the stairway. A couple of them heard the screams, saw my attacker run past them down the stairs, and turned and chased him. The other painters kept coming and found me standing in my doorway in my nightgown. Right at that moment, the maid arrived at my door.

"Someone was trying to rape me!" I blurted out.

She looked like someone had slapped her. "Oh, don't use that word!" she yelled. I felt like slapping her.

And that's when I lost it and became hysterical. I don't even remember who came in the room and asked me who to call, but I had them call Jack, and he hurried up to the room. When he got there, the tape was still on my hands. I suppose they wanted to leave the tape on to get fingerprints or something, but when Jack saw that he flipped out and removed it.

Then the manager of the hotel arrived and got the story from me. One of the painters caught the guy outside of the hotel as the police were arriving.

The truly crazy thing was what happened later in court. My attacker, a forty-one-year-old married man with children, William Daniel, who had planned to help himself to my body, was fined $50 for common assault, and that was it.

The judge apparently said, "There's no business like show business."

O Canada!

Jack and I had a long talk after that. I told him that I couldn't travel alone anymore—I had to get somebody to be with me. And I never traveled alone again.

Generally, life on the road wasn't so eye-opening. Most of the time, it was just me and Jack driving from one engagement to the next. Jack always drove because I didn't know how. A lot of times, I sewed in the car. There were stories about how quaint I was as a country girl and that I made some of my own gowns, but I never did. I just sewed sequins on them. I had a black strapless gown, and I liked to keep a row of sequins sewn across the top to sparkle in the lights. I just had to make sure I got both sides done by the time the show went on.

I also tried to keep up with my painting. I did one painting around this time called "Four Seasons" especially for Jack Rael's sister. For a while, I traveled with my paints but they were oils, which didn't dry too quickly—you had to have something to guard what you painted so it wouldn't smear. This was before the faster-drying acrylics came out. It got to be a hassle, and I began finding any excuse not to paint.

Then I gave up painting altogether for a long time because of a cocktail party at the Hotel New Yorker, which was across the street from the famous Paramount Theater. The hotel had a terrace outside this room where Mercury Records was giving the party, and I started chatting with a professional artist who was one of the guests. Someone told him that in addition to my music I was also an artist.

"Oh, really?" said the painter. "Don't you find it so relaxing?"

I looked at him quizzically and thought, *I must be crazy.* I've never relaxed in my life while painting. Much later, I realized that what he meant was something like, "Don't you forget the world while you're painting?" I took it the other way. After the party, I finished one painting that I was trying to do, but then I stopped, having formed the conclusion that I was doing it all wrong. I put my paints away and didn't pick them up again for a decade.

It was 1950, and Patti had just made her debut at New York's Paramount, a huge theater seating 3,600, which had made superstars of entertainers such as Frank Sinatra. When Sinatra performed live there in 1944, prior to a movie screening, 35,000 fans had shown up, resulting in a near-riot. Many Hollywood movies premiered there, and it would be the venue for the 1956 world premiere of *Love Me Tender,* Elvis Presley's first film.

Patti was opening for Frankie Laine, who was Mercury's leading artist and a major musical star at the time. They were originally booked for two weeks, but because of public demand, this was extended to twenty-one days. It was a testament to Page's popularity that, at a time when many Broadway houses were half-empty, Jack Rael had to cancel other bookings so she could keep playing at the Paramount.

The shows helped vault Page's career even higher, garnering her glowing reviews from critics. *Variety* praised her performance, saying she put on a better show than Frankie Laine, the headline act and Mercury's #1 star, who had recommended to the label's management that they give Page her first contract. She got so much press attention that Ed Sullivan, who already had a show on television as well as a very popular syndicated newspaper column, came to one of the shows. According to Page, he would later tell people that he "discovered" her there. She would appear on Sullivan's shows for almost two decades after that.

It was clear from the press coverage that Patti Page was evolving as a performer. When she had appeared at Cafe Society in New York in 1949, a review had called her "a chubby awkward kid," but when she appeared at the New Yorker Hotel in 1950, a critic noted that she had slimmed down, was becomingly groomed, and now handled herself with "a modest certainty."

When I first came to New York, I would go to the Paramount when I wasn't working. They asked to see my ID the first time I went. I thought, *wow, that's fantastic!* It made me feel very cosmopolitan. The Paramount was a real movie palace, and it had a great stage, too.

Ticket prices for our shows were 55¢ except on Saturday, Sunday, and holidays, and that covered both our show and the movie. The feature film began at 9:00 a.m. The musical show started at 10:30, after the movie. The band warmed up the crowd. I sang and then Frankie. The whole set was about forty-five minutes, no more than an hour, then the movie would play again and then the musical show. We would do four or five shows a day.

The movie that played during our engagement was the Humphrey Bogart film *In A Lonely Place,* but that's not how the Paramount felt during our run. I was supposed to perform three songs with no encores, then just take a couple of bows so the movie could start on time. I was thrilled when audiences demanded a fourth number at more than one show.

I found out about the accolades I received after the fact because I tended not to read the "trades" like *Variety, Cashbox,* and *Billboard.* I did like to read the writer Army Archerd of *Variety* because he was always a class act. But as a performer in New York, the writers that you wanted to mention your name in print were the popular newspaper columnists like Ed Sullivan, Walter Winchell, and Earl Wilson. When Wilson in his "It Happened Last Night" column gave me "Today's Bravo" for my stint at The New Yorker's Terrace Room, it was quite a coup. Everyone read the newspapers in those days, and hardly anyone had a television set. Newspapers wrote articles about how I'd blow off steam arguing with Jack (partially true) and that he was good to me (mostly true). They'd write that my favorite singer was Ella Fitzgerald (true) and that I loved horseback riding, tennis, and swimming (sure, but who had time?).

The year 1950 also marked the first time I played the Desert Inn in Las Vegas, which had just opened. I had played Las Vegas for the first time at the Thunderbird in 1948 when there were only two other venues: the El Rancho Vegas and the Tropicana. The Flamingo had just been built. The town really started to become the entertainment capital of the world after the Desert Inn hotel-casino was constructed. Las Vegas catered to families then, and gambling was not played up, it was just an adjunct. They had the nightclub, the hotel, the swimming pool, and people were invited to bring their families. They even offered babysitters at night so parents could see the shows. Even so, we'd occasionally get babies in the audience. I still to this day get letters that say things like "I was the little boy that sat in the front row when you played the Desert Inn, remember?"

Patti Page was appearing all over the country as never before. Later in 1950, she played the Blue Room at the Roosevelt Hotel in New Orleans with Skinnay Ennis and His Orchestra, and did two weeks at the Shamrock Hotel in Houston.

In August, she debuted at the famous Ciro's nightclub on Sunset Boulevard, in Los Angeles, a venue frequented by Hollywood movie stars such as Kirk Douglas. She was a hit at Ciro's, the crowd demanding multiple encores most nights. Today The Comedy Store sits at that location, attracting a different kind of Hollywood audience.

I did two shows a night for two weeks at Ciro's on Sunset Boulevard. Like the Paramount Theater in New York, there was a line of dancers who were part of the entertainment. Show business was a small world, as one of the girls, named

Bonnie Hunt (not the same one as the contemporary actress/talk show host), was married to my conductor, Rocky Cole, at the time.

I was interested in movies and in acting. I thought that maybe I could explore that possibility while in Los Angeles, but it didn't happen. The agency that did my bookings, General Artists Corporation, was not too hip on that idea because they made more money on me in nightclubs and theaters. You see, if I did movies then I would have to take very little salary since I was not known as a movie star.

This was a pattern that would play itself out over the course of the next several decades. Many of my career decisions—or should I say the ones that I allowed to be made for me—would be based less on what I wanted and more on what my representatives wanted—that is, how much money they would make. And as I had always preferred a low-key social life with family and a few close friends, I probably didn't capitalize as much as I could have on being in Los Angeles among influential Hollywood stars. There was no big first-time-in-L.A. reception thing.

I got a big lesson at Ciro's but not during one of my performances. I saw the great Maurice Chevalier play there. It was something I'll never forget because there was no one in the audience. Someone told me later that the lack of fans might have been because Chevalier was considered a sympathizer during World War II since he kept performing in France, even for German soldiers. All I knew was that he had been in great movies, and at Ciro's he put on a show like that room was filled to capacity. Prior to that night, I would be disappointed if places I played were only half or three-quarters full. It made me realize that it doesn't matter. Even if only one person is there for you, you give them your all.

It was another of those lucky little accidents for me, but nothing like the one that was coming that fall when Jack and I worked on creating a hit for Christmas. We got our wish, but what Santa pulled out of his bag was the biggest surprise of my life, and God's greatest musical blessing on me.

FIVE

The B Side That Sold
10 Million Copies

I n October of 1950, I recorded what Jack and I hoped would be a hit
Christmas record, a single called "Boogie Woogie Santa Claus." Mercury
wanted to put an obscure song on the B side so people would concentrate
on the A side. Usually nothing would sell at that time unless it was a Christmas
song, so the idea was to get DJs to concentrate on playing "Boogie Woogie
Santa Claus" in lieu of anything else.

Jack and I had an office in the famous Brill Building of Tin Pan Alley
songwriting fame at 1619 Broadway. Lots of music companies and those
peripheral to the music business had offices in the building. The Brill was also
the location of Lindy's, a famous Jewish restaurant. People knew each other
pretty well, and many a deal was brokered over a bagel with cream cheese or a
corned beef sandwich on rye.

We'd planned, as usual, to do four songs at our upcoming recording date,
but none of the ones we'd selected were nondescript enough for Mercury
to go on the B side, so Jack was on the lookout for something suitable. One
morning in the lobby, he ran into Jerry Wexler (a different Jerry Wexler than
the Mercury A & R man), who worked at *Billboard*. Jerry told Jack about a song

he had reviewed the night before, an Erskine Hawkins cut from the Rhythm and Blues field that had previously been recorded as a Country song. Jerry had no idea that we had a recording date coming up; he just had this idea that if a Pop singer "like Patti Page" ever got hold of the song it might be something really good. Jack paid attention to what he had to say because Jerry was very knowledgeable about music. He'd never heard of the song, so Jerry hummed it for him. Intrigued, Jack followed Jerry up to his office, where Jerry gave him a copy of the record—Hawkins's version of "Tennessee Waltz."

Jack liked the song well enough, and so did I. We added it as a fifth side to our recording schedule. The next day, we went in to record the four songs, planning to add the new song if we could fit it in. We had no time to make an arrangement; we would have to make one up as we went along.

I got through the first four tracks quickly, and we had just enough time to record "Tennessee Waltz." I wasn't worried about not having an arrangement for it because we had booked famous Jazz trumpet player Buck Clayton for the date and when it came time to record "Tennessee Waltz" we just told him to "come up with something." Joe Carleton masterminded the session and everything was very smooth. Although the labels on the records later read "Orchestra by Jack Rael" (he had a habit of putting his name on everything), Joe Reisman was the conductor. It was a sweet, poignant song, and I enjoyed singing it because I could put a lot of emotion into it. Plus, I was reminded of my country roots and the folks back home.

We happened to like the way it turned out, but nobody had high hopes for it. The records for Christmas would be released very soon, and we were just happy to have a pleasant song on the other side of our anticipated big Christmas hit about the boogie woogie Santa.

To tell the truth, I quickly forgot about "Tennessee Waltz." That changed while I was working at New York's famous Copacabana as the opening act for the comedian Joe E. Lewis, who is probably best remembered for a great supporting part in the movie Some Like It Hot. My job was to do five numbers and no more. I had been hired because of the success of "Eyes Wide Open," and I usually closed with that number.

After my last number I had to walk through the Copa's kitchen and take an elevator up to my dressing room. One night, as I walked along, people were saying "Do the waltz" or "You should do the waltz." I had no idea what they were talking about. Sing the what? I was probably shaking my head when I punched the button to my floor.

I went to relax in the dressing room. There was some time between the first and second shows. I was reading when Jack came up to join me.

"They kept telling me to do the waltz," I said. I lowered my magazine and looked at him over my glasses.

"What waltz?" he asked.

"I was hoping you'd know."

Jack grabbed a phone and asked the hotel operator for an outside line. "I know how we can get to the bottom of this," he told me. "I'll call Harry Rosen, the Mercury distributor in Philadelphia."

"At this time of night?"

"I'll call him at home."

Harry had become a friend of ours, so Jack had his home number. Had it been today, Jack would have had Harry's cell number—but had it been today, we wouldn't have been in the dark about what was going on. I watched as Jack started the conversation and his eyes immediately got wide.

"No, I have no idea what's going on," Jack said. "Really?" He motioned for me to come over and listen in. I huddled close to Jack's side.

"You've gotta be kidding!" gushed our friend in Philly. "We've ordered three times already, Jack! In two weeks! And each order was 200,000. You better get your head out of the sand!"

Jerry Wexler had been right about what might happen if a Pop singer like Patti Page recorded "Tennessee Waltz." When Mercury Records catalog number 5534 was released on November 10, 1950, it entered the *Billboard* Pop music chart the same day. It would stay on the chart for 30 weeks, hitting #1.

To keep up with demand, Mercury farmed out some of the record pressing to one of its competitors, RCA. Such a step was so unprecedented in the recording industry that it made the news, as tens of thousands of 45s and 78s of "Tennessee Waltz" piled up at an RCA pressing plant in New Jersey.

I used to go into record stores in New York and on the road and often spent a bit of time chatting to the owners. One in New York pulled me aside and said, "You cannot believe the phenomenal success of this song, Patti. I've been in the record business for years, and I've never seen anything like it." He said, "I want to prove something to you." With that, he took me to the side, out of sight, and made a prediction: "Just watch. Everybody who comes into my store will buy a copy of 'Tennessee Waltz.' Everyone. Whether they're Opera buffs or Rhythm and Blues or Country. Jazz fans, too, and they won't let you see what they bought. They don't want anyone to see them buying 'Tennessee Waltz'!"

And you know what? I stayed there long enough to see that he was right! It was almost impossible to comprehend, to be honest. It is hard to put into words the joy and gratitude it gave me to know that people from all kinds of backgrounds and with all types of musical tastes had taken this song into their hearts in such a big way.

In the midst of the frenzy that was created by "Tennessee Waltz," I was also excited because my family was coming to town! A few days before Christmas, my mother, father, sisters, and I were appearing together on the Morton Downey TV show *Star of the Family*. There was also going to be a big picture article about myself and my family in a major magazine, and we had to do the photo shoot for that, as well.

My folks weren't particularly impressed by New York. They weren't excited about being on national television, either. And they preferred the food back home. So much for Manhattan haute cuisine. When Morton Downey asked who they were most proud of, my dad without blinking said his son Charlie, who was serving in the Korean War. Well, I felt that way, too. Charlie had been taken prisoner in World War II and survived, only to keep fighting for his country when war broke out in Korea.

Nothing like family to keep you grounded.

In 1951, there were about 151 million people living in the United States. Many didn't have record players and played records only on jukeboxes. Yet on January 3, 1951, barely six weeks after the release of "Tennessee Waltz" sales had passed 1.4 million copies. A further six weeks on, sales had passed 2 million. By March, the record had sold 2.5 million copies. That meant that within three and a half months of the record's release there was a copy of "Tennessee Waltz" owned, on average, by roughly one out of every sixty people in the country.

For the whole of 1951, total sales of all records in the United States were nearly 200 million. Patti Page's "Tennessee Waltz" sold about 4 million copies in that period, which means that it accounted for one out of every fifty records sold in the country in 1951.

By late March 1951, the sheet music sales of "Tennessee Waltz" had reached 1.1 million copies. In a way, this marked the end of an era, as it was the last piece of sheet music to ever sell over a million copies.

"Tennessee Waltz" was written by Country music stars Redd Stewart and Pee Wee King in 1947 and had been a #3 Country hit for Pee Wee King and His Golden West Cowboys in 1948. While Page's recording of the song had the distinction of making it to

#1 on the Pop chart, it also reached #2 on the Billboard Country music chart. On other Country charts it was #1 and also hit #1 on the Rhythm and Blues charts.

What had originally been intended as an obscure B side was concurrently #1 on the Pop, Country and R & B charts, something no other artist in recording history had ever done. No one has been able to achieve it since, either. Not even Elvis Presley.

In the way that Garth Brooks changed Country music with arena appearances that were like those of Rock acts, Patti Page was arguably the first Country-Pop crossover artist. One rival for that title was Country artist Red Foley. In 1950, he had crossed over to Pop with his signature number "Chattanoogie Shoe Shine Boy," which was at the top of the Country charts for thirteen weeks and the Pop chart for fifteen weeks. The fact that he softened his characteristic "twang" when recording the song, and that people across America knew Red as the emcee of the weekly six-hour long Grand Ole Opry likely contributed to the song's Pop success. Another contender was Bob Wills, the king of Country swing. At one point in the 1940s, he had more fans than Tommy Dorsey or Benny Goodman, and was featured in movies, but Texas swing was distinctly different to Page's Country sound.

The sales were definitely helped by the disc jockeys. Though some DJs may have heard "Boogie Woogie Santa Claus," I don't know who ever played it. Some DJs, like Bill Randall in Cleveland, were famous for "breaking" records nationally. DJs were very important when they liked a record, and it wasn't long before I had a lady working for me fulltime to promote my records to disc jockeys.

The record became such a phenomenon that even music writers were floored. The editor from *Cashbox* magazine couldn't believe what was going on. In 1951, when a record store owner in Harlem sent in his sales figures for "Tennessee Waltz" by Patti Page, the editor kept changing the performer's name to Erskine

Hawkins for publication. Finally, the record store owner called the editor and said, "What are you doing? We got Patti Page's record up here!" And the editor still didn't believe it. What? Black people loved a Country song? How could that be?

I think that the success of "Tennessee Waltz" helped show that Country music had a wider appeal than many record label executives had believed up to that point. Maybe my crossover didn't make waves quite so much as, say, Elvis Presley, who introduced Rhythm and Blues, or so-called "black music," to a whole new audience when he burst on the scene. But I still felt proud to have helped break down barriers between Pop and Country because I believe all musical breakthroughs are important to our culture. And I hope that it helped other recording artists who came after me.

At the time, though, the media didn't have as big a sway over American culture as it does now, so we didn't really talk about the impact of a hit song crossing over from Country to Pop; it wasn't seen as culturally important at the time. I just kept singing, but I put "The Waltz" in the act, you can believe that.

The first place I sang the song publicly was Miami. My sister, Rema, came on the road with me and sang the second part, but she always sang it from a microphone backstage, never in front of the audience. I was shy; she was worse. I was in the spotlight singing the song one night and it apparently really impressed one particular customer. The owner of the club let me know the next day that they catered to the mob-famous Vecchetti brothers and that one of them had come in, heard me sing "Tennessee Waltz," and said, "Tell me about this girl singer." I shuddered thinking about it.

"What did you say to him?" I was almost afraid to ask.

The owner chuckled. "Oh," he said. "I told him, she's spoken for. She's engaged to her manager."

Thankfully, that was the last reaction I got like that. Everyone else merely applauded when I sang "Tennessee Waltz." And I learned a valuable lesson: Let the wolves think you're married.

I've thought over the years about why everyone likes that song so much. I was brought up on Country music in Oklahoma. Country music was simple, and everybody could sing along. Maybe that was part of the song's appeal. Some of the other songs on the radio, even then, were not that simple. Plus, I think the timing had a lot to do with it. It was about five years after World War II and people wanted a peaceful time, and the soothing "Tennessee Waltz" came along at just the right moment. It's amazing how ballads of longing and loss somehow leave people feeling better about the world and are so beloved. As a singer, it makes you feel like, somehow, you were there for people when they needed you.

It was popular literally all over the world. For some reason, the communist Chinese government banned the song, so in 1951 we heard that copies of the record were selling for $75 each on the black market in China! Even my brother Charlie, stationed in Korea, was affected. The North Korean Communists would do propaganda radio broadcasts to American GIs like the Japanese had with Tokyo Rose. Quoting the lyrics of "the Waltz" about losing your sweetheart to a friend, they would try to convince American soldiers that their sweethearts were cheating on them back home in the States. Communists would tell any lie to try to win. I was told about this when I played for our troops later, and I just laughed about it like they did.

In March 1951, I took two weeks off from it all and went and sang at my sister Peggy's wedding in Tulsa. As I watched the ceremony, I thought of how lucky I was. There was nothing more valuable than spending time with my family and watching my sister marry a wonderful man.

A couple months later, I paid my first visit to Tennessee to play the Loew's State Theater in Memphis. Governor Gordon Browning met the plane I came in on and announced to the press that he would make an appearance with me at the theater on one of the days that I played there. I had visions of so many people turning out for the ceremony that they'd have to turn folks away, but that didn't happen. The Loew's was a big theater like the Paramount, and the whole time I was there, I don't think that theater was packed once. It was disappointing to me, but remembering Maurice Chevalier at Ciro's, I went out and put on the best concerts I could. We had a little ceremony with the governor, and he came on stage and presented an award to me for helping Tennessee tourism.

Later in her career, Tennessee would honor Patti Page by making "Tennessee Waltz" one of the state's official songs. That put her in a small club of recording artists who had their hit songs made official state songs: Hoagy Carmichael, for Georgia, and Jimmie Davis, for Louisiana.

Since its release in 1950, Page's recording of "Tennessee Waltz" has sold over 10 million copies, making it the #1 record by any female recording artist. In today's recording industry parlance, that's "diamond." Overall, her recording of "Tennessee Waltz" ranks #3 in all-time sales, after Elton John's "Candle in the Wind" for Princess Diana at #1 and Bing Crosby's "White Christmas" at #2.

The success of "Tennessee Waltz" was an immediate turning point in Patti's career. Before the hit, she made an estimated $250,000 a year, but when she signed a new contract with Mercury in mid-1951, she was guaranteed to earn double that amount, $500,000 a year. Additionally, she would receive 5 percent of the profits from "Tennessee Waltz." While she had received $750 for a TV appearance before the song became a hit, she was offered around $3,500 per show afterwards.

In 1951, she beat Doris Day for the title of favorite girl singer in America in influential radio personality Martin Block's poll of about 56,000 people. In 1950, before the release of "Tennessee Waltz," she had failed to make it into the Top 20.

Patti's career had swiftly gained momentum. Her next song, "Mockin' Bird Hill," would sell 250,000 copies in the first twenty days, and she would have three songs in the Top 10.

"Mockin' Bird Hill" was a hit for me because of Art Talmadge, the vice president at Mercury. I was traveling to a show at the Fontainebleau in Miami and got paged at the airport in Chicago; Art was on the phone.

"Patti!" he exclaimed. "Don't take that plane! Wait out there for me. I'm coming out with a record that I want to play for you."

I canceled the flight and waited. Art showed up with a little portable record player and played Les Paul and Mary Ford's version of "Mockin' Bird Hill" for me.

"Wow," I said. "That's great."

"What's great is that people are going into record stores and asking for your version of it. They think that's you! I think we should cover it."

"Well, okay," I said, "but Jack is already in Florida and I've never recorded without him."

"Don't worry about it," Art said. "I've already set the recording date at Bob Fien's studio. Go to New York and let's do it."

So I did. I went to New York and recorded "Mockin' Bird Hill." Art loved it, but promised me that he wouldn't release it if Jack didn't like it. I flew off the next day for Miami and played a pressing for Jack, who got on the phone to Art immediately.

"I like the song," he told Art.

"Thank God," Art said. "We've already pressed 200,000 copies of the single and shipped them!"

Some people got the mistaken notion that I considered Les Paul my rival. The fact is, Les Paul and Mary Ford ended up being good friends of mine, and I couldn't have been happier when their version of their song and mine both hit the top of the charts.

Perhaps hoping that lightning might strike again that holiday season, Mercury had Patti Page release four Christmas singles at the close of 1951, including her own version of "The Christmas Song," which had been a hit for Patti's friend Nat "King" Cole five years earlier. Mercury even reissued "Boogie Woogie Santa Claus," only this time as the B side to "Christmas Bells."

In total, Patti Page released fifteen singles in 1951, having hits with "Would I Love You," "Mockin' Bird Hill," "Detour," and "And So to Sleep Again."

The record buying public had made 1951 an incredible year for me. My career felt like a galaxy in bloom, and sometimes I just had to pinch myself. I headed into the coming year hoping to expand my horizons: Another, still-young entertainment medium was calling to me.

SIX

Hits, TV, Movies, a Doggie, and Things People Say

I still had movies on my mind, and in January 1952, I did a screen test at 20th Century Fox. The test didn't work out; Hollywood prospects continued to be frustrating. It seemed that movie people didn't think "Patti Page, the Singing Rage," as I'd been dubbed by the press, could become "Patti Page, the Movie Rage."

In February, I was back at the Paramount, and "Detour" got the audience really clapping along. One reviewer called it a "hillbilly tune," but that was just fine with me. I wonder what he would have said if he knew I did my recordings barefoot!

I was not always the headliner when I played live. Girl singers had made a lot of headway, but the guys still ruled the roost and got top billing. I had a huge amount of respect for other female singers such as Kay Starr, Georgia Gibbs, Dinah Shore, and my friend Rosemary Clooney. When any of us enjoyed success, I like to think it boosted all of us female singers. I was glad for our success because male singers like Frank Sinatra, Frankie Laine, and Vic Damone had been getting all the adulation for years. These men were all talented performers who certainly deserved the accolades, but I did think it was about time women singers started getting their fair share of notice, too. When I performed, I felt like I was doing something to get more respect for the lady singers, and that's why I always tried to smile at other women in the audience.

Even a big-name male star couldn't fill up a stadium on his own back then, though. To play at a big venue, you needed several drawcards. In "The Biggest Show of 1952," Frankie Laine and I traveled around the country on the same bill, playing only baseball stadiums. Once again, I was the opening act, but I didn't mind because Frankie was a wonderful entertainer.

Frankie Laine, whose real name was Francesco Paolo LoVecchio, was a decade and a half older than me and had one of those amazing Italian voices. Frank helped pave the way for many singers who followed, delving into Blues and Jazz and even the beginnings of Rock 'n' Roll. He was all passion with his music, and I used to love to mimic him singing his big hit, "That's My Desire." With songs like "Cry," Johnnie Ray had that painful-sounding passion, but Frank got there long before Johnnie. Like me, Frank got lucky and was discovered unexpectedly. In his case, it was at a club in Los Angeles. He was invited onstage to sing a song by Hoagy Carmichael, not knowing Hoagy was watching in the audience, which eventually led to Frank's contract with Mercury. We were both passioniate about the songs we sang. When we put on a show together, we brought out the best in each other.

I learned a lot from Frank that helped me on the road to success. In my early New York days, Jack Rael and I went to a Mercury Records party that was heavily populated by well-known girl singers from other labels. As we arrived, I looked around and saw that the other girls were all wearing fur coats, and I had on a simple cloth coat. Today's thinking about wearing fur is different, and in those days it was all the fashion. Accordingly embarrassed, I was headed for the door when Frank intercepted me and convinced me to stay. Not only that, he took me onstage, praised my singing, and I got a round of warm applause from everyone, including the girls in the furs. It was a turning point for me. If he hadn't done that, I would have gone right straight home, and it might have hurt my career. The lesson I learned that night was that your own self-image might not match what others think.

Through the spring and summer I was all over the country, singing my heart out, but it wasn't without sadness. Jack's mother died of a heart attack, and my sister, Rema, and my secretary, Dorothy, both had to have surgery in New York just as I was leaving on a thirty-two-day tour. With the Internet, every move of singing stars would become public knowledge, but in those days, you didn't have a Web site on which to announce you couldn't make a playdate because of personal situations. The show had to go on, and so I did.

At this point in her career, Patti Page was performing at least 300 days a year, in addition to going into the studio to record new singles. Crowds were so great at some of her concerts that fans had to be turned away. Page was the top income earner for her agency, General Artists Corporation.

In May of 1952, Page's impact on American culture received official recognition when "Tennessee Waltz" was placed into the Library of Congress archive.

I hadn't given up on my dream of getting on television, so I was interested when I heard that NBC wanted to do a variety show and—perhaps because there were so many men hosting shows on the air—they wanted it to have a hostess. They auditioned me, and I got the job! I would be on the air for the next season running from October to May.

The Scott Music Hall, so named because it was sponsored by the Scott Paper Company, also starred a very funny and popular comedian named Frank

Fontaine and a talented dancer named Mary Ellen Terry. It also featured the Page Five Singers and the Jack Rael Orchestra (Jack hadn't lost his musical chops). We were scheduled opposite Arthur Godfrey, whose *Arthur Godfrey's Talent Scouts* on CBS was the #1 show on television, but I wasn't worried. My thought was to simply do the best I could and let the ratings fall where they may.

I got to do very entertaining bits on the show, like tracing the musical history of entertainment with Les Paul and Mary Ford, and perform duets with legendary performers like The Mills Brothers. What would become my own theme song—"This Is My Song" by Dick Charles (whose real name was Richard Charles Krieg)—originated with that show. I always loved the lyrics:

This is my song
This is my melody
This is my song
The very soul of me
Every note is a part of the love in my heart
For you
Every word written there
Is a kind of a prayer
That you will love me, too
This is my song
This is my everything
Here is my heart
The song I sing
And I know if you'll stay
When the words and music are through
I'll sing my song
For no one but you
© 1978, 1999 Lear Music Publishing

Doing a variety show with music and dance numbers and comedy wasn't much different than doing a show without cameras. And since shows were broadcast live and not taped at the time, I couldn't see the show later and so had no perspective on what I'd done except what people told me.

My uncle, who was the police chief of Claremore, Oklahoma, had a booster antenna set up just so he could get *The Scott Music Hall* on television, but my parents weren't so easy to impress. It actually took a compliment from another musician, Guy Lombardo, to persuade my parents that I was somebody, so to speak. One night I went to dinner with Jack and some of our friends at the Roosevelt, where Lombardo had a radio show originating every night. And that night he opened it with a song dedicated to me. When my mother and father heard about it, they were very impressed that I'd been honored on the radio by Guy Lombardo, the man most people listened to every New Year's Eve as his band played "Auld Lang Syne" on airwaves across the land, the equivalent in those days of the ball dropping in Times Square on television. Naturally, even though I talked to my mother every week on the phone, I didn't hear from her personally that they were impressed. It came to me roundabout, from a friend. Another time, when I called my mother to tell her I was in the latest edition of *Life* magazine and she should buy it, she replied, still as practical as ever, "But why do I need another picture of you?"

The Scott Music Hall first aired on October 8, 1952, on NBC. Each episode was a half-hour long, and it appeared on alternate Wednesdays, for almost a year.

For the second consecutive year, in 1952 Patti Page was voted the top recording artist by *Cashbox* magazine and was presented with that award live on her show. The show ran through the end of the 1953 spring season.

She continued with a hectic recording schedule and released "I Went to Your Wedding," which would eventually sell 2 million records. A fact that might be of interest to fans of the song is that Patti herself was no stranger to attending the weddings of other family members and would be an aunt for the twentieth time before the year was out.

In November 1952, I was honored to be invited to sing for President Truman at the National Press Club. After the concert, the president came backstage. I wasn't sure what to say to him, but he beat me to the punch.

"Well, Miss Page, I enjoyed the concert very much," said the leader of the Free World. "I just have one suggestion."

"Why thank you, Mr. President," I said, wondering what was coming next. President Truman had sent a scathing letter to a music critic who panned a piano performance by his daughter, Margaret. Was he going to propose Margaret as my opening act? "What is your suggestion?"

"Well..." He chuckled a little. "That 'Tennessee Waltz' is pretty good, but I was wondering why you didn't record 'The Missouri Waltz' instead!"

"Mr. President," I replied, "that's the second time I've been asked for another waltz. When I was playing the Capitol Theater in Washington, D.C., Senator Kerr from my home state of Oklahoma had his office call me backstage and ask why I hadn't recorded 'The Oklahoma Waltz.' But since you outrank him and asked me in person, you just got in line ahead of him."

I could see Jack cringe over to the side, wondering if we'd hear about this later. I wasn't worried; I figured President Truman would just laugh and forget about it, and sure enough he did. The closest I ever got to recording another waltz was "Changing Partners" in 1953, which had a line that began "We were waltzing together..."

I was now able to do things I could never have dreamed of while in high school. That summer, I went home to Tulsa and bought my father a new car.

I was also able to buy my parents a new home. I knew they wanted to stay in Tulsa, so I told them to pick out a place. They bypassed the most expensive real estate in town and opted for a new housing development instead. I suggested they get two lots and had a house built for them with a little more room. And it was a *lot* more room than the free section house provided by the railroad!

Still, you can't get respect from some people, particularly in your hometown. My mother's grounded, down-to-earth attitude to my success was one thing; antagonism was another. One man in Tulsa, who will remain nameless, said to a friend, who passed it on to me: "Took more than sangin' to buy that house." Who was it who said you couldn't please everybody all the time? I tried to laugh it off, but the comment stung.

On August 1, 1953, Patti Page appeared at the vast Soldier Field stadium in Chicago as part of *Downbeat's Star Night*. By that time she had a new hit to sing to the massive audience, "How Much is that Doggie in the Window?" Though not as emotionally impactful as "Tennessee Waltz," it is one of the songs most closely associated with the singer, appealing as it does to listeners of all ages.

I went in to do a children's album for Playcraft titled *Arfie, the Doggie in the Window*. It was only after we did the recording that Mercury said "How Much Is That Doggie in the Window?" should go out as a single. The single was released immediately and the children's album was brought out later.

Another singer, Mindy Carson, had turned down the opportunity to record this cute little tune about a girl who wants to buy a doggie from a pet shop window to keep her lonely boyfriend company when she's gone.

I must take a trip to California
And leave my poor sweetheart alone

If he has a dog, he won't be lonesome
And the doggie will have a good home
Words and Music by Bob Merrill

I did some other "Arfie" songs that no one remembers anymore like "Arfie Catches an Echo" and "Arfie Goes to School." But no one remembers that doggie's name was Arfie, either! What everyone who comes to my concerts does remember is that the dog barks on the song because they join in every time!

When we recorded "Doggie in the Window" we didn't consciously think about putting in the barks for comic effect. To a musician, it was natural to make a sound of some kind at that place because it was right on the beat, so the violin player, Max Ceppos, chimed in with the barks. When we listened to it being played back, Joe Carlton, the A & R man, said, "Oh, that sounds great. Let's keep that in there." Why not? It was a really nice dog. Then Joe Reisman, the arranger and bass clarinet player, who had been in Jimmy Joy's band, put in a "small dog" going "yip yip," which made it even cuter.

The song was an immediate hit with both kids and adults. And it got me a little more notice with the men in my audience. They'd not only bark, they'd do wolf calls when I sang "Doggie in the Window." The wacky comedy musician Spike Jones had recently parodied "I Went to Your Wedding." Next the Country comedians Homer and Jethro recorded "How Much is that Hounddog in the Window?" which I thought was hilarious.

When I worked the Paramount Theater during this time, suddenly, I not only had kids showing up in my audiences, but they'd also bring their dogs—some on leashes, some not! Mothers would corner me and say, "Why, oh why, did you record that song!?" Their kids would make them play it endlessly!

While I was writing this book, my secretary, Claudia, told me that her little granddaughter was learning first grade math and her teacher started the class by singing "How Much is That Doggie in the Window?," counting the barks.

Claudia's granddaughter raised her hand and said, "My grandma works for that lady who sang that song!" Sometimes I still think they'll be playing that song 100 years from now.

After Patti Page sang "How Much is That Doggie in the Window?" with a dog onstage on the *The Scott Music Hall*, sales of the single passed 1 million, and it rose to #4 on the charts. It went on to become the most popular song in Europe.

Companies sold huge quantities of a wide range of "Doggie in the Window" products, such as stuffed toys and children's books and bedclothes. However, as Patti's manager at the time, Jack Rael, had not negotiated to receive a share of the profits, she saw no income from the sale of those products.

In 1953, I was asked to appear in a couple of short films, perhaps the earliest type of music video. Columbia had a movie coming out called *Indiscretion of an American Wife* about a married American woman who gets involved with another man while visiting relatives in Rome. It was produced and directed by Vittorio De Sica, with dialogue written by Truman Capote, and it starred Montgomery Clift and Jennifer Jones, who were both huge stars at the time. My short movies were shown in theaters preceding the movie, like a prologue, with the aim of bringing in more business.

They put me in a glamorous New York penthouse and filmed me singing two songs, "Autumn in Rome" and "Indiscretion," both written by Paul Weston and Sammy Cahn. Unlike other Hollywood projects, this time I didn't even have to audition because Selznick Studios contacted Jack to get me to do these songs. I was thrilled, especially when I learned that something like this had never been done for a movie. I loved doing the project—they filmed it beautifully and it was great meeting David O. Selznick, who was the executive producer of the feature film.

By now, in addition to my secretary, Dorothy, I also had a fan club president, "Gertie" Gertmann, who was on salary to handle the fan mail that came to our office on 58th Street. I really appreciated all the well wishes I received from people. A New York fan club sent me a collection of autographed photos from Hollywood stars personally wishing me a happy birthday. The members of a fan club in Formosa (the name for Taiwan at the time) sent me record-shaped cards with their pictures on them. A fellow named Mick Pardoe started a fan club for me in Birmingham, England, and was trying to organize them all over the United Kingdom. I'd even received a letter from a fan in South Africa, who called me a month later just to hear my voice on the phone.

One thing I did not let Gertie do was autograph the pictures. I also didn't use an automatic signing pen like people did in those days. No matter how many there were, I would come in and sign all the photographs and everything else because I believe fans deserve the utmost respect.

Jack considered himself an efficiency expert, so he wasn't crazy about me spending time signing autographs. This might have had something to do with how he started in show business. He was in the Army, a special sergeant charged with booking twenty acts a week into Percy Jones General Hospital in Battle Creek, Michigan during World War II. The bluster he exhibited probably had a lot to do with those military days, too, and his experience getting around the rules to keep performers happy and wooing them into traveling to cold Michigan to perform. When I was in New York to appear on a TV show, I'd find hundreds of fans waiting at the stage door and, though it didn't make Jack too happy, I would sign autographs for everyone because the fans were why I was there. I think he probably would've liked it if I had taken another way out of the building.

The people who waited for autographs were always friendly and goodhearted, so it never felt overwhelming. People in the 1950s were not as celebrity-conscious as they are today. I was able to walk down the street without there being much of a fuss. Some of the younger boy singers were mobbed a little, especially in the late-1950s, but I always thought some of those screaming events were staged at the beginning of those stars' careers, even Elvis's. I could go into restaurants, and the maître d' might know me but only rarely would anyone approach me at my table. And other than very rare incidents, such as the attack in the Toronto hotel, I didn't experience the darker side of being well-known. It was a much more cordial and thoughtful time in many ways.

Live audiences certainly showed me nothing but warmth and hospitality wherever I went. I had a very embarrassing moment while performing at Rice University in Houston before 10,000 fans. Somehow I managed to forget the words to a song onstage. Normally that would be just a little minor setback—after all, no one is perfect—but this was "The Star-Spangled Banner!" I felt terrible about it because it is a song that means everything to me. Like so many of us, whenever I hear "The Star-Spangled Banner," I can't help but get teary-eyed. Those friendly Texans forgave me, and I was very grateful.

With Pop success came attention from the media, of course, and that could be good and bad. It was a real joy if the writer I was talking to was a fellow music lover. I got a kick out of sharing my collection of Langworth transcriptions with Nat Henthoff, a reporter for *Downbeat* magazine. These were sixteen-inch glass discs that radio stations had recorded on from the mid-1930s to the early 1950s. I'd held on to some of the transcriptions where I sang standards with just a rhythm section—the kind of songs I loved to sing but didn't release as singles as they weren't all that popular then. It was a real compliment when Mr. Henthoff said my transcriptions were reminiscent of Ella Fitzgerald, who was my favorite singer at the time. Of course, I made sure I mentioned my friend Rosie Clooney as my other favorite female singer. When he asked me what I listened to at home, I told him I loved the instrumental *Jazz at the Philarmonic* albums and that my favorite song was "Roses Remind Me of You." Who knows why a song affects you. It's still one of my favorites to this day.

For another article in *Downbeat*, Leonard Feather had me put on a blindfold, then he played singles for me. I had to guess who the singers and musicians were and rate the records. I identified most of them correctly, but I later learned that one recording I didn't like at all and gave only one star to was Benny Goodman. I swear it had nothing to do with that party in Philadelphia! I got the last song right because it was Ella. Honestly, I would have given Ella ten stars for any of her recordings. It was hard for me to put into words the effect it had on me when I heard her sing. Why did I feel that way? Because she'd been given a lot of bad songs to record yet sang them with such feeling that she sent me out of this world. Though I hadn't been exposed to many other singers when I first started out, I felt that if I had, Ella Fitzgerald was the one I could have really learned something from.

Unfortunately, just as they would be today, the media was usually more interested in who I might be dating or how much weight I'd put on than my favorite musicians. They were interested in things like what kind of a TV I had in my apartment. Or they would allege I was having an affair with a Jazz musician. Then a writer would somehow find it controversial that I didn't wear glasses on TV yet didn't want to wear contacts. (Glasses caused a glare in the lights and contacts irritated my eyes, so I'd memorize the scripts.) Every detail of my life seemed to be under the microscope.

Oh, I know—what did I expect? But having led a pretty tranquil life back in Oklahoma and been on the road touring most of year, it was hard to get perspective on how the public saw me versus how I felt inside. Some people who rise quickly to the top lose themselves in all the melee of fame. Perhaps it was maintaining a small circle of friends that helped me stay sane.

Patti Page was renowned in the entertainment industry for her quiet, hard-working lifestyle and for spending any spare time with a small circle of friends and her family rather than in the more common celebrity haunts of nightclubs and parties. When a popular magazine had an expert analzye Page's longhand and they concluded that she had a well-concentrated mind, shyness, and devotion to a few people, it would have come as no surprise to those who knew her best

One thing I never spent much time talking to journalists about was my love life. My attitude was to just let them figure it out if they wanted to try, and in 1954 they were trying every week.

Famous newspaper columnist Dorothy Kilgallen had me scheduled to marry motion picture executive Art Fellows while Walter Winchell said I'd eloped with someone else. I was also linked in print with popular comedian Professor Backwards. (His real name was James Edmonson, Sr., but I didn't date him under either name.) Then there was songwriter Ned Washington, who was Country star Roy Acuff's brother. (I guess the columnists wanted me with a musician). When I went out with New York Yankees slugger Eddie Robinson, they made a big deal about the fact he was from Paris, Texas, in the northeast part of the Lone Star State, not far from my native Oklahoma. I suppose people subconsciously thought that the next step for the "Oklahoma Cinderella," as the press had dubbed me, was the prince and the castle, so to speak. At least I saw a lot of great Yankees games up close. (Later, I got even closer to the Yankees via my drummer, Stanley Kaye, who was a good friend of Yankee owner George Steinbrenner. Stanley was a Yankee nut and seemed to know everyone in the organization.)

There was persistent media speculation about Patti Page's private life. In a *TV Radio-Mirror* story in 1954, the writer Macy Edwards led off with a discussion of how both "Tennessee Waltz" and "I Went to Your Wedding" were banned in Red China, then argued that Page's own life seemed "to bear out the Red propaganda," referring to Chinese communist claims that in the United States "women must resort to all sorts of devices to snare a husband." The accompanying picture was of Patti relaxing with Jack Rael on her boat, a thirty-four-foot cabin cruiser called *The Rage*.

Edwards continued: "She is beautiful, talented, famous—but still unmarried. At twenty-six, there is not even a 'sweetheart' for any girl friends to steal.'"

Macy Edwards's story in the *TV Radio-Mirror* might have seemed harsh, but some parts of it did give me a chuckle, like the bit about the Cadillac I drove that was a gift from Mercury Records. In fact, I didn't even know how to drive.

What Macy did get correct, though, was that I wanted five babies. "I've always wanted to be married," I said. "The right man just hasn't come along yet."

It was always difficult trying to have a career and a boyfriend because I was on the road so much. For a time I did have a beau, Joe Guercio, who was on the road with me; he was the first piano player/conductor I had. He quit working with me because I went on TV and wasn't on the road as much, and we didn't see much of each other anymore. I resigned myself to that since Joe and I used to argue a lot anyway. After we stopped working together, though, Joe called me up one night and said, "I found out I missed you." How could a girl reject a line like that from a man she admired? We dated about a year, and he even took me up to Buffalo to meet his family, but ultimately nothing came of it. I suppose neither of us were the marrying kind at that time—at least to each other. We remained good friends through the years, and Joe went on to run Elvis Presley's band. Today he's playing with a projected Elvis onscreen and all the musicians who backed up the King in a great posthumous stage show.

Other than with Joe, I truly had nothing serious going on in the relationship department, which might sound sad. However, I did have plenty of love, and shared plenty of love, but it was through my music.

It bothered me that the superficial items got all the press. Why was it so interesting who I was dating or that I was noticeably slimmer when I opened at Chubby's in Philadelphia? (You have to laugh at that irony!) Even Jack couldn't keep from falling into the Patti speculation trap. He told one reporter that I'd probably not make it into the movies because I liked to eat too much!

While the media were mostly focusing on the details of her private life, Patti's list of professional accomplishments was growing ever longer. She became the first woman to be awarded the prestigious Interfaith Award in Baltimore, Maryland. She continued to record and release hit singles, including "Cross Over the Bridge," and also branched out to record albums, such as *Patti Sings the Duke*, an album of songs by Duke Ellington. The musical genius himself had high compliments for her renditions of his songs.

Of all the tour dates I played around this time, the ones that made me proudest were those I did for troops at Army bases and hospitals in Hawaii. Because Jack had been in the Army, he'd sometimes put aside his love of making money and book me in places like Tripler Army Hospital in Honolulu. Jack and I walked many a military hospital corridor, hoping to bring a bit of comfort to wounded troops. There's nothing like giving back to people who are willing to give everything for the country we love.

Neither he nor I knew it then, but Patti Page was about to undergo a whole lot of change. My stage shows would be refined in ways I would never have thought. Television would become a prominent part of my career. And I would meet a man whose name would appear next to my mine in a great many columns and articles, a fellow who would finally take the "Oklahoma Cinderella" from the ball to the altar.

SEVEN

Multiple Spotlights and a Man on Two Coasts

I n January 1955, I began shooting some fifteen-minute musical shows, with five songs in each, which Jack decided to call *Songalongs*. I would do three numbers with the Jack Rael Orchestra, and the Page Five Singers would do one number. As for the fifth song, when we were shooting, we would leave a gap until the last minute, so that if there was a big hit song that week, I could cover it on the show. Or we'd bring on a special guest.

Frankly, I wish they still made fifteen-minute shows like that. In retrospect, it was sort of a precursor to MTV. It was great fun, although demanding—we filmed the show in a studio in New York, shooting two episodes in a day.

Jack Rael produced Patti Page's *Songalongs* with Lee Cooley, who was the producer of a long-running TV show hosted by Perry Como. Also on board was Joseph Santley as producer-director. He had worked on shows such as the *All-Star Revue* and a TV series by Mickey Rooney. Most famously, he had created Jimmy Durante's signature ending to his show—Durante walking away into fading spotlights, and saying, "Good night, Mrs. Calabash, wherever you are," which brought a tear to some viewers' eyes.

In a sponsorship deal that would be unimaginable today, the show was backed by Chesterfield cigarettes, who also sponsored Perry Como. *Songalongs* was produced in association with Screen Gems Studios and aired on CBS, which was owned by Screen Gems. In total, 104 episodes were filmed, and screened twice weekly for fifty-two weeks. It was a $1 million deal for Page and her manager, and it was sold in syndication to 175 cities by Rael and General Artists Corporation. It was eventually also screened in Australia, Canada, and England.

Rael insisted that the shows be recorded using the new Perspecta sound system, which was becoming popular in Hollywood. Standard TV practice at the time was to record shows using black-and-white kinescope equipment, which meant filming the live footage off a video screen. For *Songalongs*, though, the live studio performances were shot directly on film, by Hollywood professionals. It was a wise move, as unlike many kinescope recordings of the time, the *Songalongs* look and sound as good today as they did when they were made. In recent years, they have been aired on a cable network and were part of a DVD collection released by VIEW Video.

About the time we began filming *Songalongs*, I began to feel that something was missing from my stage shows and that I could be giving the audience more. I became certain of it when I went to see Betty Hutton's show at the Palace Theater in New York.

Betty had become a big movie star after the release of *The Miracle of Morgan's Creek* in 1944. After starring in *Incendiary Blonde* the next year, she was Paramount Studios' #1 female box office star. My publicity agent, Frances Kaye, wanted to make sure I was seen attending the Betty Hutton show at the Palace and had a limousine pick me up so that I'd make a big splash arriving. Me being me, however, I had the limousine driver drop me off a block away so that I wouldn't pull up in front of the theater where all the newspaper people and cameras were. Some of them managed to catch me going in, anyway, and some of them took pictures, but there wasn't the big entrance Frances had tried to arrange. I tried to explain how nervous I'd felt about running the gauntlet, but still, she was absolutely livid with me!

Betty Hutton's show was fantastic and the choreography was spectacular. I wanted to meet whoever had staged the show. I spoke with Jack and one of my agents at General Artists Corporation. They disagreed with me that I needed something extra in my show, but to humor me they set up a meeting with Betty Hutton's choreographer who I soon learned was her ex–husband, Charlie O'Curran.

I had an engagement coming up in about two weeks' time at the Fontainebleau in Miami, and we brought Charlie in during rehearsals to make some changes to the show. Charlie added a very nice touch, the spinning mirrored ball overhead that I've used all these years when I do "Tennessee Waltz," which gives the impression of a dance hall. He advised me on what songs I should do, what I should talk about in between songs, how I should move my hands, things like that, so that I wasn't just standing straight up and singing. I'd always used hand movements since I started singing, but Charlie got me to exaggerate them theatrically. I wouldn't truly realize how much I had changed them until I opened in Miami.

It was the same way when I realized I was dating him. At first, I didn't even know that he was trying to get me to go out with him. All I knew was that he was a man about town with a great line of patter. Like some of those old romantic comedies you see, at first we had a bit of animosity between us because I thought it was awful that Charlie had been married twice. Before Betty Hutton, he'd been married to another Betty who was now the drummer Buddy Rich's wife.

But that's how I met Charlie, just me and him and a rehearsal pianist he brought along to a little studio that I hired. Charlie was a dark-haired Irish-American from Atlantic City, New Jersey. He was lithe, suave, and had a smooth manner that I suppose came from decades of dancing. Every time we rehearsed, he would come in and toss a new matchbook on the piano from the El Morroco, the Stork Club, 21, or any other of the hottest clubs in town. I thought, oh wow, this must be someone. And that's probably exactly what he was trying to get me to think.

It didn't take me long to see that Charlie was a very talented man. To the day he died, I felt that way. There was a part of me that he reached that had never been brought out by anyone else. The more we met and talked about what I would like in my act, the more we were attracted to each other. He began telling me about his upbringing, from the time he'd danced for pennies on the boardwalk in Atlantic City to doing dance marathons with his friend Nick Castle to his work in the movies. We laughed and shared ideas, and soon he asked me out.

"Of course not," I said.

"Why?" he asked. "Is it being seen with a divorced man?"

"I'm not used to clubs like that," I stammered. "The Copacabana, 21... wherever it is you go."

"Well," he said, smiling, "do you ever eat dinner?"

So Charlie took me to a restaurant one night. We were kind of feeling each other out, vying for each other's time, and we were very attracted to each other.

What was I doing thinking of romance? I had a lot going on. And I knew how it would go; if I got too tight with a man, Jack would feel a little threatened. Jack and I had a good relationship, but he protected his meal ticket at all times.

Charlie kissed me for the first time after one of my shows at the Fontainebleau. Later that evening, he was sitting outside my hotel room door and his explanation when I found him there was that he just wanted to be near me. He had all the right moves, all the right things to say, and I was smitten.

The introduction of Charlie O'Curran into Patti's world had a profound impact not only on her private life. The subtle changes he brought to her stage shows received high praise from the critics and ushered in a new phase in Patti's career. *Variety* reviewed one of her performances at the Fontainebleau Hotel, Miami, and concluded: "Charles O'Curran, stager, can take a bow from the change that takes Miss Page from the at-mike straight-singing recording click, and transforms her into a fully rounded performer...This is a new Miss Page, one who has been restaged, restyled carefully and intelligently."

Her work in the studio also continued to bear fruit, and she had her 22nd hit single, "You Too Can Be a Dreamer."

After Charlie entered my life, it wasn't long before I started seeing comments in print like "She's svelte and elegant now." One writer that year said I was "slenderelegant." Was it love that made me look better? Whatever it was, I welcomed the comments. I shared my diet with one of the publications that always wanted to know about my weight:

Breakfast: ½ grapefruit or 1 glass unsweetened grape juice; 2 eggs, any style (no butter); Melba Toast; black coffee (no sugar).

Lunch: Green salad or cottage cheese salad or fruit salad (no dressing); Melba Toast, black coffee (no sugar).

Dinner: Unlimited lean protein dish, broiled or boiled (no condiments or as little as possible); stewed tomatoes; salad (no dressing); stewed or fresh fruit; black coffee (no sugar).

It might not match up with nutritional knowledge today, but with people apparently watching my every bite, I'd try whatever I thought would work in 1955.

My home base was New York but Charlie lived in Hollywood because he was working on films at Paramount Studios. Whenever he came into town he would call me and we'd go to 21 or someplace like that. I was impressed that everybody knew him.

In February, I was guest hostess of *The Perry Como Show* for three weeks. It suited me to stay off the road for almost a month. I was able to spend some time with Charlie, and when a writer asked if I had any "special heart interest" I said yes. I figured that would make more interesting reading than another article about how much I liked to clean my closets. (I really did, but it got old being asked about it).

In March 1955, the Chinese communists finally lifted the ban on "Tennessee Waltz," allowing it to be played in what was then the world's most populous nation.

It was now becoming apparent that Patti Page was one of the hardest-working performers in the entertainment industry. One reporter calculated that in nine years she had sung a total of 61,000 songs. Another noted that fifty of her records had sold no less than 300,000 copies each. In July 1955 came a rare sign that she might be pushing herself a little too hard, as she was admitted to hospital with a case of strep throat. It didn't keep her down long; soon after she was released, she threw herself into publicity appearances for a Mercury promotion in *Hit Parader* magazine for her song "Too Young to Go Steady," called "Patti Page's 'Too Young to Go Steady' contest."

Yet Hollywood continued to elude her. In August, she auditioned for the lead in the movie *South Pacific*, which had been a smash for Mary Martin on Broadway. She rehearsed the hit song "I'm Gonna Wash That Man Right Outta My Hair" and even lost fifteen pounds especially for the part but was not successful.

I liked getting out to Los Angeles to see Charlie when I could, and on occasion I'd squeeze in appearances on shows with people I liked, such as *Steve Allen in Movieland*. The press was beginning to follow Charlie's and my every move, speculating on our relationship. Once when I flew out to see Charlie, we were spotted together at the Luau Club in Hollywood, and soon it was in Earl Wilson's column that Charlie and I were serious. Army Archerd made a mention in *Variety* that Charlie and I were an item later that month in New York City. When Charlie was reportedly spotted out for the evening with singer Roberta Linn at the Mocambo nightclub in Los Angeles, "Where's Patti?" was the headline. A month later, someone reported that he was seen out with dancer Lois Ray and others. Saving face for me, Jack told a reporter that he was "98 percent sure" Charlie and I would marry. And when Charlie was with me at a venue in Canada, Louella Parsons, one of the two most influential columnists on the West Coast and a friend of Charlie's, made sure to report it. Another reporter noted that Charlie visited me when I played Las Vegas in October. Walter Winchell seemed to love mentioning Charlie and me: Charlie visting from the coast, our being seen together in Palm Springs, and our supposed "solid wedding plans."

Charlie might have been in Betty Hutton's shadow when he was with her, but as my boyfriend he couldn't stay in the background and that was fine with him. I soon realized that Charlie liked socializing and being in the spotlight much more so than me.

Then on Thanksgiving, Charlie showed up at my apartment on Central Park South and brought along a live turkey!

"I brought this all the way from California for you," he said with a big smile, "because I just had to come and see you."

I don't know if he actually got it when he got to New York or if he brought it all the way from California as he said, but I fell for it. I don't remember what happened with the turkey, but Charlie got to spend the weekend.

The 1950s were a time of exciting advancements in television that we now take for granted. I was in awe of Edward R. Murrow, who had made a name for himself as a correspondent in World War II. (The movie *Good Night, and Good Luck*, starring my friend Rosie Clooney's nephew George, was about how Murrow took on Joseph McCarthy in the early 1950s.) So I was honored—and a little overawed—when in February 1956, I got to appear on his celebrity interview TV show *Person to Person*. What was innovative about the interview was that Murrow was in his TV studio, posing questions to two interviewees in their own places, thanks to the new coast-to-coast coaxial cable. I was living at 220 Central Park South. I'll never forget how Murrow's crew disrupted that whole brand-new lovely building to come in and set up for the interview. They had to get permission from every tenant, but nobody was unhappy that such a popular show was being filmed in their apartment building. The show was on live, and I felt like a fan and a celebrity at the same time.

In the middle of March, I recorded *Manhattan Towers*, an album of eleven songs by the great songwriter Gordon Jenkins. It was a musical tribute to Manhattan Island with a thread of romance running through. I did it in an attempt to get the lead in a TV show of the same name, but that role went to someone else: Helen O'Connell.

When I wasn't recording or touring I could keep myself amused with the "Patti and Charlie when?" press speculation. Earl Wilson swore we were going on a honeymoon in Italy. Then we were supposed to get married on Labor Day. Mike Connolly, the "Rambling Reporter" columnist for *The Hollywood Reporter*, said Charlie and I had called off our engagement, and yet another said that

Frank Sinatra and I were a "coosome twosome" when we were both playing in Las Vegas. Rumors like that were as fake as the promotion I did for Oldsmobile about the car they gave me to drive on personal appearances. It sure looked good, but I still hadn't learned to drive!

In May, I sang for President Eisenhower at the White House Correspondent's Dinner. James Cagney was also part of the show. I wondered if, like President Truman, the man affectionately known as "Ike" would have a musical request. After my performance, I got to my room and the phone rang. It was a man from the Secret Service. *Oh boy*, I wondered, *was the president on the way?*

"Hello, Miss Page," said the Secret Service man. "I know you would probably like to get the president's autograph, correct?"

"What?" I remembered mentioning something like that to Jack on the way in. Wow, had they overheard me?

"Well, would you please not ask him tonight?"

"Umm, sure, I guess so," I said, and I hung up.

Well, I suppose they had everything wired for anything. They were keeping tabs on anybody that was going to be around the president that night. I was amazed. I never asked him for an autograph but then, he didn't ask me for mine, either.

That summer I was asked to host a summer replacement show for Perry Como while he took a well-deserved break. Perry received an Emmy award for his show in 1956, and nobody could make entertainment seem as effortless and cool as Perry. Few critics believed that a mere girl like me could "carry" a show, but I didn't pay much attention to them.

Called *The Patti Page Show*, it was broadcast live Monday, Wednesday, and Friday and was sponsored by Oldsmobile. My schedule was a bit crazy. By 6:30 in the morning I was hailing a cab to 20th Century-Fox Studios in New York City. I'd be busy until 10:30 getting ready for the show, and then at about 10:30, I'd rehearse a number with the Page Five Singers. After that, more often than not, I'd do an interview with a writer. I might get a few minutes for lunch and do more work on the show until mid-afternoon, when we'd do more numbers. By 6:00 p.m. we'd wrap the show and then I'd be done with my day like a normal person, right? Not really. Usually I'd be off to the studio to do some recording, then have a snack afterward with my people to talk about record promotions. And then, in bed by midnight, and up at 5:30 the next morning to start again.

After her stint as Perry Como's replacement on TV, Patti Page played live dates in Atlantic City, then flew to California for a short vacation with Charlie O'Curran. Next, she performed in the twenty-seventh annual Chicagoland Music Festival at Soldier Field, where a crowd of 80,000 people gathered for a two-hour show also featuring the leading tenor of the Metropolitan Opera, Richard Tucker, and Broadway musical geniuses Richard Rogers and Oscar Hammerstein. When asked by a reporter for the *Chicago Tribune* what she attributed her success to, she replied, "The right voice, the right song, the right manager, the right arrangement, the right conductor, the right recording engineer, the right company, the right press agent, plus about 98 percent luck!"

She was continuing to have lucky breaks that would secure her place in television. At the end of August, she was brought in as a substitute host for Ed Sullivan. She would be the only female host Ed Sullivan had on his long-running show and would make a total of seventeen appearances as a guest on his show.

Ed Sullivan wasn't a performer, and with his poker face, he was impossible to read. You'd hear from someone else that he liked you, and the only reason you'd hear was because Ed wanted you on the show. He didn't care if you were a hit or not; if he liked you, you were on. I remember one night, before I sang, I introduced the song "Father, Father" as being derived from the Jewish song "Aily, Aily." I sang, and it created a very somber and lovely atmosphere in the theater. After I had finished, I was standing in the wings as Ed marched out onto the stage and said, "In all my years of doing this show I don't believe I have ever experienced something like this." *Wow,* I thought, *what a compliment.* And then he said the name of a monkey act that was on next. That was what he'd never experienced before! I thought I would die. Everybody's face was aghast; they didn't believe it either. But Ed really loved those circus acts!

In August 1956, Charlie was suffering from a respiratory ailment that was caused by a car accident. It made me wonder about the wisdom of a bi-coastal relationship. As much as I was used to traveling, I began thinking about changing the situation.

On one of my trips to Los Angeles around this time, I auditioned for the lead role of Helen Morgan, a popular singer of the 1920s and 1930s, in the MGM biopic *Why Was I Born?* It was always nervewracking going up for a Hollywood part, but I got a little shot of confidence when Louella Parsons wrote that she thought I could sing Helen's famous song "My Bill" just like Helen used to sing it and that I was a "fine little actress." I wore a black wig for the audition with director Michael Curtiz, tried to keep Louella's words in my mind, and tried to forget that the very popular actress Jennifer Jones was also up for the part.

Well, I didn't get it. Some people in the press said it was because I was considered too heavy to play Morgan. My public relations lady countered with a story that I had turned it down because MGM had a "no TV" clause in their film contracts. The truth was, I didn't turn down the part because they didn't offer it to me. Helen Morgan was played by Ann Blyth.

Supposedly, writer/producer/actor Jack Webb of the hit TV show *Dragnet* fame saw my Helen Morgan tests and wanted me for his leading lady in a movie he was doing called *The Drill Instructor,* but you won't see my name in the credits of that one, either. Hollywood continued to be a disappointment for me.

After a while, the columnists quit speculating on the status of my relationship with Charlie until one of them, George Clarke, finally declared that "a source as close to the horse's mouth as a bucket of cats" had informed him that Patti Page would never marry Charlie O'Curran. Clarke said we'd continue to be close friends and that we had a relationship built on mutual respect and esteem, but marriage was out of the question.

Charlie and I didn't ignore the newspapers and the rumors. How could you? As the Christmas season approached, I think we finally got tired of it all. We were staying during the Christmas holidays with our friends Nick and Millie Castle at their home in Palm Springs, and one day we just decided to go to Las Vegas and get married. We flew to Vegas in the private plane owned by Charlie's friend, Ray Ryan, the owner of the El Mirador Hotel in Palm Springs. With Ray and his wife pitching in, the whole event was a whirlwind. My family members came, friends arrived from Chicago, there were dozens of Charlie's friends, and my publicity agent, Frances, came out from New York and handled the promotion for it.

Promotion for a wedding? Well, why not? People had been writing about the possibility for a long time. Why not give them the truth to put in the papers?

On December 28, 1956, Charlie and I married at the Las Vegas home of Wilbur Clarke, the owner of the Desert Inn. It hadn't looked like it was going to happen that day, though, because after we went to Las Vegas City Hall and took a test and bought a marriage license, Charlie was put in jail! I was frantically trying to get him out and couldn't understand the charges. Finally, Louella Parsons "sprung" Charlie and we learned the whole thing was a big gag put on by Charlie's pal, Ray. Much later in the day, the ceremony was conducted by Las Vegas District Judge A.J. Henderson. Charlie was forty-two and I was twenty-nine. He wore a braided evening suit, and I wore a beautiful peaches-and-cream outfit. Although some press reports erroneously said it was my first marriage, I knew better than to wear white. It was Charlie's third marriage. Since he was Catholic, I suppose that should have told me something, but you miss a few things when you're in love. After a reception, we flew back to Palm Springs on Ray's plane and checked into the El Mirador Hotel.

The big festivities started the next day at the hotel. I remember being overwhelmed by all of the famous people that were there, people who Charlie knew. Even though I was used to meeting the most famous people in the music business, Hollywood had a fantasy appeal to me, and the circles Charlie came from still seemed like something out of my realm. I felt like a princess who had finally moved into the castle. We stayed there through New Year's Eve. What a way to bring in the New Year!

It was a short honeymoon that ended on January 4, 1957. Charlie was starting work on the Elvis Presley movie *Loving You* at Paramount on January 7, staging the dance numbers. I had to go back to New York to appear on the Perry Como Show on January 12. That's show business. There was no big announcement on the show that I was now Mrs. Charlie O'Curran. In fact, no one mentioned it until I somehow managed to slip "O'Curran" into a line, and Perry commented on it with a smile.

What I wanted from my marriage was to have my husband close by my side and five children—even a couple of sets of twins. I wanted an established home that we could decorate. And most of all, I wanted confidence in my husband, along with his confidence in me. Life wasn't much use for a woman without the man she loves, I believed.

Finally, the "Oklahoma Cinderella" had married her prince. What she hadn't counted on, in earlier days when she'd dreamt of such things, was having a prince who lived on one side of the country while she lived on the other.

And in 1957, I would get even busier, making maintaining a marriage even harder. Still, I knew there had to be a way to make it work.

EIGHT

Jack, Charlie, and Changes

I celebrated my ten-year anniversary with Jack Rael as my manager on October 20, 1956. We had a good working relationship, and I was grateful for all that he had done to help me have a singing career. But of course, like most things in life, it wasn't all perfect.

Jack and I had a unique arrangement—I gave him 50 percent of all my earnings. As far as I knew, only Kate Smith with Ted Collins and Elvis Presley with Colonel Parker had similar 50/50 management deals. Most managers took 15 percent or 20 percent. I had no regrets about my deal with Jack. The fact is, he never asked for the 50 percent. I offered him that myself because it seemed fair. He was there in the beginning, picking out songs, telling me what to do, and I never questioned his decisions.

He'd spent his own money to help me when I started out in Chicago, and when we moved to New York he also loaned me money to get by. My first year in Chicago I never made more than $200 a week. Jack's first contract with me gave him anything I made over $500 a week, so his bank account went down to $100 at one point. Taking me to his hometown of Milwaukee, he booked me in the Towne Room but that paid only $70 a week. My first twelve records for Mercury didn't do much. It was only after "Confess," in 1948, that my salary went up to $500 a week, and Jack started earning money from being my manager. Then he got me my first *Downbeat* cover, but it was only after "With My Eyes Wide Open, I'm Dreaming" the next year that my salary went up to $1,000 a week. Given the lean early days we had, and that Jack toughed it out long enough to make things happen to launch my career, it seemed to make sense that I would split everything with him.

I had never been a good money manager because I'd never really had any. So I relied on Jack. When the big money started coming in, I didn't know that we weren't handling it right, that we weren't investing like we should. We had an occasion to buy the franchise for McDonalds for all the boroughs of New York other than Manhattan, and we didn't take it. The singing team of Steve Lawrence and Eydie Gorme told us about a building for sale on 59th Street, park side, Central Park South. We could have bought it for $100,000, but Jack did not believe it was the right thing to do. It might seem hard to believe now that we didn't see the potential there, but Jack was not a gambler. He just didn't believe in putting something down in hopes of a greater return, not even in Manhattan real estate. He didn't want money to be tied up.

I regret I didn't pay more attention to finances for other reasons, too. When my records were hitting the top of the charts, my income was in the highest tax bracket. Unless you really knew what you were doing, or had someone who knew the ropes in regard to investments and taxes, you didn't get to keep much of what you earned. I don't think I got the tax breaks I should have. Later, I would also discover that there were some discrepancies in our finances that Jack didn't catch that he should have caught as a manager. That's all 20/20 hindsight, though. I was not a financial genius, and neither was Jack.

I was the first to acknowledge the role Jack had played in building my career, but I have to admit there were times when it bothered me that he'd toot his own horn about it. I didn't have a problem with it if he publicized one of the many things he had genuinely done to help me in my career, but sometimes things that just weren't true ended up in the papers and became accepted fact. For instance, reporters seemed to continually give Jack credit for the echo chamber of "Confess" and the canine yips in "Doggie in the Window."

He also took credit for finding all my songs, but it was more collaborative than that, with an A & R guy at Mercury and myself involved in picking the songs, too. One or two days a week in our office in the Brill Building in New York, song pluggers would come in and play songs for Jack. Sammy Cahn used to demonstrate his tunes, as did Jimmy McHugh, Mack Gordon, and other great songwriters. Jack had one or two days by himself with songwriters in our office in New York and then if he liked something, he would bring it to me to hear. The same would happen with the A & R man at Mercury.

Jack wasn't the only one looking for publicity; most of the people around me inevitably made their way into the press. *Downbeat* published an article that had them all arguing over who made me a star, with Jack claiming it was only because he got Art Talmadge to sign me at Mercury that I made it, and Frances Kaye claiming publicity did it for me, etc. The amusing part about it was that the article was "by Patti Page" but most of those pieces were Frances Kaye's concoctions. Though my press agent wrote most of the articles, the ideas for them came from me.

I vividly remember that Jack once told a reporter, "Let's face it, without her I'm a bum." On one level it was just a silly overstatement, kind of funny, but now that I think back on it, perhaps it showed a feeling of inadequacy in him that I hadn't realized. Certainly I think it showed it wasn't just me relying on him for management but that his life was bound to mine, too. I sometimes joked that I was his "meal ticket," but in some ways, I think it went deeper than money. In a way, Jack had begun to think he was Patti Page, not Jack Rael. He felt that he didn't have to tell me certain things because he'd already received all that information *as Patti Page* and decided against it. It must be a natural thing for some managers to think and act as though they are the people they represent because I have learned over the years that I'm not the only artist who's ever experienced that. And Jack receiving half of everything I earned was an even bigger reason for him to think he was me.

I remember once Jack and my secretary, Dorothy, and I were in the car driving to some engagement. I'd been dozing off in the backseat. I woke up and listened to their conversation for a while, and I could see that Jack knew I was awake because he glanced in the rearview mirror. They were talking about an upcoming election. Finally, I said, "Don't you want to know who I'm going to vote for?" I felt like saying just anything, to get out my feelings about the world. I wanted to do more than just go onstage and sing, you know?

Well, Jack just laughed and said, "Thank you for that, Rage. Now go back to sleep."

Patti Page, "the Singing Rage," personal opinions unnecessary. Little things like that bothered me.

One thing I regret was being swept up in my career in my twenties, working so much that I didn't enjoy my success enough. Jack wouldn't stand for any playing around, so I didn't get a chance to go through my twenties dating normally. I followed Jack's rules because I thought that was the way it was done. After all, I'd hardly dated before going on the road as a singer, so I didn't really know any alternative. Maybe if I'd had a more normal love life, Jack and I would actually have had an even better working relationship. I tended to let my emotions build up, and then I would unload them on Jack at times. I regularly got upset and moody the last day of any job. Perhaps because of my meager upbringings and the lean times in Chicago and New York, I had some subconscious fear of not having a job to go to. Then again, perhaps these outbursts were because all work and no play made Patti a dull girl.

Regardless, all these things happened because I let them happen. If Jack took advantage of me, it was because I let him take advantage. I didn't know the business end of the business. I wasn't an entrepreneur. I just sang. Tell me to sing, and I sing. I just got in the car and we drove to wherever I was going to sing next or we flew to wherever I was going to sing next, and that's how it worked.

Now I had a husband who had his own ideas. I quickly learned that he differed with Jack on the creative direction of my career. And Jack's reactions to Charlie were somewhat reminiscent of his conflicts with my first husband. Although I was always receptive to Charlie's ideas, I tried to discourage any friction between him and Jack. I had always told the inquisitive press that Jack was too good a manager to marry, and I meant it.

I had begun to learn that Charlie could do things for me that Jack couldn't do, and that he knew the business in ways that Jack didn't. Jack didn't know how to invest, and he only knew how to take the money the music industry decision-makers offered him. He didn't believe in taking anything for longevity; he did it for the money he got now. If we weren't paid the money up front, Jack wouldn't let me do it. He didn't believe in doing things on a contingency, for a payoff that might come later.

In contrast, my husband was thinking about a future with me, and what life might be like years down the line. From the time I hired him, Charlie also offered me career advice. He was from the old school of Hollywood. He knew about promotion and felt I should be more involved in that. Oddly enough, he didn't believe television would last, but I think that was because he wasn't doing much himself in television. He was still doing movies, choreographing, staging, and directing.

It was hard for Charlie not to challenge Jack. He was a musical director with Elvis Presley on most of his movies and Colonel Parker was always around, so Charlie knew what strong managers were like. Charlie wouldn't hesitate to give his opinion and I would take it to Jack, and Jack knew where it came from, so he'd often dismiss it. I was caught in between and it got tiring as I was always trying hard to keep the peace.

One aspect of Patti Page's marriage with Charles O'Curran that it would have been hard for Jack Rael to fault was his revamp of the staging for her live act. Reviewers were continuing to notice the improvements and refinements he had advised her to make. The first time Page played the Desert Inn after her marriage, a reviewer wrote that she displayed "canary talent to heights unreached before"—"canaries" being a term common at the time for female singers. The success of Page's show was, he wrote, "partially due to the expert staging by her groom, Charles O'Curran. Dramatic lighting and wise pacing blend well with the wholesome, girl-next-door friendliness of Miss Page's delivery." The writer particularly applauded the "unusual effect" of the revolving mirrored ball O'Curran had introduced into the show when his wife sang "Tennessee Waltz."

In the entertainment industry there is no shortage of opportunities for friction between husband and wife. It's no wonder so many entertainment couples get divorced because it can be hard to have a normal family life. For instance, Charlie loved to talk showbiz, but my mom and dad had little interest in entertainment beyond enjoying my singing. (My dad always cried when I sang "the Waltz.") When I played, I might have major showbiz personalities like Louella Parsons or Gracie Allen sitting together in the audience. Maybe those names mean little to people now, but they were big celebrities then. Charlie would be all showbiz with Louella, Gracie, or whomever else might be there—but then, if my parents were in the audience, they'd be more interested in talking about when he and I were going to give them some grandchildren. Guess which conversation he found more comfortable? Also, I don't think my folks were crazy about the idea of Charlie and I living on different coasts.

It seemed I was always doing some social balancing with the people in my life.

Charlie and I went on our real honeymoon in the summer of 1957, months after we got married. We took a voyage to England on the *Ile de France*; it was the famous ship's last voyage. The honeymoon was quite an experience, a beautiful trip, and the first time I'd been away from my manager, my secretary, and business in general in a long time. My records weren't popular in England because they were held in customs for six months before being released, which gave all the English singers a chance to record the songs and make them into their own hits. There were two or three English recording artists who had a hit with "Tennessee Waltz." Later on, Mercury smoothed out the problem causing the delay, but at the time, I expected we would be able to see the sights on our own, barely being recognized.

When we got off the boat south of London, there were all kinds of reporters on the docks, and I wondered what famous person was on the ship. Well, it turned out it was me! My *Songalongs* were running in England, something I hadn't known. What we thought was going to be a very peaceful trip became kind of hectic. I had reporters vying for interviews and I didn't know anything about the English press, a group that could be pretty catty. To my relief, I was treated fairly, and I was thrilled to know that my show was doing something over there.

We went to the Old Vic Theatre to see Vivien Leigh, Laurence Olivier, and Anthony Hopkins in *Titus Andronicus*. As you might imagine, the performance was magnificent, but when they played "God Save the Queen" I got up and started to leave the theater. Charlie stopped me just in time. I didn't know that you showed your respect to the Queen before leaving. Plus, I guess I was dazzled. I'd read that the Old Vic was the thing to do while in London and the whole evening took on fantasy proportions for me.

Charlie was Irish, so the Emerald Isle was next on our list. As Ireland came into view from the plane, I gasped because I had never in my life seen anything greener. It was late in the day but still light, and I remarked on that as well. Charlie tried to make me think the day was extended because I was coming in, that they'd manipulated the sunlight just for me. I laughed at that line of blarney, then again when someone mentioned that it was the longest day of the year. We loved Dublin and spent some happy times riding out in the countryside and seeing the gypsies known as "the travelers."

From there it was on to Rome. It was nice to be anonymous and in love, strolling through the Coliseum, the Spanish Steps, and the Vatican.

When we flew back to the States, I had a smile on my face and a happy husband by my side.

NINE

Spinning Toward
Hollywood

My next television venture was called *The Big Record*. It was a one-
hour show on CBS, designed to compete with *Your Hit Parade*, a
music program that had started on NBC in 1950. It was fabulous
hearing the opening from the announcer each week. As two spotlights swept
the floor at the front of the stage, he would say, "Here's the girl who keeps
The Big Record spinning—the star of our show, Miss Patti Page!" I hosted
the program, and it featured the Vic Schoen Orchestra. The lineup of stars
who appeared on *The Big Record* was amazing. The artist didn't have to have a
Pop record. It could be anybody that ever put anything down on vinyl: opera,
instrumental, anything. We had opera stars like Joan Sutherland, Broadway
stars like Julie Andrews and Ann Miller, and Jazz stylists like Nancy Wilson
and Tony Bennett. One show I remember vividly was with Sammy Davis, Jr.
and Benny Goodman. Sammy, Benny, and I did an energetic dance number
to "Birth of the Blues" with Sammy taking the lead. And one night we had
Margaret Truman on as a guest, playing the piano. Naturally, she played "The
Missouri Waltz."

The atmosphere in the studio was great, and it was a delight to get together with other entertainers and have a blast performing the music we loved. But there were rare occasions when it wasn't one big mutual appreciation society backstage. Vic Damone appeared on the show one night, and Vic was my biggest "unfan" as far as I was concerned. Shortly after I moved from Chicago to New York, I opened at the New Yorker Hotel on the same night Dinah Shore opened at the Waldorf. When a reporter asked Vic which show he planned to take in, he said, "Where do you think I'm going? Where will the press be? They won't be at the New Yorker." It was a slap in the face because Mercury considered its important artists to be Frankie Laine, Vic Damone, and me. I had never quite forgotten his slight, but I always thought he was a consummate entertainer.

I learned a lot about production from doing *The Big Record*. Every Monday morning, the producer, the director, and I talked about what song we would do with each guest and how we would stage it. If there was any promotion I had to do, I did it before the guests started coming in on Tuesday, which was when we a had run-through, music rehearsals, and ironed out the cues. There was no lip synching unless I had a part that required me to do two or three voices. The show aired from 8:00 to 9:00 p.m. on Wednesday night, and since there was no videotape at the time, there was no pre-shooting of any of the numbers.

The Big Record had a great crew. The director, Jerry Shaw, later worked in Hollywood on dozens of game shows, starting with *Hollywood Squares*. At one point, our producer was Jack Philbin, the former executive producer of *The Jackie Gleason Show*. And in the small world of showbiz, our conductor, Vic Schoen, was married to Marian Hutton, the sister of Betty Hutton, Charlie's ex-wife.

One thing I had to get used to was all the costume changes. In that one-hour period, I would have at least four or more changes. It meant a lot of extra work outside the studio, just over my outfits. I'd go to stores like Saks or Bergdorf Goodman to look at gowns. A designer would go down into the garment district and bring other selections back to my apartment or to the studio for fittings. There was a different wardrobe lady at the studio for the day of the show. Of course, I just loved it. When you are young, everything is exciting and wonderful, but the clothes and costumes were a real treat.

Things always ran pretty smoothly but I only had forty-five seconds to change completely from head to toe. It was a flurry of activity, and I couldn't blow it. This was in the day when the unions were just getting started in New York—they were as new then as television, and that could cause confusion. For example, where do you draw the line on what's a prop and what's wardrobe, and who is allowed to hand it to you? I had to deal with makeup, the designer, my hair person, maybe five people all at once doing their job on me. Sometimes I had to take something out of their hands and do it myself to save time—like putting in my own bobby pin. Union rules could get in the way of forty-five second changes from top to bottom!

It wasn't just me that would get flustered by the pace of things. One night I was following the cue cards, talking as I walked toward the camera, and one of the cue card guys fell in the orchestra pit. I didn't follow him onto the trumpet player but with a sweep of my hand I managed to get the producer's attention about what had happened. I couldn't stop; the show was live! That was the fun thing about television then.

The first night of *The Big Record*, as soon as I left the studio, I called my folks to celebrate, but they weren't home. They'd gone to services at the Church of Christ. I called later and my mother said she was just about to call me—which would have been a big thing for her.

"You were wonderful!" she gushed. I felt like a schoolgirl with straight As on a report card.

"Thanks!" I cooed. "Let me ask Dad what he thought about it, will you?"

I could hear him grumble about taking the phone as Mom explained my question; I tried not to laugh. "Well," he said, "I thought it was good."

"Great!" This was a high compliment from him as he was a man of few words.

"What did you like about it?" I asked, like little Clara Ann looking for Daddy's love.

"Well," he drawled, taking his time. "I sure liked that Eddie Cantor."

The Big Record first aired on September 18, 1957, and ran until June 11, 1958. It was shot in the famous CBS Studio 50, in the middle of New York, only a couple of blocks from Patti and Jack's offices in the Brill Building. Other shows produced in that same studio include *The Ed Sullivan Show, The Honeymooners,* and several quiz shows such as *What's My Line?* and *Password.* It is now the home of *Late Night with David Letterman.*

The Big Record commenced at the time when CBS—or "the Tiffany network" as it was then nicknamed—began broadcasting regularly in color. It was the first variety show that the network broadcast in color. This was prior to the advent of videotape, and the shows were saved on black-and-white kinescope, then the standard practice. So, despite the fact they were seen by the original television audience in color, they can now only be viewed in black-and-white.

On Wednesday nights, after the show finished at 9:00 p.m., I'd spend about an hour signing autographs. And then I would rush to LaGuardia and catch the overnight flight to Los Angeles. In those days you didn't have the airport security precautions we have to go through today, so I didn't have to be there any time except before the doors closed. Lucky for me, TWA had a plane with sleeper capabilities. I would catch the 11:00 p.m. flight for Los Angeles and be there for Thursday, Friday, and Saturday with my husband, then I'd catch the plane back on Sunday night for New York, sleeping on the return flight. I'd arrive in New York about 6:00 in the morning, go to my apartment, change, then hurry to the production meeting for the new week's show. When you're young you can do those things.

Sometimes I visited Charlie at movie locations, too. In early January, 1958, I went to be with him in New Orleans, as he was working there on what was probably Elvis Presley's best movie, *King Creole*. I think Elvis was so good in the movie because he knew he was going into the Army. He'd been drafted and had to get a sixty-day extension from his draft board to finish filming before he was inducted into the U.S. Army.

I believe that Elvis had fantastic potential as an actor if he had done more than all those movie musicals. I compared him to John Barrymore, Drew Barrymore's grandfather. I really thought he was that kind of an actor. I wasn't shy about telling him that, either, because it bothered me that he didn't do more serious roles. Elvis had so much more talent than all those movies let us see. Charlie's pal, Hal B. Wallis, produced the movie and the director was Michael Curtiz, who'd turned me down for the Helen Morgan movie. We never said anything about that. Supposedly, Elvis Presley said to Curtiz after the filming, "Now I know what a good director is." Wish I'd had the opportunity to say that to Mr. Curtiz!

Charlie and Elvis loved each other. And I was a fan of Elvis's singing, too. I let "The King" know, only to have Elvis tell me that I was his mother Gladys's favorite singer!

I loved doing *The Big Record*, but in March 1958, the length of the show got trimmed to thirty minutes because the first half of our hour competed with the latter half of an hour-long hit NBC show called *Wagon Train*, which starred Ward Bond. I believe another reason was the cost. Our weekly budget was more than $100,000, which made it New York's highest-budgeted live show. The next week I got a very bad case of laryngitis. I think it may have been connected with the stress I was feeling. As well as my show being trimmed, that month I'd been in talks with producer Jerry Wald about the lead in a musical for 20th Century Fox and didn't get it. And in a rare move, Jack had put some of our money in a real estate investment—the President Madison hotel, in Miami—but it hadn't done so well and he sold our interest in it the same day the show was cut down to thirty minutes. There was a lot on my mind.

I got over my laryngitis quickly. I had to because the last week of that month, I had a special wedding to go to. My secretary, Dorothy Birdoff, married her beau, Abe Safier. I was going to miss Dorothy. I had been in Las Vegas playing at the Desert Inn when I'd first hired her. She had flown out to join me on the road. I remember it well because it was the day in 1952 when Queen Elizabeth II was crowned, and I recall watching it on television.

In June of 1958, *The Big Record* was canceled. I wasn't the only singing casualty of television around that time. My friend, Rosemary Clooney, and even Frank Sinatra himself had TV shows that failed in 1957. Still, I had really enjoyed doing that show.

One chapter of Patti Page's television career may have come to a close, but in 1958 she continued to receive extraordinary accolades. In June, *Cashbox* magazine declared her the Most Popular Female Vocalist of 1958. The 30th Annual *Disc Jockey Poll* named her Favorite Female Vocalist. Returning briefly to Tulsa, she received an Honorary Doctorate of Art from the University of Tulsa, and she was also a Grand Marshal at the Miss America pageant in Atlantic City.

I went back on the road, doing state fairs all the way out to Wyoming. It was just the beginning of that sort of thing for me; later, I'd do many more. Sometimes, Charlie went with me. The crowds all wanted to hear "Old Cape Cod," which I had recorded the previous year. The song was penned by Claire Rothrock, an amateur songwriter and a resident of Cape Cod. She brought the song to me when I was playing at Blinstrub's Village nightclub in Boston. I loved it, and I took the train back to New York and recorded it. Even though it has lush instrumentation by an orchestra, we did it surprisingly fast. Suffice it to say that the musicians in New York were fantastic. I did the main vocal in New York, then added the other two voices in California when I flew out to see Charlie. It became one of my biggest hit records. Over the years, I've heard from kids who say their parents fell in love to that song, and the Cape Cod area real estate turned into a booming business where there hadn't been much of one before. The people at the fairs also loved a song called "Money, Marbles and Chalk," which was my first Country hit, in 1949.

Although I never went to all the big show business parties, I have always loved meeting people, which sometimes had unexpected consequences because people I met would bring me songs I could turn into records. One was Claire Rothrock, and another was Mike Merlow, who wrote a song I recorded called "Fibbin'." Mike was a waiter at The Tender Trap, a place in New York that Charlie and I frequented.

My dad also wrote a song for me. There was no music, just the words, and he sent it to me in a letter and asked me to come up with the music or have it written. The result was my Country tune "Who's Gonna Shoe My Pretty Little Feet."

Patti Page was not absent from viewers' television screens for long. She began hosting *The Oldsmobile Show* in the fall of 1958. This time she was on ABC, her third network. No other television personality had had their own show on all three networks, a record that remains unbroken. *The Oldsmobile Show* first aired on Wednesday, September 24, 1958. The weekly variety show ran from 9:30 p.m. to 10:00 p.m., and featured Rocky Cole, The Jerry Packer Singers, and once again, the Vic Schoen Orchestra. It was produced by Ted Mills; the choreographer, Matt Mattox, hailed from Tulsa. In contrast to her previous TV show, *The Oldsmobile Show* had a smaller budget, $40,000 per episode.

The first episode, with guest stars Walter Pidgeon and Walter Hayden, aired to good reviews. One reviewer called it "as engaging a 30 minutes as we've seen on TV in a long time. It is a smooth, polished variety program that skips along in friendly fashion with a deceptive simplicity that belies its skillful behind-the-scenes handling."

At this point in her career, Patti had put out ten gold records—meaning they had sold over a million copies each—and in total she had sold around 40 million records.

At *The Oldsmobile Show* the pressure was really on us to be good because we were up against the very popular *I've Got a Secret* with host Bill Cullen and a panel of celebrity guests. I think Oldsmobile backed me because they were competing with Chevrolet, the sponsor of the popular *The Dinah Shore Chevy Show*, which most people remember because Dinah said "See the U.S.A. in your Chevrolet!" on every show. I got to sing "It's a thrill to take the wheel, of my merry Oldsmobile!" on my show.

I had more of a say in the overall production and staging of *The Oldsmobile Show* than I had on *The Big Record*. It was less of a hectic pace than the previous show, and the guests were the best: Nat "King" Cole, Gene Krupa, and Carl Reiner were some I remember well.

When I was doing *The Big Record*, the executives liked that I didn't mind ad libbing, turning a mistake into a laugh. The situation was a bit different on *The Oldsmobile Show*. One time in particular, I wished I was the producer because if I had my way, we would have made the most of that funny ad libbing. Eydie Gorme was a guest on the show that night. We were doing a number, and the idea of the bit was that Eydie would start her song and a curtain would rise and reveal me standing there, and I would join in singing with her. It was all going well. Eydie began the song, the curtain went up and revealed me to the studio audience and the cameras—and then it dropped. I just kept singing.

Well, you can't let a curtain stop you!

I kept singing as I crawled under the curtain and went downstage. We went all the way through the duet singing and it was hysterical, the audience was cracking up. After Eydie and I finished our number, the audience went wild.

"Cut!" said the director. "Take your places for the opening of this scene!"

This was the first year the networks had used videotape, and so they rewound the tape and reshot it, forever losing the hilarious bit we'd just done. I looked at Eydie and she looked at me and we shook our heads. I thought that was just awful. Many times when Dick Clark would do a blooper show, I remembered that bit and sighed.

I worked with other entertainers on the ABC network, too. When Bing Crosby did his very first TV special that October, I was a guest star along with Dean Martin and Mahalia Jackson. I'd just done Bing's TV show the week before, so I saw a lot of "Der Bingster" those two weeks. It was a happy time for me.

I was up for an Emmy for Best Actress for a Continuing Musical or Variety Series for *The Big Record*, even though the show had been canceled. I didn't win, but I certainly appreciated the recognition of being nominated. I hoped I might get nominated again for *The Oldsmobile Show*, which I thought was better. Well, you know what they say about the best-laid plans of mice and Pop singers.... The last airing of my Oldsmobile show was March 16, 1959. Another summer of fairs was coming up.

As well as doing the TV shows, I continued to go into the studio regularly to record. One of the songs I did that year was "Goodbye Charlie." It had nothing to do with my husband; the last thing I was going to tell him was goodbye. Happily, I was right around the corner from some very big changes that would put me in a position to tell him hello every morning.

TEN

At Last, the Movies, and a Book, Too

My parents had their fiftieth wedding anniversary in 1959. Dad was seventy-one and Mom was sixty-nine. They'd married on July 5, 1909 in Dyer, Arkansas. How amazing, I thought, they were still just as happy together after five decades. No wonder they call it "golden." Charlie and I flew into Tulsa from Los Angeles after midnight, just in time for the celebration on Sunday. Fittingly enough, there were fifty that went to church that morning before going back to my parents' house. There were twenty-six grandchildren there; unfortunately, none of them were courtesy of Charlie and me.

As we were gathered in my folks' pleasant, six-room ranch style home I thought that Mom and Dad had the perfect life. Mom gardened and spent time with Dad, and they had five of their children living in Tulsa near them. Maybe that's why I wanted five children of my own. I thought that was a reasonable amount. After all, Mom had said she'd wanted an even dozen and had to "settle" for eleven.

My dream to start my own family might have still been elusive, but on the professional side, one of my longest-held career hopes—to be in a feature film—was finally coming to pass. And what a film it was: *Elmer Gantry* with Burt Lancaster. As so often seemed to happen, this role relied in part on good fortune as it hinged on movie producer Joe Pasternak seeing me sing at the Desert Inn in Las Vegas. Pasternak wasn't a producer on *Elmer Gantry* but after he saw me perform, he recommended to the makers of the movie that I play the role of the choir leader for Lancaster's title character, the evangelist preacher Elmer Gantry. To my relief, there was no screen test involved—I was hired on the condition that I would do an album connected with the movie, including a dozen hymns and spirituals that I sang in the picture. The movie was produced by Burt Lancaster's production company, and they thought the album would help with the promotion of the picture. I loved singing those gospel songs so I was happy to do it.

The director, Richard Brooks, really didn't want me. I was told he had said, "Patti Page, what kind of a name is that?" I do feel he resented the fact that Burt Lancaster and Ben Hecht told him to cast me. His resentment may also have come from pressure put on him by the star of the film, Jean Simmons, who he was having an affair with at the time and who would later become his wife. I couldn't say for sure what his issue with me was as I'd never quite figured out Hollywood. I thought Brooks did a pretty good job, but he was an egotistical guy. I didn't like the way he directed and treated people, but the movie was something I wanted to do.

And everyone kept telling me it was the right thing to do, logically because Doris Day had started as a singer and she was now the #1 movie box office attraction. I think a lot of people assumed that all singers should go that route because Doris had been so successful. As if every girl singer could do it! Of course, you couldn't just snap your fingers and be a movie success. That didn't stop people from thinking it, though. Movies were something I'd always wanted to do, but I have to admit that I did feel a certain amount of pressure because of all the expectations and preconceptions about singers who wanted to act.

The first day on the set I spent watching Burt Lancaster and Jean Simmons.

Burt was amazing. You could tell that he studied every night when he went home; that he would practice, above and beyond what was expected. Just about everyone knows the scene in the movie where Burt comes running into the tent and takes a flying leap and lands on his knees and starts preaching. There wasn't any stunt double for that!

I never worked on the same days as Shirley Jones, though. We knew each other as casual acquaintances from the music business and got to know each other better later.

No one really gave me many pointers about acting. Once in a while, Richard Brooks would tell me to do this or that but it was mostly about movement—where to go and what to say when I went there. I waved my hands a lot because I played Sister Rachel, the director of music for Lancaster's evangelist.

I was on the set a lot during the four months or so it took to do the picture and really enjoyed it. I was as much in awe of watching everybody as I was of my being there. I had to pinch myself a few times to believe I was on the same set with Burt Lancaster and the other stars. Being cast in a lead role meant I had lunch with all of them every day. I loved the camaraderie and just listening even though I never knew what they were talking about half the time.

Burt Lancaster, I learned, played bridge and he found out that I was a bridge player, too. I was invited to play bridge with him and his wife along with Ben Hecht and others. I felt they were out of my league, so I didn't play. Even though people would come up to me on set and tell me they loved my music, it still didn't make me feel that I deserved to be there. I don't know why. Maybe it was because when I went to the movies I was watching people thirty feet high. I was as intimidated as any other fan.

The film was shot at Columbia Studios in Hollywood and night scenes out in the Valley in Burbank. Fittingly for a movie about a fiery evangelist, there is a scene of the burning of a tabernacle, which we shot on the pier in Santa Monica. Watching it go up in smoke was especially fascinating, but I loved the filming of everything. Burt was pretty on fire in that movie, and that's why he won the Oscar. I also thought Jean Simmons was phenomenal, but she wasn't even nominated. Nevertheless, the next year at the Oscars, it was *Elmer Gantry* take all. The awards that were given to that movie were just unbelievable.

Elmer Gantry came from a novel written by Sinclair Lewis in 1927, which hadn't been well-received by evangelists. One pastor wanted Lewis jailed and another wanted him lynched. Some evangelists also didn't like all the romantic liaisons the main character has in the story. (We certainly learned more about that kind of thing in later years, with preachers like Jimmy Swaggart.) I didn't feel the theme of the movie was problematic to my personal beliefs because the movie wasn't anti-Christian though it was anti-evangelistic. It drew attention to the type of people who were later indicted, like Jim and Tammy Bakker.

I wasn't brought up in an evangelical church. Ours was more staid, a "don't flaunt it" type of Christianity, but I kind of liked the fervor displayed by Burt's character in *Elmer Gantry*. My mother would take me to different churches sometimes when I was little. Not that she was searching—as a Christian she was more sedate—but I think she kind of liked that fervor, too. I remember when I had the mumps and she thought I wasn't getting better, so she took me to a tent revival to be healed. And sure enough, I soon began to feel better. I guess I was healed!

Being in Los Angeles for such a long time during the making of *Elmer Gantry* made me think I would like to live there permanently. California was beginning to be as important to recording as New York, and Columbia had great recording studios on Sunset Boulevard. I was interested in doing more movies, too. I discussed it with Jack and GAC, who at the time agreed to help me find more film roles. Later, though, I felt like they did little about it. On days when I hadn't been on set during the shooting of Elmer Gantry, I was in the recording studio, but I couldn't play any live music dates. Let me tell you, the film salary was a pittance compared to my music income. (I would later be paid "residuals" from the film, but I didn't realize that at the time.) That showed me why Jack and GAC didn't want me to do movies.

One column reported that I was wanted for a role in *Butterfield 8* with Elizabeth Taylor but I couldn't do it because of a booking. Funny, I don't remember being told much about that. I suspect that Jack turned it down on my behalf because it wouldn't have paid as well as singing. It always came down to the money with Jack. It was a pity not to be involved because the movie got a lot of notice and Elizabeth won an Oscar for her role.

One of the songs I recorded that year was "What Will My Future Be?" How appropriate it seems now, looking back. I know I loved the weather in southern California, and I also loved going to Dodger games. Charlie and I would see them with Nat "King" Cole and his wife, Maria, and everyone was a Dodgers fan. In fact, on the set of *Elmer Gantry*, people seemed as much interested in how the Dodgers were doing in the World Series that year as they were in making the movie. I would run through lines with Burt and then on a break the first thing he would ask was how the "Boys in Blue" were making out on the ball field. Despite my reluctance to socialize like most people in Hollywood, I could see myself fitting right into the social scene there. Charlie and I had discussed it quite a bit but had yet to make a firm decision.

Sales of singles were down in late 1959, the normal seasonal trend, and boy singers were still selling better. The latter was likely because the majority of record buyers were girls, 75 percent of them, in fact.

As the calendar turned to 1960, I put on another "hat" with the publication of my book *Once Upon a Dream: A Personal Chat with All Teenagers*, which was aimed mostly at those young girls who bought the majority of records. The book was published in response to Pat Boone's own guide to teenagers, by the same publisher, Bobbs-Merrill. They wanted a girl to "answer" Pat's book because it had sold very well. Pat was a teen idol with hits like "Love Letters in the Sand,"

and the girls adored him. Back in the 1950s and 1960s, hit songs would be "answered" by a corresponding song sung by a member of the opposite sex. For example, my good friend Rosemary Clooney's hit "Come On-A My House" (a song she had to be talked into recording) was answered by "Where's-a Your House?" by radio and TV personality Robert Q. Lewis. Both of them did well on the charts. If answer songs worked, why not an answer book? Bobbs-Merrill picked me, I suppose, because they thought I was the female equivalent of Pat Boone in the minds of teenagers, and Pat and I were good friends.

Although I had a writer to work with, it took up a good bit of my time because I wanted the book to offer useful guidance for the teens who'd be reading it. When I told them about how I'd gotten my first break, obstacles I had to overcome in my teens, and my thoughts on a happy marriage, I wanted it to be solid advice that they could apply to their own lives.

My main message was how to get along in life no matter your social strata. They'd read the articles about my 150 pairs of shoes and the matching handbag for each pair, 300 dresses, and mink coats I owned. I wanted my readers to believe they could achieve success, too, and not merely in a material way. I wanted them to know that I had spent too much time in my life worrying about stupid things.

I figured readers would laugh when I described that I'd made people sick when I learned to cook blanquette de veu in cooking school because the wine sauce was too rich. Onion soup and Caesar's salad on my next assignment had been fine; anyone could make that. And I didn't mind talking about my battles with weight. Maybe my well-publicized battles with weight had struck a chord with them and that's why I tended to get a good reception from teenage girls—they could relate.

The publisher did something interesting by setting up a book tour in which I and a number of other authors visited five cities by train. The other authors I remember most were Robert F. Kennedy, Dr. Joyce Brothers, and the author of the novel *The Longest Day*, Cornelius Ryan. Bobby Kennedy was the Attorney

General of the United States at the time, and Dr. Joyce Brothers was the most well-known psychologist in the nation. *The Longest Day* was a bestseller, which would become a big movie in 1962. I found the whole thing a bit embarrassing. We would all sign copies of our books at the same time at adjoining tables at a bookstore, and often there would be just a few people lined up for the other authors but my line would sometimes stretch out the doors and down the block a little. It was like people lined up for a concert.

"I should be a singer," Mr. Kennedy said to me one day.

In August of 1960, Patti Page made the big move from New York to California to live with her husband Charlie O'Curran. She had been living in a well-appointed and stylish apartment at 605 Park Avenue, whose décor had been featured in numerous magazine articles. Though she had been offered the chance to buy the apartment in the past, she had chosen to rent instead.

Charles O'Curran had been living in a far more basic furnished bachelor pad on DeLongpre Avenue, near Fountain Avenue, in Hollywood. While in Los Angeles to shoot *Elmer Gantry*, Patti had found the couple a place to rent on Sunset Plaza Drive, just north of Sunset Boulevard. It had been redone for the owners, actors Anne Baxter and John Hodiak, by renowned cutting-edge architect Frank Lloyd Wright, who was Anne Baxter's uncle. It provided a stylish, secluded, and quiet retreat off the Sunset Strip.

When Patti decided to live in California permanently, she contacted famous Hollywood real estate agent Elaine Young, with a view to buying. Patti fell in love with one of the first houses Young showed her, a Gerald Colcourt–designed home at 603 N. Canon Drive in Beverly Hills with a price tag of $110,000.

The house at N. Canon Drive reminded me of what I'd always heard of beautiful English homes: white clapboard with dark green shutters, a used brick trim, and a white picket fence. I thought it cost a lot of money and that I couldn't afford it. It just so happened that the man who owned it was the publisher of the song "My Jealous Eyes," which was on the B side of "Doggie in the Window." With that kind of coincidence and the way I adored it, I took the plunge.

With plenty of living space, the beautiful southern California weather, and the then relatively unhurried Los Angeles streets (compared to Manhattan), the contrast was just unbelievable. If I'd ever been a Cinderella as reporters had originally said about me, I felt as though at last I had the prince and the castle with a white picket fence.

Well, almost everything. I didn't have the royal family, but I was working on it.

To my surprise, in 1960 I was cast in another movie. I played Liz in the movie *Dondi* starring David Jannsen. The movie was based on a popular comic strip about an adorable Italian war orphan who stows away on a ship returning to New York after World War II with U.S. sailors onboard. Once they reach dry land, Dondi gets lost and, as they say in Hollywood, "hijinks ensue" until one of the sailors, Dealey, played by David Jannsen, takes Dondi in. Liz was Dealey's girlfriend. It might not have been the greatest movie made that year, but it was fun, and I liked doing the title song, too. They even talked about a sequel called *Dondi Goes to the Moon* but we were spared that one.

In late October, I got a letter about something new in Hollywood: a Walk of Fame. I was one of the first 75 inductees to be recognized for our contributions to the entertainment industry with our own stars on the sidewalk. Each star would feature a symbol representing the performer's art; I would have a record in the middle of my star, at 6760 Hollywood Boulevard. That was it, just a notification, no ceremony with cameras rolling. They celebrate the star installations a little differently these days!

Jack Rael had been investing in real estate in 1959, but I didn't hear much about how that turned out. He'd also dabbled in the TV packaging business with a musical quiz series idea but hadn't gotten very far with it.

We decided to form our own production company together. I was headlining in the Versailles Room at the Riviera in Las Vegas when we announced the formation of Argap. The plan was for me to appear in some of the "properties" that we controlled, meaning stories for movies, including a movie version of "Tennessee Waltz" from a story by Marie Nordlin and a romantic comedy. Jack was talking with both United Artists and Allied Artists about releasing any movies we made.

Meanwhile, I kept doing guest appearances on Dinah Shore's show and then on Garry Moore's very popular comedy variety show. Charlie was staging my Vegas shows, and reviewers were taking notice of aspects of the staging like having the color of the spotlights match my outfits onstage. It might not seem like much given today's electronically amazing shows, but we did what we could.

Sometimes, little slipups provided nice touches at my shows. Once at the Riviera, I walked onstage and realized that my slip was slipping below my dress. I immediately started backing up toward the curtain, which drew a laugh, and I explained what was happening. My hairdresser, Lee Trent, pinned my slip up from behind the curtain and as he finished I said, "Thank you, Mona!" I couldn't let my audience know that a man had reached under my dress. Can you imagine anyone caring today?

By this stage of my career, I had gained more confidence. Despite objections from my management, I'd stood up for my idea to develop my live act and I'd picked Charlie to do the staging, and it had paid off with positive reviews and more-satisfied audiences. Finding and marrying a man who loved me didn't hurt, either—nor did getting an increasing amount of control of my television shows.

Maybe my gradual rise to success, and then my slow and wearisome ascent to appearing in movies, helped me achieve a measured outlook on it all. Perhaps that's one of the problems for top performers today: With 24/7 television and the endless Internet, someone can become a massive hit in the shortest time possible. When there's tons of money to go with it, the artists lose perspective on what that success means, and they are simply unable to cope. If that had happened to me, I don't know that I'd have had such a long career.

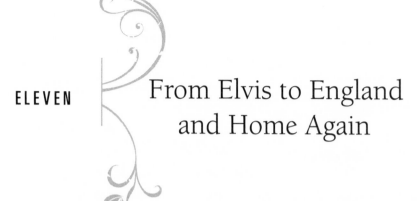

ELEVEN

From Elvis to England and Home Again

Charlie was doing another Presley picture, one that Hal Wallis was producing in the fiftieth state, called *Blue Hawaii*. When I realized I could spend a week with Charlie on Kauai, I made my schedule work around it.

I'd gotten to know Elvis a little because many times when I played Las Vegas, he'd fly his mother Gladys out to see me. Since I worked Vegas four times during the year for four-week engagements, sixteen weeks gave him plenty of opportunities. There was always an occasion to bring his mother to see my show. Gladys had a reticence about her; she didn't want to be involved in conversations and especially didn't like to answer questions about Elvis. She adored him but didn't like to thrust her opinion of him on anyone.

While Gladys was watching my show, Elvis would play the slots outside the room where I was singing. If you believe it was possible, he was still being able to be a little bit inconspicuous around the casino, and I think he wanted to take advantage of that. In Hawaii, he couldn't even get out of his hotel room. I hated to see him lose his privacy.

After shooting was finished each day, we'd all have dinner and then we used to sit around and sing—all the old songs, whether they be Gospel or Pop or whatever. Elvis and others from his group played the guitars. The Jordanaires would harmonize. We'd all join in and just have a big songfest. This would go on for maybe an hour after dinner, and then Elvis always seemed to have some girls to go visit. We'd sing church songs and then Elvis would commune with the choir, I suppose you could say.

Despite his pleasure proclivities, I think Elvis was basically very religious. There's no handbook for being a superstar. He was brought up with all the basic values I was, and he came up from poverty like I did. His upbringing played a major part in his life and probably that's what ultimately did him in after Gladys died in 1958. With her gone, I think he developed a guilt trip about some things he had done and how he had displeased his mom, whom he adored. She would never have approved of his shenanigans and drugs. When Elvis saw me, he'd get a lump in his throat or even tears in his eyes because he associated me with Gladys.

I got to be in *Blue Hawaii*, but this time I was an extra. Just as a gag, I took part in a big wedding scene where the major characters are all coming down a waterway in canoes, up to where they step out near the minister and some beautiful bridges. You won't see my name in the credits, but if you look, I'm there in the film, in a boat with one of Elvis's cousins.

I flew away from the island state and went back on tour, flying to an island nation. It was the first time I'd been to England since Charlie and I had been there on our honeymoon. My new single was "Dondi" with "A City Girl Stole My Country Boy" on the flip side. The English critics were as fickle as their American counterparts. Some liked "Dondi" while others loathed it, and some liked the "City Girl" song while others panned it.

One of the most important venues to play was the Pigalle Theater Restaurant in London, a supper club whose expansiveness reminded me a bit of Blinstrub's in Boston. It was too bad Charlie wasn't there. He had written a song for me, "I Never Met a Singer Who Didn't Want to Dance," and it was a big hit with the crowd and the critics. They also loved how I made my way to each table as I sang, something I'd never done before Charlie got involved in the staging of my act. It was made much easier by a new invention I was wearing that night, a transistor mic, which made for much less bulky cables than when I started out as a performer. I got a kick from trying out new things like that.

The grand dame of torch singers, Sophie Tucker, was in the audience that night, so I went and saw her perform the next night at Talk of the Town. Other singers in the audience were Shirley Bassey and Alma Cogan—girl singers sticking together!

In the spring of 1961, I found myself in a much different environment. I was back home in Tulsa, making the rounds, visiting with contestants in the Miss Dairy Queen contest and offering them career advice, appearing at a National Dairy Association luncheon, and signing books at a local store. I got to visit with my parents and sisters, Hazel and Ruby Celeste. It was wonderful. I felt like I could be Patti Page and Clara Ann Fowler at the same time.

That year, my TV work was mostly guest appearances on shows like *The Garry Moore Show*. I also got the chance to do some dramatic acting on the popular *Bachelor Father* TV series in an episode called "A Song is Born" with Jimmy Boyd. The "Huck Finn" actor-singer's career path and mine were destined to cross many times. The episode was (can you guess?) about a singer. I'm sure I was cast for no other reason than that I was a well-known singer. It wasn't any different than it is today: People have a name and media executives want to take advantage of it. (Still, I like to think I had some talent!) It was a one-time thing, like a *United States Steel Hour* episode I'd done in 1957 called "Upbeat" in which I also played (I'm sure you've already guessed) a singer. At least *Bachelor Father* wasn't broadcast live. On the *United States Steel Hour,* if you forgot your lines, you had to make up something and still stay within the story. It was like doing a Broadway show on television. It was nerve-wracking.

I was all over the place that year. I could be autographing books one day, acting in a TV show the next, then appearing at a nightclub across the country two days later. I was always "on" because, as any well-known performer will tell you, each time you appear in public, you're judged in that context alone. If you're not nice at a book signing, people might think less of your records, and if you're not perceived to be as excellent in live performance as you are on a recording, critics will say you're a phony. And if you're photographed with someone, that can be seen as an endorsement of that person. When I played the famous Latin Casino in Cherry Hill, New Jersey in the summer of 1961, I was worried because the city's Democratic city committee had bought out the house of one show to stage a political rally. Governor Hughes and all the state's Democratic bigwigs were there. Would everyone assume I was a Democrat? (Most people assume that about entertainers to this day.) Would I be asked to endorse anything? Luckily, the entertainment columnist of the local paper mentioned the politics but left me out of it.

Patti Page's dramatic TV roles brought good reviews from influential entertainment writers such as Louella Parsons.

A Closer Walk With Thee, a gospel album Page recorded in New York in 1960, sold well, as did the *Elmer Gantry* album. However, in 1961 she recorded only a few new singles and they did not climb the charts.

The slowdown in her recording career seemed irrelevant when she flew in to the Philippines in August 1961 for concerts with singer Jimmie Rodgers, most famous for his hit "Honeycomb." Crowds of teenage fans were awaiting their arrival at the Manila International Airport, and a motorcade had to be organized to take them into the city. Page did twelve nights of performances at the Araneta Coliseum, which seated 36,000 people. Page thrilled the audiences in Manila by especially learning several songs in the local language, Tagalog.

I was interested to discover that Tagalog was actually the #3 language of my now home state of California, after English and Spanish. One of the favorite songs for the Philippines audiences in 1961, ironically for me as I was away from my husband, was "Goodbye Charlie." During one of the shows, I was reminded of my own history when I got to welcome two girls onstage who had competed for the title of "Local Patti Page." The Manila Broadcasting Corporation's *Big Show* sponsored the contest. The girls were talented and cute as a button. Now I knew what Bob Hope felt like that night back in Tulsa.

In November, I cut my first sides at Bradley Studio in Nashville, Tennessee. This would begin a forty-year relationship with the capital of Country music. After having recorded in Chicago first, then New York, then Los Angeles, I was amazed at how Nashville did things. I fell in love with the musicians there. Like me, most of them didn't read music. Musicians and singers went back to an old tried-and-true method of reading music by the numbers. I would have loved to learn it, but I didn't know where to start. I didn't use a number system, but I could look at a song and tell where the note went. Like me, they just went and did it, not spending a lot of time to get the tracks down. And like me, most of those people were from the country. We got along very well. I usually did my own background vocals, but this time I had the Jordanaires as backup singers. It was a real thrill to have them on my first true Country and Western tracks.

Patti Page's first foray into the Nashville recording scene resulted in the album *Country and Western Hits.* Shelby Singleton at Mercury was so impressed with the track "Go On Home" that he ordered acetates pressed and sent to local disc jockeys the same day it was recorded, and a further 100 to DJs all over the country the next day. "Go On Home," with "Too Late to Cry" on the flip side, was the first single released from the album, and it put Patti back on the Country charts, rising to #13.

Next on the agenda was movie number three of my career (if you don't count *Blue Hawaii!*). This time, I was shocked to learn that producer Martin Ransohoff actually wanted me to gain twenty pounds for the role. The picture was *Boys' Night Out* with fellow Oklahoman James Garner about some men who are having their mid-life crisis and rent an apartment along with a beautiful young woman for the purpose of romantic liaisons. The problem, they discover too late, is that the young lady is a sociology student doing research on the sexual habits of middle-class men. No, I wasn't the beautiful young woman; that part was played by Kim Novak. They wanted me to gain weight so I could play a somewhat dowdy Southern wife of a funny character actor named Howard Morris. Marty Ransohoff and the director, Michael Gordon, had an idea that a Southern housewife should be plump!

Given how much the press had loved to talk about my weight going up and down in the past, I was hardly keen to purposely plump up. But I took the part because it was a great cast and I knew it would be a lot of fun. I got to work with people like Tony Randall, William Bendix, and Zsa Zsa Gabor. This time, I got co-star billing with James Garner, Kim Novak, and Tony Randall. There was even more camaraderie on the set than on the shoot for *Elmer Gantry*, perhaps because it was not so serious a movie. I loved the story of a gang of men who ride on the train into New York together, leaving their wives at home, and how the wives gang up on them when they find out what the scheming husbands are trying to do.

Oddly enough, I couldn't look fat enough to suit Marty and Michael. They finally opted to put me in frumpy, shapeless dresses. I was happy that I didn't have to eat fat foods to suit them.

Michael Gordon had directed Doris Day in *Pillow Talk*, and I was a little wary of what he would think of me, another popular singer branching out as an actress. I found out one day when he took me aside on the set.

"Patti," he said, "I don't think you'll ever be a big movie star."

Gulp. Well, I could tell he had a reason for saying that, and he hadn't said it unkindly.

"And why is that, Michael?" I asked.

"It's because you don't know where your key light is," he replied, and he showed me what he meant.

The key light is the most important light for any actor. It highlights the subject, and all other lighting in a scene is configured around that light. By not being aware of the key light, I wasn't helping the camera focus on my character in the scene. Without that kind of awareness, I was breaking the connection with the audience to some degree. It was quite a lesson to learn, a bit of craft no one had previously taught me.

When the new year turned, I debuted at The Dunes in Vegas, and all seven of my sisters appeared onstage with me in a family reunion, which was very special. Jack, meanwhile, seemed to be making progress for the "Tennessee Waltz" movie we'd talked about for so long. We'd signed a writer named Audrey Thomas to write a screenplay based on the song, and Charlie and I celebrated with Jack and his wife, Rack, songwriter Mack Gordon's daughter Racquel.

As it would turn out, however, I had much more important projects to bring to fruition—projects that had nothing to do with my career. Unexpected but happy opportunities were about to deliver my fondest dream yet.

TWELVE

Finally, A Family!

In March of 1962, Jack and his wife got a big scare when an elevator they were in at the Fourteen Hotel in New York skidded down ten floors. Steve Lawrence and Eydie Gorme were also on the elevator, and Eydie was pregnant. Luckily, all eight people on the elevator were fine.

I was so happy for Eydie but I envied her being pregnant. Charlie and I had been trying for a long time, and the situation was really beginning to bother me. We had talked many times about having kids, and it was part of the reason I had moved out from New York. For all our talk, it just never happened. I had seen multiple doctors to see if there was something physically wrong with me, but each time I checked out okay. I always wanted Charlie to be tested and find out if he had a problem, but he resented the idea. He would not get tested, just wouldn't. I knew I'd never change his mind about that. His first wife had gotten pregnant and that was all the proof he needed. I was tempted at times to get in touch with her and ask about that, but it just wasn't the kind of thing you'd do in those days. Charlie resisted testing because he was terrified and would have seen it as a blow to his manhood if he found out he was infertile. My husband would not have been any less a man to me if it turned out he had a problem that was stopping us getting pregnant—I just wanted to know so we could plan for the future.

I had waited long enough. One day, I let Charlie know at breakfast. "Let's adopt some children, Charlie," I said softly. "It doesn't look like it's going to happen between us."

My husband was, sorry to say it, a typical male. "We've talked about that," he said, sipping his coffee. He kept reading the entertainment section of the paper, then added, "You know I want my own."

I just dropped the subject. How many times would I have to discuss it? I'd made up my mind, though. I'd always wanted five children. If I had to adopt them, I would. What I wanted most of all was the opportunity to try to give some kids a great life that was full of love. In time, Charlie came to see how much it meant to me and we started looking for a child to adopt.

The options were limited in California. Charlie was Catholic but because I was not, no Catholic agency would work with us; legally, I wasn't married in their eyes. We got a lot of offers about black market babies. It was the time when a lot of that was going on, but we wanted no part of something illegal. I talked to anyone I thought might be helpful about adoption because I didn't know where to go.

In June, I was performing at the Vapors Casino in Hot Springs. I played there quite a bit and when I'd go on the radio to promote my show, the DJ would invariably ask if Charlie and I had children. I'd always say no, but we're trying and hoping, and we may want to consider adopting. When the booker at the Vapors heard me that week in 1962, he told me about his lawyers, who were in charge of adoptions for the State of Arkansas. He and his wife had adopted a child through them. He suggested I go to Little Rock to see them and learn what was involved in adopting from Arkansas.

I made an appointment and drove up to Little Rock. I met with them, and they were just super. They told me that once in a while they had a baby that wasn't spoken for and that they would be glad to let me know the next time

THIS IS MY SONG

a baby was available.

I walked out of that office with a greater sense of hope because I felt that for the first time, someone had truly understood my dream of adopting and was willing to help make it a reality. It was only a few months later that I got a call on a Monday morning in October informing me that the most beautiful little girl had been born that Sunday, October 21. Would I like to adopt her?

Charlie and I booked the first plane that I could find for Little Rock. I called my mother and my sister, Trudy, before we left for the airport, and they were as excited as I was, if that was possible. Our plane stopped in Wichita on the way to Little Rock, and Trudy met the plane and brought me a new baby kit of sterilized nipples, bottles, and milk.

I was so excited that I've had trouble ever since remembering the exact details of what happened after we arrived in Little Rock. What I do know is that we went to the hospital and saw this beautiful baby, and as it happened, when Charlie saw her for the first time, his heart was lost. Until that time it had been very hard sailing to get him to accept the idea of adoption, and everything had happened so fast. After he saw his future daughter, though, he was sold.

The doctor who delivered the baby explained to us that the little girl was from a young couple who were in over their heads. The dad was a basketball player at the University of Arkansas, and the mom was only sixteen years old. The young couple's parents had gotten together and decided they would take care of adopting the baby out. None of the grandparents wanted to see the baby, but Arkansas law didn't allow a mother to give her baby up for adoption until she'd seen the baby. That had already taken place, the papers had been signed, and that's when I had been called. It was a tragic situation but I understand how terrifically hard it might have been for them to raise a baby.

The afternoon after we arrived at the hospital, we were able to take the baby with us. She was only three days old, and we named her Kathleen, a good Irish name, with the middle name Patricia. I adored her immediately. We took Kathleen Patricia back to the hotel where we were staying, and thank goodness my sister had bought me those few things because it meant I could feed her the instant she needed it. I went shopping and got enough necessities to get us home, and suddenly, I realized we were a family.

We had a beautiful four-room suite upstairs at the house on Canon Drive that I called the children's wing. It was still in my mind to have five. There was a beautiful little bedroom with a built-in bed and paintings on the wall. It looked like something from a fairy tale. It had been built years before, as though it was destined for our family, and that became Kathleen's nursery.

Before the baby, we had dogs in the house—a terrier called Window (nicknamed "Windy") who'd come from New York and another one called "Other One" because we'd never settled on a name. They weren't quite sure what to think of Kathleen, but they were excited because they could sense how happy Charlie and I were.

For the first six weeks, I didn't do anything but stay right there at home with my daughter and be her mother. Still, I knew I couldn't maintain that cozy cocoon for long, so I proceeded to look for a nanny to travel with us. I hired Jackie Smith, a lovely girl from England who was only eighteen years old and beautiful on the inside and out. She had never taken care of a new baby before. "I've only got six weeks head start on you," I told her. "We'll learn together!" That's what we did, and it worked out very nicely. Jackie immediately became very close to the baby and me. I adored her, but Charlie didn't particularly like Jackie.

Charlie had a habit of criticizing people. Later, I realized there was a lot of jealousy there. I didn't really want to think that, but it was true. Charlie resented Jackie repeatedly doing the right thing, and subconsciously felt Jackie was getting closer to me than he was. Jackie became very close to me, like a girlfriend really, even though she was much younger. I simply think Charlie didn't like the fact that not one but two new people were now competing for my attention. Until then, he had been the center of my world.

Charlie wasn't working at the time. His career had narrowed down to the

Behind the scenes on The Big Record (1958)

With Burt Lancaster in a scene from "Elmer Gantry"

On stage with fellow KTUL performer Al Clauser (1945)

Performing with the
Jimmy Joy Orchestra
(1947)

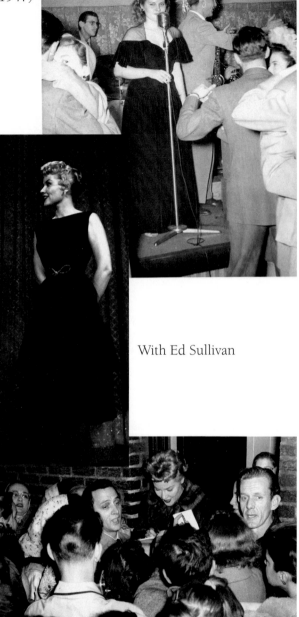

With Ed Sullivan

At the stage door of
The Big Record sign-
ing autographs for
fans (1958)

"Boys Night Out". Anne Jeffreys (left); Janet Blair (center); Patti (right)

Contest winner Clara Ann Fowler with Bob Hope at Avey's Coliseum in Tulsa, OK (1943)

Rehearsing for The Big Record (1958)

With my friend Rosemary
Clooney

With Elvis Presley and
The Jordanaires (Charlie
O'Curran on Patti's left)

With David Janssen and
David Kory in a scene
from "Dondi"

Checking out
my gowns in
a small New
York dressing
room

Very early
recording
date with
Jack Rael
(glasses)
and the
musicians

Performing
with The
Four Lads
on The Big
Record

Making music with my
friend Frankie Laine

Guest appearance
on "The Joey
Bishop Show"
with his co-host
Regis Philbin
(1966)

Singing to the troupes
during a tour in Viet Nam

With Mom
& Dad

Singing Christmas music
with Perry Como and Eddie
Fisher (picture used on
cover of TV Guide)

With Danny,
Kathleen &
Charlie

With Jerry, Page and Sarah

Winning my first Grammy
(1998)

The whole
Fowler Family
at mom and
dad's 50th
Anniversary.

point where he had a job only if there was a Presley picture that Hal Wallis wanted him to do or when I needed advice on my shows. When he'd do a picture with Hal Wallis he was a big man for a while, and that would last him for half a year or so, at least as far as his ego was concerned, and he could live on that. His down times, however, got to be very draining on me, and I had conversations with Charlie where I threatened to leave, even before we had any children. I ignored the red flags that I saw popping up because of my dream to start a family. And then once Kathleen came along, I was too busy doing everything I could to make life perfect for our daughter.

I took baby Kathleen on Regis Philbin's show, which was local in San Diego at that time, but tried to stifle the media to a large degree. That was because of the adoption rules at the time. I was told that during the first six months of an adoption, the birth mother had the right to change her mind and reclaim the child. For the second six months, as we understood it, both the adoptive and birth parents had the same rights. At that time, either couple could go to court and claim to be the best parents for the child. After a year without challenging the adoption, the birth mother no longer had the right to try and reclaim the child. So, Charlie and I were sort of walking on eggshells the first year, especially that first six months. I was concerned about what might happen if I got national publicity and the birth parents saw me holding my beautiful baby girl adopted from Arkansas. My lawyer suggested that we not have any pictures taken, so there would be no media exposure that might trigger someone to say, "That's my baby."

The agency gave us a choice to either share our identity with Kathleen's parents or not. We chose not, and so we also didn't seek the identity of the birth parents. To this day, I do not know those folks, and as an adult, Kathleen has chosen not to try to find her birth parents.

I returned to work, recording several new singles and another album, including the title song for *Boys' Night Out* and a cut I particularly like called "Most People Get Married." I played everything from the Arkansas Poultry Festival at Robinson Auditorium in Little Rock, Arkansas, in August to *The Pat Boone Show*, a TV special, that September.

Peter, Paul, and Mary were guest stars on Pat's show and sang their huge folk hit "If I Had a Hammer." Watching the folk trio, I couldn't help but think that music was changing in very distinct ways. But I had no idea how drastically it would change—and soon. Pat, myself, and comedian Phil Harris represented the "old guard" of show business. When Pat and I did a medley at the end of the show, it felt like old, comfortable times.

Whenever I was away from Los Angeles, Jackie and Kathleen would travel with me. Charlie worked on Elvis's movie *Girls! Girls! Girls!* at Paramount with Hal Wallis, so except for the beautiful additions to our family of Kathleen and Jackie, life was pretty much normal. And of course our friends spent more time at our house—everyone had to see the baby. Kathleen was the biggest celebrity on Canon Drive.

That Christmas with the new baby was very low-key. We stayed at home because we didn't want any publicity. One sad thing was that Charlie's mother was in ill health and could not come out to meet the new baby. In fact, she would never meet Kathleen. Charlie's father had abandoned his family when Charlie was young, so he was out of the picture, but I had hoped that Charlie's mother would be involved in Kathleen's life. At least Kathleen had received a very warm reception from my side of the family. Our first Christmas was a wonderful, cozy little time that really taught me how special it could be to finally be a mom.

In January of 1963, Charlie went to work on another Elvis picture, called *Fun in Acapulco*. Meanwhile, there was talk of me doing my own TV show again, but the "conventional wisdom" of the networks had devolved to the belief that women couldn't carry a show anymore. Their idea was that women comprised the majority of the TV viewing audience and that women preferred seeing men on television. I didn't go for that because women were my best audiences in nightclubs. I contended that the audience was interested in the content of the show, not whether the star was a man or a woman. I told anyone in the industry who would listen that taking people like Rosie Clooney, Dinah Shore, and me off television was short-sighted.

I often couldn't understand and found it hard to predict male thinking in the television industry. When I was a guest on *The Ed Sullivan Show* and was going to perform *Boy's Night Out*, Ed wouldn't let me sing the last line, "What boys are after, girls are after, too." He said it was too risqué! Yet I'd sung the same line on Pat Boone's special, and there wasn't anyone in show business more family-conscious than Pat.

It took years for women to come back strong as forces on television, and today they basically rule. Will there ever be anyone on television more powerful than Oprah Winfrey? Sometimes I wonder what TV would have been like, had network executives been a little more open in the mid-1960s.

During the early 1960s, Patti Page was offered parts on several television shows—a situation comedy, a Western, and a series about three women working for a fashion magazine—but she and her management felt the roles would have been a backward step for her TV career.

Yet she did remain a major television personality. In May 1963, she appeared on her sixth TV special with Bob Hope and was paid $10,000, or a hundred times what she'd received for her first stage appearance with Hope in Tulsa, in 1946.

As time went on, I didn't have to keep Kathleen away from the cameras so much. She was about eight months old when I was preparing to leave on a six-week concert tour that would take me to the Philippines, Korea, Vietnam, Hong Kong, Singapore, Australia, and Japan. But first, with Mother's Day approaching, I couldn't turn down a request to do a full cover story about our new family for the magazine *Woman's World*.

The day of the photo shoot turned out to be one of the strangest days of my life. The photographers arrived at 8:00 in the morning and started setting up. Kathleen had been a dream from the beginning, a lovely baby who didn't cry much at all, so Jackie and I were baffled when she started crying and kept it up that whole day. We changed diapers, made sure she was fed, took her temperature, but everything seemed like it was just fine. We managed to get some good pictures, but were about at our wit's end. Then, at 4:00 p.m. she stopped crying just like that. Nobody knew what to think. The photographers got some more shots, then wrapped up and went on their way. About two hours later, I got a call from Oklahoma. My dad had died at precisely the moment Kathleen stopped crying.

I'd bought my parents a rocking chair at a place in New Hampshire where I'd worked, the Farragut Hotel, where all the acts stayed when they played right in Rye Beach. They sold gorgeous rocking chairs and I sent one to each of my sisters who had their own place and one to my mom and dad. That Friday before Mother's Day, Dad died in that chair. He had pneumonia and had never been one to check himself into a hospital if he was feeling rough.

Kathleen had met my father one time, the week before the photo shoot, when

I'd worked in Hot Springs again. My mom and dad always came to see me when I worked there because it was within easy driving distance from Tulsa. I'd thought Dad was getting a cold, but I didn't think much of it when he and my mom said goodbye and drove back to Tulsa. They left on Wednesday morning. I closed the engagement that night and flew back to Los Angeles for the photo shoot that Friday.

I was scheduled to leave for Japan on Monday, but on the news of my father's passing, Charlie and I left Kathleen in Los Angeles with Jackie and flew to Oklahoma. It was so strange, flying out for my father's funeral after seeing him laughing and happy only a few days before. I consoled myself with the fact that he had seen all his girls except my little sister, Peggy, at my concerts in Hot Springs, and on the way back home he and my mother happened to meet up with Peggy and her husband on the highway to Hot Springs. What were the odds, in the days before cell phones, of them passing one another on the highway and stopping to talk? It was eerie. All I could attribute it to was the hand of God. The only sibling my father hadn't seen that week in Hot Springs was my brother, Charlie, the one who had been in the service in Korea. He was living in Youngstown, Ohio, which was a little too far to drive.

I had never talked to Dad much about my career, or anything else, really. He just wasn't a big talker. When he was proud of me for something, I would usually find out the same way I learned it was okay for me to join the Jimmy Joy band—via someone else. My father didn't have that many friends and what railroad friends he did have, he didn't see much after he retired. Someone in our family would always tell me how Dad felt. When he hadn't seen me for a while, my father would just look at me and cry. I felt so grateful that he had been there in Hot Springs the whole week.

I'm sure that both my parents were always a little bit amazed by how my life turned out and wondered how God had always seemed to put me in the right place at the right time so I was able to do what I really loved—sing for people. I couldn't answer that, but I knew my Dad was now in a place where he could find out. My dad playing guitar while his girls sang had contributed a lot to my becoming a singer. I hope that it had made him happy when I recorded the song he wrote, "Who's Gonna Shoe My Pretty Little Feet," on one of my Country albums. He had been a wonderful man, and I would miss him. I thought about the way he had always cried when he heard me sing "Tennessee Waltz," and I shed silent tears on that flight to Tulsa.

THIRTEEN New Pages
for Music and Me

My family had to almost force me to leave Tulsa after Dad's funeral. My tour had already been postponed by two days. They convinced me that there was nothing anyone could do, including me, except get on with our lives. It was sensible advice, but they had to persuade me. I felt this time that it wasn't the show that should go on, but family life. They were right, though. When I saw the faces of the U.S. soldiers in Okinawa light up at hearing songs that reminded them of home, I knew I'd done the right thing, something Dad would have wanted.

Page had long had fans throughout Asia. In fact, in Japan, "Tennessee Waltz" had been the first American record to catch on, and a restaurant had been named The Tennessee Club after the tune. A Japanese singer had even recorded "Tennessee Waltz" in Japanese, making her a star.

During her 1963 tour, Patti also played for American servicemen in Hong Kong, at the

NCO Club and the U.S. Officers Club. Many of her appearances were for one night only, except for a three-day stint at the Sankei Hall, in Tokyo. In the Philippines, she played to audiences of 1,500 to 2,000, and to larger crowds in Japan and Hong Kong.

At the City Concert Hall in Hong Kong, I got deafening applause and squeals of delight with every number. These people really knew my music. And as I walked out in the audience, as I now routinely did during my show, some of the young men seemed to swoon over being near me. Now I knew what Frank Sinatra and Elvis felt like with the young women!

Our traveling group consisted of me, Charlie, the baby, Jackie, Jack, and my hairdresser, my pianist, and my guitarist. Though it might seem unexpected, having a baby along made the trip more exciting. I had Kathleen to play with during the day! She was precious, the perfect baby. It was heartbreaking to be separated from her, but I couldn't keep her with me all the time. I was playing in many locations on the tour and didn't think it would be wise for her to be up and down in so many airplanes in such a short span of time. After my performances in Japan, I sent Jackie and Kathleen to Australia ahead of us. We played the other locations then took a flight from Hong Kong to Australia and ended up getting the same pilot that had flown Kathleen and Jackie "Down Under." He and the stewardesses told us they'd never seen such a good baby on a flight. Kathleen had slept soundly and didn't cry. I felt very proud.

I played Australia for two successive weekends at the Chevron Hilton. In the week between my performances, we got to see a little bit of the country, and I found the Australian people to be as friendly as my people back in Oklahoma. The whirlwind tour was about six weeks long, so by the first part of July 1963 we were back in the States.

Life just seemed better with the new addition to our family. I'd cut my touring down to about forty-two weeks a year and was loving spending time with the baby. I also got to spend more time with my family back in Tulsa. I was all over the country in the next few months—San Francisco; Sparks, NV, just east of Reno; Houston; and Boston—but I was back in my hometown, Tulsa, for Kathleen's first birthday on October 21 and took a few more days, enjoying being off the road.

One day while I sat with Kathleen in my lap in my mother's living room we were watching television because the president was visiting Dallas. Coverage of his motorcade wasn't being broadcast nationally because there was no satellite transmission at that time, but we could pick up the Dallas stations and were watching it live. I was feeding Kathleen a bottle trying to put her to sleep. Then the narration of the events became hysterical as we watched the horrible events unfold before our eyes. President Kennedy and Governor Connolly shot in their open limousine! The First Lady scrambled on top of her husband, trying to protect him, but of course it was too late.

It was mind-boggling. From then on, everyone was glued to the television. All of the networks concentrated on nothing else, from the assassination itself to Johnson being sworn in as president to Jack Ruby killing Lee Harvey Oswald in the jail garage in Dallas. The entire country was in shock. Shows were canceled and theaters were closed, all of which I thought was a mistake. Instead of keeping them open to get people's morale up, they closed them.

It was a strange Thanksgiving and Christmas season in the United States that year. No one understood how such a thing could have happened. The job I did best was singing and hopefully cheering people up. And back in Los Angeles, that's what I tried to do. As the New Year turned, I hoped that the social malaise that seemed to be hovering over the country would lift.

Fortunately, it wasn't long before it did. Entertainment played a role, but in a way I could never have predicted.

In January 1964, I was playing the Latin Casino in Philadelphia, and Charlie and I took a day off to attend the christening of the son of friends of ours, Joe and Evelyn Niagara. Joe Niagara was an important disc jockey in Philadelphia, so the christening was filled with people from the press and entertainment industry, including Chubby "The Twist" Checker. Like my husband, I tended to spend time with behind-the-scenes people such as disc jockeys. I'd always liked DJs ever since the early days of my career when I had to meet a lot of disc jockeys in their studios. They were so competitive, and if you didn't impress the right DJ first in a city, you were dead because the others wouldn't consider you important and play your record—Bill Randall in the Cleveland area was one example. When you did a show with a DJ, they'd talk to you on air between playing your latest single and maybe a commercial. The whole thing would take only five or ten minutes at the most but could sell a lot of records in the area. Later, I'd do shows by phone. Once, I did almost three dozen of them in a day. One DJ, Joe Smith, eventually became the head of Warner Bros. Music.

But no DJ in America could make an act the talk of the nation the way Ed Sullivan could on TV. On February 9, 1964, while I was playing in Philadelphia, Ed introduced four boys from England that I'd never heard of called The Beatles. I'd never seen such craziness on television, the girls screaming so loudly you could barely hear the music. I wasn't around when all the girls were crying and screaming for Sinatra at the Paramount, but I'd seen what it was like for Elvis around the ladies, and I'd heard how they would shoot him from only the waist up the second time he went on *Ed Sullivan*. That was mild compared to the girls' reactions to The Beatles, who were just four little kids to me. Their haircuts were a bit different, though not as different as they would become in a few short years. I imagine there's many a parent who would have loved musicians to be like The Beatles were when they first came out rather than all the strange acts that followed during the hippie era.

Watching those girls freak out on television made me think, *Oh my God, what's happening to our world?* It makes me laugh now, thinking back to how wild the whole scene looked. The Beatles later did two more shows with Ed, with their performances on the third show taped beforehand. By the time they were done, American music would never be the same, and neither would American girls.

I could only imagine what it was like to get that kind of reaction from audiences. A reporter for the *L.A. Times* had written a crazy article in 1962 saying that I had been walking down the street in Miami Beach a few years before and a rubber-necking guy in a convertible wrecked his car because I distracted him. According to the article, the man had sued me for $50,000 because he couldn't take his eyes off me. That was flattering, but it didn't happen.

With fans, it's just the nature of females to be more emotionally demonstrative. I remember stepping onstage at the Capitol Theater in a strapless orchid-colored gown and hearing wolf whistles among the cheers, but generally, boys never went that wild in my audiences. I kind of wish they had! It was always girls following boys. When the 50s teen idol boys came in, like Frankie Avalon, they were the ones that the girls chased. I was never in that "being followed" class. I had fans, girls and boys, but none of them screamed and cried like they did with The Beatles.

That was in a different day of celebrity. Today, girl singers like Britney Spears and Miley Cyrus are just as likely, or even more likely, than boy singers to be followed by fans and photographers. Then, any girl singer could stroll to the store and not be bothered, but the boy singers couldn't. They were followed everywhere. And The Beatles were virtually held prisoner in their hotels by fans.

I got to see The Beatles in Las Vegas courtesy of my friend, Kappi Ditson Jordan, who handled my record promotion publicity. She also did travel arrangements for performers and, lucky her, she was handling all of The Beatles travel throughout their first American tour, working with their manager, Brian Epstein. I was scared to death at that concert! The Beatles played in a big auditorium and Kappi and I were sitting in the middle of the place. Having only seen the "Fab Four" on television, I didn't realize just how frantic those fans were in person. So, silly me, I'd brought along the baby. Girls were standing on the seats and screaming so loudly I couldn't really hear the music. At one point, I thought they would come climbing over the seats behind us to get closer to the stage and there might be a stampede. They were pushing toward the stage and the guards, stationed at the end of every aisle, had to keep them back.

Kathleen wasn't particularly disturbed by the crowd, but I was. And since we couldn't hear that much of the music, Kappi and I got out of there early. Thankfully, there weren't any reporters around to take pictures and write "Patti Page Walks Out of Beatles Concert!"

To me, John, Paul, George, and Ringo were just cute, enthusiastic young boys. The potential of their eventual fame just didn't occur to me yet. I had Kappi get word to them that if they wanted, they could get away from the crowds and use the tennis court and pool at the house where I was staying in Vegas, but they never showed up. And why would they? I'd seen what women did around Elvis—for The Beatles, this was magnified four times, at least!

When The Beatles "invaded" they played the theaters and coliseums. It amazed me when they packed Shea Stadium. I had played Soldier Field in Chicago, one of the largest stadiums in the world, but I had never played there alone. One time at Soldier Field we had six headliners on the bill: me, Eddie Fisher, Frankie Laine, Nat "King" Cole, Ray Anthony's orchestra, and Billy Mays's orchestra. We did a tour of five cities, playing the arenas. The Beatles could pack those places all by themselves. My peers and I thought that it was fabulous to generate that many fans, but since The Beatles were an import from England, there was also a feeling among performers of "How dare they come over here and do that!"

We were aware of the huge changes they were ushering in, but I'm not sure The Beatles were aware of it. How could they be? America was new for them. One thing I know: Pop music made a dramatic change. We already had Rock 'n' Roll, but this was different. Nobody could really pinpoint what "it" was—we just knew things were going to be different. Not long after The Beatles made their debut, other groups started coming across the Atlantic.

I got my own dose of "the British invasion" when I appeared on *The Ed Sullivan Show* the same night as the group Gerry and the Pacemakers. They, too, were managed by Brian Epstein. The brilliant Stevie Wonder was also on his show doing his hit "Fingertips," as well as a popular comedian named Bill Dana who did a Mexican character named "Jose Jimenez" that he'd never be able to do in these politically correct days. The Pacemakers were dressed in suits like The Beatles had worn, there were four of them, and the girls swooned over their hit "Don't Let the Sun Catch You Crying."

Perhaps inevitably, my music was changing, too. I had switched record labels and was now on Columbia. The 1960s were all about albums, and I felt that while Mercury did a good job of selling singles, they just didn't know how to push albums. The 1960s were the beginning of Nashville being the Pop center of the world, too, and Columbia thought that was the place for me to go and record. I liked their thinking.

Patti Page is best known for her most popular single releases such as "Tennessee Waltz" and "How Much Is That Doggie in the Window?" But avid fans and aficionados are aware that in her early days with Mercury, in 1947 and 1948, she recorded albums in which she explored genres for which she is less well-known. A notable example is the Jazz album she did with guitarist George Barnes and his group.

On her new record label, Columbia, she proved that she was still one of the industry's most focused and hardest-working singers, recording three albums in 1964 alone. When she wasn't recording or touring, she made TV appearances. In late March she was featured on *Hollywood Palace* with a number of traditional acts—George Burns as host, Carl Reiner and Mel Brooks, Sergio Franchi, and the Lennon Sisters from *The Lawrence Welk Show.* In April, she was back in New York, playing the Empire Room at the Waldorf-Astoria Hotel. It was a lively time to be playing in the Big Apple as the city was packed with people from around the world flocking to the World's Fair.

After we'd adopted Kathleen, I wondered if I might then get pregnant; I'd heard of that kind of thing happening with couples. But it didn't happen. Any test I took to find out if I had a physical problem continued to give me the all-clear, and Charlie still would not have any tests done.

Then one day a man who was a dear friend to Charlie, the famous Hollywood clothier Sy Devore, was over at the house with his daughter. Sy's little girl was adopted, probably five or six years older than Kathleen, and she said to her father, "Why couldn't you have adopted someone for me to play with so that I wouldn't be alone all the time?" Here she was visiting with cute little Kathleen and she realized what she was missing out on because she didn't have a sister or brother. This got Charlie and me thinking.

"I don't want Kathleen to grow up like that," I told Charlie over dinner that night. "We've got to adopt a sister or brother for her."

"I think you're right, hon," Charlie said.

And that's how our son came into our lives. I called up the same lawyers in

Arkansas, and it wasn't long before they called back and said there was a little boy expected, would we like to adopt him? Naturally, I said we'd be there. A year and a half after Kathleen, our son was born on June 22, 1964. We flew down to Little Rock to bring him home. He was no relation to Kathleen, and all we knew about his birth parents was that his mother was married to a man serving in Vietnam. She got pregnant while her husband was away, and she wanted to adopt the baby out. We named our son Daniel Benjamin, in honor of my father, whose name was Benjamin. Danny was the cutest blonde-haired boy.

Later, when Danny grew up, he wanted to find out about his birth parents, but unfortunately I didn't have a lot of information to help him. I knew the doctor who delivered him, the same one who had delivered Kathleen in the same hospital, and that was about it.

The thought had crossed my mind that maybe my mother wouldn't accept adopted kids as well as her other grandkids that were her own blood. My mother loved all her grandchildren and doted on them, though, and treated my kids just like the rest. I did notice, however, that Charlie didn't seem as happy about Danny as he had been about Kathleen. It was just something I felt, and I didn't see it as a red flag at first. Charlie was pretty "show business." In front of the right people, if it was the right moment to be proud of his son, he was, but I don't remember too much bonding between Charlie and baby Danny and that would have bad repercussions later.

Since I was working so much, I took the kids with me constantly, up until when they started preschool, and we had fun. We had Jackie with us, and I'd learned how to shape my professional schedule to suit the children. I always tried to fly at night when they were sleepy. Since I worked late, I would get up about the time the kids were having lunch. They would nap, then Jackie would take them for a walk, leaving me some space to do an interview if necessary. Otherwise, I'd be on the walk, too. When we were at home, I'd care for them in the afternoon. After they started preschool, they'd get back around 4:00 p.m.

and I would be with them until they went to bed. When we were on the road and I was busy, Jackie would keep them busy and happy by going to the zoo and doing other activities like that.

It wasn't difficult being on the road, even with two kids. Rental services could provide everything you needed, from diapers to playpens, strollers, and cribs. Kathleen never complained when I took her on airplanes in a canvas fold-up basket with all the essentials—formula, disposable diapers, and a change of clothes—stuffed in an airline bag. That arrangement suited Danny just fine, too. They did get a bit pampered, I admit— Kathleen's wardrobe grew almost as big as mine, and Danny had more cute new outfits than I think he felt comfortable in.

I learned patience from being a mother. I could be out all day and come back tired, knowing I'd need sleep if I expected to do an evening show, then when I'd see my kids and start playing with them, all thoughts of sleep would be forgotten. Before the kids, I would get impatient about little things. After they were in my life a while, the family values I'd grown up with thanks to my hard-working parents and older siblings came rushing back to me. I regained perspective.

FOURTEEN	Golden Statues and Changing Dreams

My love of singing and of the movies would come together in a most unexpected—and welcome—way in 1964. Late that year, I flew to Nashville to record a song inspired by a movie that had just been made, starring the great Bette Davis. My song "Hush, Hush, Sweet Charlotte" was *not* featured in the movie of the same name, but it did end up being nominated for an Academy Award for Best Song, and I sang it at the Oscars. Show business sure does move in mysterious ways.

There was a version of the song in the movie, sung by Al Martino, over the opening titles. The music was by Frank DeVol, who had done the score for the movie. Mack David had written the lyrics, which gave audiences a taste of the grisly story at the heart of the movie.

Chop chop, sweet Charlotte
Chop chop till he's dead
Chop chop, sweet Charlotte
Chop off his hand and head
To meet your lover you ran chop chop

Now everyone understands
Just why you went to meet your love chop chop
To chop off his head and hand
© 1964 by Frank DeVol and Mack David

No one had yet done a commercial recording of the theme song, though. Bob Johnson, who was an A & R man at Columbia, called up Joe Pasternak, who produced all the Academy Awards shows at the time. Bob offered that I would record "Hush, Hush, Sweet Charlotte" if Joe booked me on the Academy Awards show to sing the song. Joe agreed, so I recorded "Hush, Hush, Sweet Charlotte" after the movie was released and sang the song at the Oscars.

For my version, Mack David wrote lyrics that were quite a bit different.

Hush hush, sweet Charlotte
Charlotte, don't you cry
Hush hush, sweet Charlotte
He'll love you till he dies

Oh, hold him darling
Please hold him tight
And brush the tear from your eye
You weep because you had a dream last night
You dreamed that he said goodbye
He held two roses within his hand
Two roses he gave to you
The red rose tells you of his passion
The white rose his love so true

And every night after he shall die
Yes every night when he's gone

The wind will sing you this lullaby
Sweet Charlotte was loved by John
© 1964 by Frank DeVol and Mack David

In addition to the single, Patti also released a *Hush, Hush, Sweet Charlotte* album on Columbia in 1965, which was reissued and combined with her *Gentle on My Mind* album in 1968.

The film *Hush, Hush, Sweet Charlotte* received seven Oscar nominations, more than any other horror movie up until that time.

Page sang "Hush, Hush, Sweet Charlotte" at the 37th Academy Awards on April 5, 1965, at the Santa Monica Civic Auditorium. The combined audience—those in the auditorium plus TV viewers watching the Oscars broadcast at home—was the greatest she had ever reached at one time. The song went to #1 after her performance, but it was "Chim Chim Cher-ee" from the movie *Mary Poppins* that won the Oscar for Best Song.

As The New Christy Minstrels sang "Chim Chim Cher-ee" on the show, I fondly recalled Julie Andrews appearing on *The Big Record* so many years before. It was appropriate that she won that night. After all, not only had her song been in her movie, so had she! Julie was also nominated for Best Actress for *Mary Poppins*, and she won that Oscar, too.

To me, it was just the perfect evening—to be able to sing on the Oscars stage with the audience dazzlingly dressed and knowing millions of people were watching at home on TV. A while later, I got a letter from producer Joe Pasternak in which he thanked me for appearing and for "adding to our Hollywood image of real glamour." I saved that letter!

Charlie's buddy Hal B. Wallis was nominated as producer for *Becket* but he lost to Jack Warner and *My Fair Lady*, which won a lot of golden statuettes that evening. (*Mary Poppins* also won an Oscar for Best Music Score, Substantially Original, and *My Fair Lady* won for Best Scoring of Music, Adaptation or Treatment.) Becket won an Oscar for Best Screenplay based on material from another medium. We were very happy for Hal that evening. And I was proud to be associated with *Hush, Hush, Sweet Charlotte*.

The funny thing about the Oscar program back then was that it started with "The Star Spangled Banner." Can you imagine that happening now? Times have changed—and not necessarily for the better. Maybe my old friend Bob Hope being Master of Ceremonies had something to do with that opening. For a fellow who was born in England, he was amazingly patriotic.

I got my own "Oscar" in January of 1965 while performing at the Ivy at the Sands in Las Vegas. During my closing show, the famous comedy team of Allen and Rossi interrupted my act to present me with a comic version of the little golden man because they said I'd been cheated by the Academy. I appreciated that very much because the "Oscar" Marty Allen carried on stage was at least six feet tall!

As Page's single "Hush, Hush, Sweet Charlotte" was reaching #1 on the charts, she was reaching out towards a new horizon in her career: She was about to take to the stage in a musical. Page had the lead role in *Annie Get Your Gun* at the Dallas State Fair.

The part of Annie Oakley had been written by Irving Berlin for Ethel Merman to perform on Broadway. Betty Hutton, Charlie O'Curran's ex-wife, had taken over the role for the movie, released in 1950. Productions of the musical had been entertaining audiences across the country since it began touring in October 1947, in Dallas, Texas, with Mary Martin playing Annie.

Annie Get Your Gun was the first time I'd ever done anything like a musical, and the prospect terrified me. Time and time again, I put off learning my lines. I would just take the material out and look at it once in a while. I knew the words to the songs but I didn't rehearse them. I guessed I just thought it would go away! No doubt I was afraid of how I might be received since it was a completely different medium for me.

I'd had the material to study for around three months, but it wasn't until a week before I had to report in Dallas that I began familiarizing myself with the part. Every waking hour I could take away from my children I spent in a studio in the back of my house learning all the songs and the dialogue. And that was far from easy. In *Annie Get Your Gun*, Annie's onstage 85 percent of the time.

On the way to Dallas, I dropped the kids off in Kansas to visit with their Aunt Trudie. She always took care of the kids in the family and was the one everybody else could count on to help out. I had two nights with her in Wichita for a little rest, then I flew on down to Dallas so I could concentrate twenty-four hours a day on the show during the next week of rehearsals. It was times like this that I loved the fact that I was part of a big family.

Ethel Merman and Betty Hutton were boisterous; that was their style. I took a completely new approach to Annie. I did a quiet Annie, one that had a little less oomph. We performed for two weeks and kept the usual Broadway schedule of eight performances a week. It wasn't easy because I was worn out from the rehearsals and all the tension—perhaps because I'd had to learn it all in a week. It was my own fault, but then everything in my career—good and bad—was my own fault.

By doing that musical, I learned something important about performing onstage. One night after a performance, the director knocked on my dressing room door and asked to have a private word with me. He explained that I was getting upstaged by other cast members. I was naive about the ways of stage actors and actresses. I'd gotten too involved in the play, trying to make it too real, I suppose, and I was getting overshadowed. Others were capturing the limelight by positioning themselves at the front of the stage.

"Patti," he said to me quietly, "tomorrow night, I want you to just walk to the front of the stage and deliver your lines. These New York actors and actresses will never try to upstage you again. Try it, you'll see what I mean."

I had been so involved in the story itself—and of course, the music—that I hadn't thought about being in the right place so the audience could see me. It was like my problem with the key light on the movie set. I had to be more concerned with my position on the stage.

So I did what the director said, just like I had on the set of *Boys Night Out*. When I walked to the front of the stage that next night, it worked. A couple of the actors looked a little shocked, but they didn't try to upstage me again.

I was glad that I'd made the decision to play Annie a little differently as it resulted in the best review I'd ever got in my career; the reviewer thought that I brought some life and truthfulness and sincerity to Annie. I was thrilled. What I hadn't realized until playing Annie was how emotionally involving it would be. After one performance in Dallas, I got a standing ovation, and it made me so overjoyed I cried. I was still crying when a reviewer interviewed me backstage.

Patti Page's performance as Annie Oakley received high praise not only from audiences and critics but also from her fellow cast members. The reviewer for the *Dallas Times-Herald* who interviewed a tearful Patti Page backstage quoted her co-star Jack Washburn as saying she brought out "a new quality in Annie." Another Dallas reviewer said her performance was "a study to remember." Joe Brady in *The Daily Oklahoman* wrote "Our Patti Page Wows 'Em at State Fair Music Hall."

The main thing in my life in those days was my kids, though, and I was happiest whenever they were with me. When I was playing in Reno once, Danny was in the audience when I started singing "the Waltz." He cried out, "That's my Mommy!" and the audience cracked up. So did I. They had to take him out of the room because he wouldn't stop talking about his mommy singing.

I wasn't sure of what route to take next in my career. I thought about doing more musicals. Offers had begun coming in even before I finished in Dallas, such as an invitation to appear in *Can Can* in San Francisco. But I decided that, what with my kids and husband, maybe I should simply stick with what I did best—touring and putting on concerts and aiming to make people happy with my music. So for the next couple of years, that's what I set about doing.

FIFTEEN

Old Haunts, Brand-New Places, and Home

My procrastination prior to *Annie Get Your Gun* taught me a lesson. Before I opened at the Sands in Las Vegas that year, I decided to get a little more rest and not make any major changes in my show. I didn't want to work myself into a tizzy again over rehearsing something new. Besides, I wondered how prudent it was to have a work schedule like mine while trying to raise children, nanny or no nanny. When performing, I'd get to bed no earlier than 3:00 a.m., then be up as early as possible to be with my children as much as I could.

Then there was all the travel. Doing a concert for Emperor Hirohito in Japan might sound exotic and wonderful—and it was—but ask anyone who travels the world on business about jet lag, and they'll have a lot of stories of exhaustion.

Patti Page's Far East tour itinerary in 1965 was not as extensive as it had been on her previous tour, with fifteen stops in places such as Tokyo, Hong Kong, Formosa (later named Taiwan), Australia, and a number of performances for servicemen in Okinawa and other U.S. bases. Along with her this time were husband Charlie, manager Jack, musical director Rocky Cole, hair stylist Lee Trent, and drummer Kenny Hume.

Page continued to have a dedicated fan base in Japan, where "Hush, Hush, Sweet Charlotte" had hit #1 in the charts. Columbia put out a Japan-only album entitled *Patti Page in Tokyo*.

When Page played the "City Hall" arena in Hong Kong, she added something new to her performance, singing a song that was popular at the time, "Boll Weevil," and accompanying herself on the guitar.

In 1966, she embarked on another international tour, starting off in Germany. From there she went to Bangkok, Thailand.

In Bangkok, I gave one of the oddest performances of my life, singing with King Bhumibol Adulyadej of Thailand, who plays the clarinet. I joked to my husband that it was "Patti and the King" instead of "Anna and the King."

Five-minute versions of my fifteen-minute TV show *Songalongs* had played in Thailand, and the King told me that from those snippets, he had learned English. The King was actually born in Cambridge, Massachusetts while his father was attending Harvard Medical School but the family had left the U.S. before he was old enough to talk. He asked me to his palace, where he played some songs he had written. Then we expanded the set, with Rocky on piano and Kenny on drums. With His Highness playing along, I sang "This Is My Song" because that's what my royal host remembered seeing on the TV.

I was scared to death. Not knowing all the customs, you never know exactly what might happen in a foreign country or how you should behave. We had been instructed on protocol, what to do and not do in the presence of Thai royalty, and the King's chief of staff was there as well as the U.S. State Department protocol man, but I was still nervous. The King told us that his songs were from what he called his "gay file," and we weren't quite sure what to make of that. At least I didn't laugh.

As we got into "This Is My Song," the King came in on the clarinet in the background, and he held his own as a musician. Our "concert" ended on a happy note for all concerned. It was a once-in-a-lifetime opportunity.

As any parent will attest to, once kids come along, your priorities change. My favorite audience was back in Beverly Hills: my kids. I wanted to be by the pool and romping with them in their playground or pulling them around in the miniature rickshaw I'd brought back from Hong Kong. My family life changed the kind of press coverage I got. Now the press wanted to know what kind of recipes I favored and how the kids were. There were photo shoots with Kathleen and Danny and the occasional article about Charlie and me now that we had a family. More than ever, newspapers and magazines wanted to interview me about being a domestic diva. My tastes had always been for good simple family meals rather than gourmet fads. I loved turkey dinners so much that I cooked them several times during the year, not just at Thanksgiving. Two parts cornbread, one part white bread, sautéed celery, onions, sage, and seasonings for the stuffing, that's what I liked.

I even got one of my favorite sweet potato recipes published once, or should I say, the recipe I borrowed from my mother's extensive collection of

Southern cooking. This one was a holiday favorite in the Fowler household when I was a kid:

Yam and Apple Casserole

(six servings)

3 medium size yams or sweet potatoes

3 green Pippin apples

3 tablespoons molasses

3 tablespoons butter

¼ teaspoon salt

6 marshmallows

¼ cup pecan halves

In shallow, well-buttered casserole, place slices of peeled (raw) yams or sweet potatoes, alternating with layers of peeled apple slices. Combine molasses, butter, and salt; heat and pour over yams and apples. Bake at 350 degrees for about one hour or until yams are tender. Top with marshmallows and pecan halves the last half hour of cooking. Serve with roast turkey or other fowl.

Try it, if you dare. This was the type of cooking I'd been brought up around, and maybe it helps explain my weight battles that reporters had been obsessed with for all those years. There were two rules at the Fowler dinner table: You could only have one helping, and you just ate what your mother put on your plate. We were poor and we knew that was the only food we were going to get for a while. But as you can see from this recipe, those meals—especially the dishes we had during the holidays—weren't exactly diet foods!

Being a parent made me look at certain aspects of life a bit more closely, too. There were definitely issues I was more concerned about now. When I watched TV news and read the newspapers, following what was going on in the culture, I wondered what kind of world Kathleen and Danny would be inheriting. I wondered if the long hair that was becoming so popular on boys and men, and the sounds enjoyed by The Beatles generation, were healthy. I thought of Kathleen, who had taken to walking around en pointe, with her toes curled under, like a ballet dancer. She hadn't had lessons, it was just something she'd started doing. I had thought maybe it wasn't healthy but the doctor told me to never stop a child from doing anything that "came natural." Maybe the younger generation of performers like The Beatles and other bands were also just doing what "came natural," but I was worried about the drugs that I'd heard about—a lot stronger stuff than Benny Goodman's boys and a room full of marijuana smoke.

Some record executives shared my concerns, but they weren't saying or doing anything about it. I remember one executive for Columbia told me that he wouldn't let his kids be involved with "all that stuff," including the music of The Beatles, which Columbia distributed. I was amazed at the hypocrisy of it—The Beatles were helping pay his bills. I was on the same label, but my opinion didn't matter unless it was about my own music.

I was troubled by some of the attitudes expressed in Rock music. I had sung for too many groups of soldiers to turn my back on them now, and I wouldn't sing protest songs. I didn't like the new morality of the era. That was just how I felt, and in retrospect, I can't say that I was wrong or intolerant. I simply had values that I cherished and an eye on the future of the generation who were listening to the music of the hippie era.

Now that I had kids, it made me even more appreciative of all that my mom had done for me and my brothers and sisters. I talked to Mom every week on the phone, and tried to get to see her as often as I could. I celebrated my birthday in November 1967 by flying to Tulsa to give her the keys to a new house. After my father's death, she'd been living in Oklahoma City. My sister, Peggy, and her husband, Mack, lived there, and I'd helped them build a house there with an adjacent apartment for Mom. She'd also spent time living in Wichita to be near Trudie and Louise, but now that she was getting up there in years, she wanted to go back to where her friends were. So, I bought her a small new house close to my sisters, Ruby and Hazel. She was eighty-five when she moved into that house, which would be the last one she lived in. I had a wonderful birthday with family and friends, enjoying seeing my mother settling into her new place, among the people she loved.

As Patti Page's publicity increasingly began to center on her home life, in 1966 Columbia reissued a family favorite, her 1959 album *Christmas with Patti Page*. And in 1966 she ventured away from her Pop and Country sounds to a more traditional and classical style, for an album titled *America's Favorite Hymns*.

In the summer of 1966, she was invited to sing with the Metropolitan Symphony of New York, ninety-one musicians in all, in Lewisohn Stadium. The only other Pop artist who had ever sung there was Page's old friend Pat Boone. But the ever-adaptable Page was equally at home soon after playing a two-week stint at Detroit's Rooster Tail club.

In February 1967, Patti Page received official recognition from the State of Massachusetts for the contribution her recording of "Old Cape Cod" had made to the state. While she was appearing at Monticello's in Framingham, Patti was presented with a citation from House Speaker John Davoren, who was accompanied by State Treasurer Robert Crane for the presentation. The next month, she was presented a plaque by John A. Volpe, the governor of Massachusetts, in recognition of her contribution to the Massachusetts Tourist Institute.

Page appeared for a week on *The Hollywood Squares* in February 1967 and on her own TV special—aptly called *Something Special*—in May, backed by a children's choir. That month she also appeared for the first time in Calgary, Canada at the Jubilee Auditorium.

For a musician, the release of their *Greatest Hits* album is usually a time to reflect, but when Page's came out in 1967, she had little time to pause and contemplate the past, as she was still busy singing those songs and new ones. Regardless of the changes that were taking place in popular music in the late 1960s, Page was still packing in large audiences. In a four-week run in September 1967, she set an attendance record at the Fiesta Room of the Fremont Hotel in Las Vegas, breaking the record previously held by the popular comedian and actor Red Buttons. Two of the songs she played at the Fiesta Room, "Near Me" and "After Hours," were penned by the King of Thailand. During the period she was playing there, the recording industry held a ceremony to present her with an award for selling more singles than any other female recording artist, for "Tennessee Waltz."

Page had hit the record charts five times in 1966, but now it was in the Easy Listening category where she was making her mark. "In This Day and Age" reached #15 and her version of "Almost Persuaded" made it to #20. In the summer of 1967, she had a double-sided hit, with "Same Old You" and "Walkin'-Just Walkin'" both reaching #16 in Easy Listening. In February of 1968, her version of "Gentle On My Mind" hit the *Billboard* Top 100 and rose to #7 on the Easy Listening charts. This all encouraged airplay for her version of "Little Green Apples," from her *Gentle On My Mind* album.

In February of 1968, while I was playing at the Paradise Island Casino in the Bahamas, one of my favorite places to play, Blinstrub's in Boston, burned down. It was the second largest nightclub in the nation, and I loved playing there. My sister, Ruby, had married a man from Boston, so every time I played at Blinstrub's, I invited his family to come see me, which made my memories of the place just that bit more special. It was a down-to-earth place with mismatched tables and chairs, and you just felt cozy despite its size. I loved the audiences at Blinstrub's, who always made me feel truly welcome. The owners didn't have a cent of insurance on the place. Jack and I couldn't believe it.

Patti Page held the all-time attendance record for Blinstrub's, which was located at 300 Broadway in South Boston and owned by Stanley Blinstrub. She had attracted big crowds to the club since the first night she played there, when lines stretched down the block. A host of big-name nightclub stars appeared at Blinstrub's: Pat Boone, Nat "King" Cole, Bobby Darin, Sammy Davis, Jr., Jimmy Durante, Connie Francis, Arthur Godfrey, and Johnny Mathis were among some of them.

It never occurred to anyone that such an institution as Blinstrub's could ever be lost, but isn't it that way with so many places and people in our lives?

That was never more clear to me than on June 5, 1968 when Robert F. Kennedy, who had just won California as a candidate for the Democratic presidential nomination, was fatally wounded at the Ambassador Hotel in Los Angeles. It was after midnight, and he died a little more than a day later at Good Samaritan Hospital. I was shocked at the news; he'd been such a nice man when I'd known him on the book tour. In June of 1967, he and Ethel had invited me to a dinner dance gala event for the benefit of the Children's Recreation Foundation at the El Morocco in New York. It was a black tie affair and I'd never seen the Senator look as buoyant as he did that night. RFK's death hit my friend, Rosie Clooney, much harder. He was a close friend of hers, and she was there at the Ambassador Hotel when it happened. Rosie was traumatized for years afterward.

Life went on, albeit more sadly for a while. I had been performing for over twenty years. Where did it all go so quickly? I should've asked Al Clauser back in Tulsa because he was celebrating forty years in show business. It made me think back to those days when I sang with Al and the boys, traveling with them on weekends in a twenty-nine-passenger bus. And it occurred to me that maybe the stars had been in the right place when I was born because

I'd been lucky to start out with top musicians. Al was the first person with a Western string band to play on the radio, and he'd appeared in movies with Gene Autry.

It seemed fitting that in June 1968, I got to go home for a concert where it all began. I performed at the Tulsa Civic Assembly for a crowd of around 7,500 people. When the audience gave me one standing ovation after another, I had tears in my eyes. I was just overwhelmed to be embraced so lovingly by fellow Oklahomans.

For Danny and Kathleen, the real thrill came the next month, when I made my debut at Disneyland, headlining in a show called *On Stage U.S.A.* at the Tomorrowland stage. This was the beginning of a long association with "The Happiest Place on Earth."

In September of 1968, Jack and I celebrated our twenty-first anniversary as a team. I was staying at the Americana in New York and performing at the Royal Box, a world-famous nightclub in the hotel. The telegrams poured in. Showbiz people—the great ones, anyway—never forget the little things. One that gave me a real laugh was from Steve Lawrence and Eydie Gorme, who had sent all their best wishes to "the most successful shut-in in the business." I once went to watch a late-night show in Vegas featuring Steve and Eydie. It was very unlike me to be out on the town, and Steve, flabbergasted to see me in the audience, introduced me to the crowd as "the most famous shut-in in show business." It was great hearing from all my old friends, including Tony Bennett, who asked me to be his guest at his opening at the Waldorf's Empire Room in October.

I was still on the road when Charlie and I celebrated our twelfth anniversary that year. I played in Moline, Illinois and then in Syracuse, New York. In late December, I played the Sullivan show, singing "Happy Birthday, Jesus" just as I'd done the year before.

In January 1969, I did a five-week tour of South Africa, the first time I had ever been to that beautiful country on the tip of Africa. The first night we arrived in Johannesburg, Englebert Humperdink was just finishing up a tour there and he had a party up in his hotel suite. I was invited with all my crew and I remember looking out over the city from the balcony and noticing the moon while talking to Englebert.

"What if my kids are seeing the moon right now?" I said to Englebert. "Wouldn't it be great if I could talk to them and they were looking at the same moon?"

He laughed and said to me, "Patti, you know you're in the Southern Hemisphere, right?"

I laughed; I hadn't thought of where I was on Earth. Not only does the moon look different from the Southern Hemisphere, there was something like a ten-hour time difference, and for the kids it probably wasn't even nighttime yet.

I played in Durban, East London, and Port Elizabeth before moving on to an engagement at the Three Arts Theatre in Cape Town. I liked Cape Town very much because the skies were overcast when I arrived, and it was much cooler than the other cities, which were sweltering during the Southern Hemisphere summer. It was an exhausting tour. While recording something for a radio broadcast at the Sea Point Hotel in Cape Town, I fell asleep sitting in my chair. I'd done two shows in Port Elizabeth the night before and been up until 4:00 a.m., then had to get up early to hurry off to Cape Town. Nodding off was a reminder of how much I was pushing myself. It was refreshing playing for Cape Town audiences, though, and one reason was because they loved my version of "Little Green Apples," which had been a disappointment to me back in the U.S.

I was honored in South Africa by an audience at the House of Lords. I still have the place settings from a meal with some of the South African dignitaries. At the time, Richard Nixon was just going into office and because they were all very much into the machinations of world politics they wanted my opinion.

"What do you think of the new president?" I was asked.

"In America, we never cry over spilled milk," I blurted out. I have no idea why I said that, but thankfully it was off the record and never made the papers.

I enjoyed being in South Africa, but I was appalled about the way blacks were lesser citizens there. I couldn't help but think about all the great people I had known—my dear friend the late Nat "King" Cole, for one—who would have been denied the chance to shine if they'd lived under apartheid. It was still in force at that time. I was proud that during my tour I played in a venue where there was a mixed audience; I'm not sure that had ever been done in the country up to then.

Back in the United States, I was as busy as ever, playing live dates, recording, and spending time with my family. In June, I was playing at the Fairmont Hotel in Dallas when it all caught up with me. I had to check into Methodist Hospital in Dallas after suffering shortness of breath in my hotel room. I was still a smoker, but it turned out my breathing problems weren't caused by smoking but by exhaustion. I was tired, had been overworking, and frankly, I hadn't been eating very well. Kay Starr, who was supposed to appear after my booking finished, filled in and played the show I wasn't able to give. I did appreciate a little break once in a while, even if it took God telling me something.

During her engagement at the Fairmont Hotel in Dallas in June 1969, Patti Page was made an "Honorary Citizen of Texas."

A person who had always found it hard to slow down, after briefly receiving treatment for exhaustion, Patti was back to her regular schedule almost immediately. She returned to the concert circuit and appeared on several television shows, such as another Bob Hope special and the very popular afternoon talk show *The Mike Douglas Show.*

On November 4, 1969, she joined thousands of other Oklahomans to celebrate the thirty-first annual Will Rogers Day in Claremore, the hometown she shared with Rogers.

There was a special reason I went to the celebration of Will Rogers Day in Claremore in 1969. The city was renaming Second Street, changing the name to Patti Page Boulevard. I took part in a wreath-laying at Will's Memorial, a parade down Will Rogers Boulevard, and a big free barbecue at the Will Rogers Round-Up Club. My mother and five of my sisters were able to join me that day, and I was very happy they could be there. Following lunch, I cut the ribbon on my new street, which was just an amazing feeling. The Oklahoma Military Academy also named me an "honorary cadet," I took part in a radio broadcast over KWPR, I had the honor of leading a crowd of a thousand people on the Memorial grounds in the singing of "America," then we spent forty-five minutes parading down Main Street. What a day it was.

January 25, 1970, marked a milestone in Patti's TV career—her seventeenth, and final, appearance on *The Ed Sullivan Show*. She sang "La La La," "Winter World of Love," and "Something," her version of a hit song by The Beatles. Other guests included Little Anthony and the Imperials, comedians Robert Klein and Norm Crosby, and in somewhat of an Ed Sullivan tradition in Patti's eyes, a circus act, Klauser's Bears.

On the recording side of her career, her Country song "I Wish I Had a Mommy Like You" entered the *Cashbox* Country Top 60 charts early in 1970.

In the middle of all that was going on for me professionally, my attention was focused on what was going on at home. Charlie was tested and found to have a lung tumor. Thank God, it wasn't malignant and was treated successfully, but it did shake us up.

It reinforced that family, as always, meant the most. That summer, I decided to limit my appearances to fairs in Seattle and Minneapolis and the King Castle at Lake Tahoe. Being on the Sullivan show was great, but it was nicer to hear my daughter say, "Oh Mommy, I'm so glad you're here," when I picked her up from school. My kids were the reason I recorded "I Wish I Had a Mommy Like You." We bought a beach house in Malibu around this time, mostly so that the kids would have a nice place to hang out on the weekends with their friends.

Considering the astonishing social changes America was going through, I'd gotten through the 1960s fairly unscathed. What I didn't know was that for me the 1970s would make the 1960s seem like fairly placid times. In 1970, I would record only one album, titled *Green, Green Grass of Home*. I had a beautiful home in Beverly Hills with green grass, a white picket fence, and a fairy tale look, but as the decade began I had no idea that things were about to change in a fairly drastic fashion for the "Oklahoma Cinderella."

SIXTEEN

A Word I Never
Wanted to Sing

Things with Charlie and I were not going very well. Charlie wasn't working—no one was making movies with dance numbers—and he refused to get work in TV like his good friend, Nick Castle. In retrospect, I think he just didn't want to face reality: After Elvis quit making movies with Hal B. Wallis and Paramount, Charlie's work with Elvis was done. The last movie they'd done together was *Fun in Acapulco* in 1963. Even after Elvis resurrected his own career with the "comeback special" on TV in 1968, Charlie didn't believe in television.

Charlie still worked with me on my live shows. He was very egotistical about it sometimes; if I changed something without telling him, like the songs he had picked out, he didn't like it. When he'd show up at the Desert Inn in Las Vegas he'd tell the lighting man off. It almost got to the point of Jack banning him from places where I was working. Even though Charlie's work had helped me feel more confident onstage (which Jack would never admit), Charlie was a regular source of trouble.

I was conflicted because Charlie had come up with remarkable touches for the show. One bit he created was pure genius. He hid an autoharp inside the piano and at one point in my show the lights would go down and I'd stroll to the baby grand to sing "Danny Boy"—dedicated to my son, of course. I'd run my fingers over the autoharp and it appeared to the audience that I was making the sound off the piano strings. The autoharp can be the kind of instrument that when you hear it, you'd think an angel was playing their harp. Tears would fall from the eyes of people in the audience. What a beautiful touch it was.

Jack never wanted me to hire anyone other than him, including Charlie. He would contest Charlie being given this or that information about my career. I didn't know what the reason was—it was only much later that I would realize it was because Jack was afraid of what would happen if I ever got smart about business. Jack started a lot of the confrontations with Charlie, but for years I just wouldn't let the truth surface in my mind. Charlie and Jack were both vying for complete control of me. I was so naïve that I thought it would all just work out. In my heart, I thought it would because I wasn't favoring one over the other. They each had their place. Charlie was my husband and Jack was my manager. I thought that they could keep their places, but they couldn't; they both wanted to be involved in everything. I never liked confrontations, so I just pretended it was all right. I didn't want to believe that they weren't really getting along. But the tension between Charlie and Jack did not abate. Finally, I just told Charlie that maybe he shouldn't hang around when I worked.

At first, when Charlie worked with me and set up the Vegas shows, he got paid, but after a couple of years he did it just as my husband. After all, we had a joint checking account, and I was making most of the money. By 1970, I was paying for everything. This caused a lot of problems because Charlie took it as a blow to his masculinity, and he didn't need any more blows in that area— he had already beaten himself up enough about not fathering children. Many times, I would say to him "Get a job, any job." He was doing the same dance Jack Skiba did. He'd pretend he'd go to work and then go down to the auction houses in downtown Los Angeles and spend the whole day there. Sometimes he bought things—a table, or different artifacts—sometimes he didn't. Our house was filled with "stuff." He was an artist and had very good taste, and he knew good things when he saw them. He claimed he wanted to become a decorator, but nothing came of it. Meanwhile, Nick Castle was busy doing the hit show *Laugh-In* with Rowan and Martin. The contrast couldn't help but damage Charlie's pride.

One day I said, "Just go out and drive a truck. I don't care what you do, I just need to keep some respect there."

He didn't like that at all. I usually didn't say much, so when I said that, it was heart-wrenching. I knew he wouldn't drive a truck. I just wanted to get my point across that he should do *something*, whether in show business or elsewhere. Charlie did stay home to look after the kids when I had an interview to do or an appointment to make, but even his staying at home got to be problematic. He didn't get along too well with any of the help because he was a little too demanding, while I wasn't demanding enough.

During the difficult moments, I tried to understand Charlie on the basis of his background. He was brought up poor just like me. His family was blue-collar Irish in Atlantic City, New Jersey. He started working professionally with Nick Castle on Atlantic City dance marathons where people would dance for twenty-four hours at a time to outlast other dancers and win a prize. Maybe because he'd done well with his movie choreography, Charlie just kind of believed he would always be dancing in the movies or directing. Fact was, he'd worked steadily doing movie dance direction since 1943 and it was a shock to him that movie choreography work dried up for him in 1963. He was very talented. He just didn't have faith in himself and perhaps didn't know how to go about finding a new career. And so he covered that with bluster, and as he got older he thought it should all just be given to him because he was so talented.

Charlie sometimes seemed just oblivious to what was right and appropriate for a guy with a wife and kids to protect. One night, Charlie's friend from his Atlantic City days, Skinny D'Amato, came by our house in Beverly Hills with a friend in tow, Sam Giancana, the infamous and well-known Mafia boss. In truth, the man had a very gentlemanly air to him. Nevertheless, I couldn't stand having him in the house. I got Charlie to "help me in the kitchen."

"How dare you bring someone like that into our home?" I blurted out. It was obvious I was plenty upset.

Charlie seemed unconcerned: "Honey, Skinny didn't mean anything by it."

It was all I could do to bite my tongue.

Later during their visit, Giancana was mocking Skinny because Skinny's wife, Betty, who was a friend of mine, wouldn't "give him permission" to go on a trip they had planned. He was belittling not only Skinny but Betty, too. I told Mr. Mafia, "Don't talk about my friend Betty like that." Giancana looked surprised. I got the distinct impression he wasn't used to anyone answering back, especially a woman.

In March 1970, Patti Page traveled to Nashville to sing on *The Johnny Cash Show*, which was on the ABC network. The show combined traditional Country music stars with the latest young Rock artists. Included on the show with Page that night were Tony Joe White of "Poke Salad Annie" fame, Sonny James who had the classic Country hit "Young Love," and one of the original Sun Records rock 'n' rollers, Carl Perkins.

Johnny Cash introduced Page as the artist who "imported the waltz from Europe to Tennessee and a whole lot of people put down their guitars, fiddles and dobros and listened to one of the prettiest songs heard anywhere."

Singing "Tennessee Waltz" had special meaning for me that night on *The Johnny Cash Show*. I felt like I was being embraced by a whole new generation of Country music artists and fans.

Johnny and I did a duet of "My Elusive Dreams," which segued into my "Cross Over the Bridge" and then "Detour" followed by "Gentle On My Mind." I was happy to see Johnny happy and steady with a hit TV show. When I'd cut my first sides in Nashville in 1961, it was at a time when Johnny was known for not showing up for his record dates and performances. He recorded in the same studio that I did—when he made it to his recording dates—and it had been terrible knowing about his troubles.

I also did a solo number called "Put a Little Love in Your Heart," a kind of bouncy hippie song that was a massive hit for Jackie de Shannon. The producers wanted current hits performed on the show, which was understandable. What they didn't know was that the song had first been offered to me to record—so chances were, it could have been my own hit that I was singing that night.

One day a music publisher brought Jackie de Shannon to my house in Beverly Hills. She came with her guitar and sang "Put a Little Love in Your Heart," and I was flabbergasted by how good it was and the way she sang it.

"Why are you offering this to me?" I asked her.

Jackie smiled quizzically and looked at her publisher. Then she said to me, "What do you mean, Miss Page?"

"You should be doing that beautiful song yourself, Jackie," I explained. "You do it so perfectly. You'd have a huge hit with it. That's what I mean."

As they made their way out the door, they left me a tape of the song for me to consider, but I could tell from the look in Jackie's eyes that she'd liked what I said. She took my advice and it was a smash, hitting #4 on the *Billboard* Pop music charts.

In the summer of 1970, I tried to spend more time at home with the kids because I enjoyed it but also because I was worried about what might go on at home if I wasn't there. Charlie had a habit of firing people when I was on tour, and our nanny, Jackie Smith, was one of them. On one of the occasions when I hadn't brought her and the kids with me on the road, Charlie got into an argument and let Jackie go on the spot, after years on the job. I was heartbroken and tried to hire her back, but she didn't want to come back; she just wasn't comfortable.

I got someone tougher and more able to put up with Charlie. Marie Costello was a fan of mine from Philadelphia who I'd kept in touch with. Marie had repeatedly mentioned to me that if I ever needed anyone to take care of the kids or the house, I should think of her. I did at that point, and she was happy to have the opportunity. She moved out from Philadelphia, and would be with me for a very long time.

We had housekeepers who took care of the heavy cleaning, and Charlie mostly left them alone, except when something wasn't done perfectly, according to him. At least he was a good cook; but the problem was, he didn't understand my dietary concerns. He thought I could eat anything, like he could. He cooked a lot of delicious but fattening foods and thought I could eat them and not put on weight. He was naturally thin and just didn't understand how some people can get overweight.

I drove the kids to playdates and parties whenever I could as I'd learned to drive after the move to California. My schedule was so busy that I'd had to take lessons between shows at an old racetrack in Las Vegas. I passed my driving test in Los Angeles and finally felt like I wasn't living a lie after all those years of appearing in commercials for Oldsmobile that gave the impression I knew what I was doing behind the wheel.

Mostly, I could walk to everything from where I lived in Beverly Hills. The kids went to a Catholic preschool and had to be driven there, but when they started going to public school they could walk because it was only two blocks away. Kathleen and Danny had been christened Catholic because Charlie was Catholic. The religion situation was a big problem between Charlie and me and something that I came to regret. He had been raised Catholic but wasn't much of a churchgoer. I had them baptized—at the Good Shepherd in Beverly Hills—because I had promised myself that they would be raised in the church. As I was Church of Christ, not Catholic, that got me in trouble with the Catholic priest, who wanted me to convert to Catholicism.

Some friends, the Grinnells, tried to help me out by formally requesting that I be enrolled in the Carmelite Apostolate of Prayer, an elevated level of Catholic devotion, with the Sisters of Mt. Carmel Novitiate. But I couldn't see myself as a Catholic. The problem was, if I became a Catholic, I would have to divorce my husband because he'd previously been divorced without the church's blessing.

These were the days when it was really difficult to go outside your own religion, especially if you were Catholic. When John Kennedy ran for President in 1960, a great many people thought he couldn't be elected due to being Roman Catholic. Charlie's and my religious differences had also been a problem with my family. When my mother heard I was getting married, her blessing was "I'll take it to my grave," referring to the fact that Charlie was Catholic.

Though other artists were now taking their turn at the top of the Pop charts, it was clear that Patti Page remained firmly in the public consciousness. In 1970, two weeks in a row, her name was an answer in the *New York Times* Sunday crossword puzzle. Groups across the country regularly bestowed her with all kinds of honors, such as "The Yellow Rose of Texas" and the "Daughter of Mark Twain" awards. (The Twain award was an interesting one in that he, like Patti, was one of the few people who had adopted an existing pseudonym and made it famous.) Page even received publicity for her love of bridge when the world champions, The Aces, wrote in their newspaper column about a "saved hand" she'd played successfully.

In February 1970, though, came a sure sign that Page was taking a more relaxed approach to publicity and to her show business image. Pictures were published in *The Tampa Tribune* that were unlike any the public had ever seen of the immaculate songbird: They showed her smoking.

The fact was, I smoked two packs a day, and my kids hated it. They'd seen anti-smoking commercials on television and begged me to quit. Even when they would get in my car and say, "Oh, Mom, this smells awful!" it didn't stop me. By allowing photographers to snap pictures of me smoking—which I'd never allowed before—maybe I was letting people know about it on purpose, in a subconscious way. Maybe, deep down, I thought that when the pictures became public, I'd feel that I had to do something about my smoking. I would eventually succeed in quitting but not just then. Smoking relieved my stress, which was continuing to build up in my marriage.

I did an interview for an article in *Family Weekly* magazine, which came out in May 1970. The kids appeared in it with me because I told the story of their adoption. I went out of my way to be gracious to Charlie, describing how he had initially said no to my ideas about adopting, then relented after four years. Describing our home life at the time of the decision, I told the writer, "Ours was a good marriage." I didn't say, "Ours is a good marriage."

Hoping the article would help parents with adopted kids, I shared a story I'd told my kids about a lonely mommy and daddy who kept searching until they found the prettiest little girl and handsomest little boy to be their children. Kathleen had made us all teary-eyed when she retold the story at a supper party for our friends, ending it with "and I'm that pretty little girl."

It was a lovely look into our family, but the pictures featured only me and the children; Charlie wasn't shown. Things were happening at our house that I hadn't shared with the magazine. There was a lonely mommy and daddy, all right, and they were living with each other.

The longevity of my career and the happiness of my kids had always made me feel blessed. I have to admit, however, that I was becoming a bit more realistic about a lot of things in life, especially marriage.

After seven years with Columbia, in November 1970, Patti Page returned to her previous record label, Mercury. She began recording new tracks and went back to her Country roots. She tried her hand at writing songs, teaming with her pianist and conductor Rocky Cole and her stylist Bruce Vanderhoff on an original Country tune, "I'm Scared to Death You'll Go." It appeared on her first Mercury Country album, *I'd Rather Be Sorry,* in 1971. Embracing her Country singing background paid off for Page, as *Variety* selected a single from that album, "Give Him Love," as one of the Top Singles of the Week, and the song did well on both the Country and Easy Listening charts. It made the ASCAP Country Music Award Winners list in 1971. (ASCAP is the American Society of Composers, Authors and Publishers.) In May of 1972, Page received a Chartbuster Award from ASCAP for "Things We Care About" because it broke into the national charts.

Looking at the certificate I was awarded by ASCAP, I found myself thinking about what it was that I really cared about personally. I tried not to think of aspects of my life that I was unhappy with. As usual, I just poured myself into my work. Between spending time with my kids, recording, and playing Vegas, Disneyland, and clubs around the country, the early years of the 1970s seemed to be flying by in an instant. I had returned to my old haunt the Desert Inn in Las Vegas early in 1971. My special guest star was the black comedian Godfrey Cambridge. (I couldn't help but wonder what the South African House of Lords would think about that.) I loved the openness of Vegas and was happy to sign a two-year contract to play at Hughes hotels there.

Las Vegas was changed forever in 1972 when movie star Marlene Dietrich put on a show and made headlines because she was paid $25,000 a week. No star had ever received a Vegas payday like that. The most I'd ever received was half that. Dietrich was worth it. Her show was just unbelievable—a huge, gorgeous event. I recall it as the first time a star came in and had a show built around her, choreographed like something out of a Busby Berkeley movie. She opened high above the stage—or should I say *appeared*—and we watched in amazement as, singing in that great deep, lusty voice of hers, she slowly descended a winding staircase. She reprised her bit in *The Blue Angel* and went through all sorts of numbers with all kinds of costumes. Marlene's run changed everything in Vegas. It was a beautiful show, but I knew I wasn't capable of anything like it, and Charlie wasn't going to try to design it.

Charlie and I had our fifteenth wedding anniversary in 1972. There wasn't much of a celebration. Charlie wasn't working and didn't seem to want to do much to change that and things were a bit tense.

Charlie would always seem logical when I got home from being on the road and he told me that he'd fired more staff. People were hired to do certain things and, according to Charlie, they weren't doing them. Charlie's demands were almost impossible for staff to meet, and the way he addressed his complaints to them was out of kilter. He had such a temper that he would just fire them on the spot rather than give them two weeks' notice or a chance to fix things like a normal employer,

I was paying the bills. I could have put my two cents in, and I don't know why I didn't.

I would talk about the situation with people who knew Charlie well, like Nick Castle's wife, Millie, but the conversations always ended with her saying something like, "Well, you know Charlie" or "You know how he is."

In those days, people wouldn't say much about other people's behavior and seeing a psychiatrist had a terrible social stigma. Just like he felt he didn't need to get tested when we couldn't conceive, Charlie never would have seen a psychiatrist or therapist because he didn't think he needed it.

I couldn't talk to his family. I was close to a couple of his sisters, but to them, Charlie was the talented one in the family and the baby. They all adored him so they always built him up. Charlie could do no wrong in their eyes.

That was the situation. I tried really hard to keep it together, but the relationship kept deteriorating.

Nobody caught on much. I believe Jack sensed something, but I didn't want to discuss it with him. That February I attended the bar mitzvah of Jack's son, Gordon Mack. It was quite a party with Alan King, Don Rickles, Steve and Eydie, and Doris Day. I was hardly about to confide in Doris about my marriage, but you might have thought we'd share our experiences as Pop singers, but we didn't. Business was business, and in those days we didn't talk about it so much at social occasions like that. You'd think, though, after all those years that Jack and I had worked together, I could confide in my manager, but I didn't trust the prospect. He hadn't wanted Charlie around from the beginning, so I assumed that a discussion with Jack about my marriage problems would have been clouded by an "I told you so" attitude from him. So, I tried not to let him know. When I did concert dates or big events, I was simply the smiling, joyous performer, "The Singing Rage." There was a little rage, all right.

Finally, after one of my appearances in Vegas at the Riviera, Charlie remarked about the fact that I had put "Allegheny Moon" in the act as a stand-alone song when normally I sang it as part of a medley of hits. He mentioned something about the way I sang the song, and then he questioned my putting it in the show without getting his approval because as far as he was concerned, he was still in charge of the way I did the show. Charlie said the song was a bad choice of material for the show.

A lot of people who came backstage after my shows would mention that their favorite song was "Allegheny Moon." That's why I'd thought maybe I should perform the whole song, by itself. When Charlie said it was a bad choice, I thought, *After all these years, not even my husband is giving me credit for anything.* And that feeling welled up, along with my emotions about him doing no work and being a domineering "Mr. Mom" who fired people on a whim.

I thought of how Charlie was the one that everybody wanted to be around because he was such a very social person and dressed great—in suits I'd bought him. I thought of how he wanted to go to all of the parties and I didn't want to go and how he wanted to go to all of the openings and I didn't want to go.

And my mind jumped from that to thinking about how I'd always struggled because I was never that outgoing social type; schmoozing had always made me uneasy and uncomfortable. Even though I had always known it was part of the business, I had been naïve enough to think that talent was enough.

I thought of how I always kept quiet. I never knew that by keeping quiet I was trying to gain control until later, after many visits to therapists. I never meant it to be that way. I didn't want to have to try to control my husband.

There I was, at the end of my husband's visit in Las Vegas, and he wasn't respecting my opinion at all. I was the one paying the bills. I was the one that gave us a family and made sure they had good care, even when Charlie fired people the kids liked. How many times did I have to leave an engagement for a day, to go back home and interview someone new for the house? All of these things just exploded in my mind at once.

"You just lost yourself a family," I told him. Those were my final words to him that visit.

At least, I think they were. It was so painful, so many painful thoughts bursting forth in my mind at once. There may have been more words exchanged, but that's the phrase that sticks out in my mind. It all came down to one word— divorce—a word I never wanted to even think about, much less say.

The kids were at home with Marie, the nanny. After I ended my run, I drove back to Los Angeles, expecting the worse. I learned that when he went home, Charlie had started making things up, like I had had too much to drink that night and was talking crazy. Charlie was on the counterattack. He knew that I'd had it when I told him that he'd lost himself a family.

I relented, and we talked. He and I went to see a lawyer friend of ours, Michael Clemens, a friend of Charlie's from the Nick Castle days. He knew how rough divorce could be, and he suggested that we should try counseling or anything that could maybe reconcile us and keep the family together. I offered to do counseling, and to my surprise Charlie did, too, but somehow, we just never got to the point of finding the right counselor. Or, I should say, we found them but we never saw them. After a couple of weeks, it was obvious that it wasn't going to work out, so I finally asked him to leave.

Naturally, it hit the press pretty quickly. One article said I hired three private detectives to move him out of the house. Instead, he just moved out, and after he did I got my own lawyer, Guy Ward, who started advising me on what to do, like keeping Charlie out of the house. Charlie wanted to be able to come and go without restriction, so when I filed for divorce I also filed for a restraining order that stated he wasn't allowed in the house unless it was okayed by me and the powers that be. I didn't want to keep the children away from him, but I knew they had to go with one of us. That's how it was done in those days, and almost always, they went with the mother.

In the divorce proceedings, Charlie asked for a house down the street from me so he could be close to the kids and that I buy it for him. He wanted custody of the kids and child support. How could he want all that? I was the one who went out on a limb to adopt the children, made all the inquiries, lived with his lack of gainful employment, put up with him firing people. It just didn't seem fair to me.

Naturally, the kids were very upset. Kathleen was ten and Danny eight and a half. During the trial, they didn't get many details from us, certainly not from me. I kept them shielded from such a negative atmosphere as best I could.

I would go talk to Jack's wife and get my woes out. Jack didn't gloat about Charlie being gone, and he was happy to testify in the trial. He was good with his testimony, too—very helpful. He didn't like Charlie, and he let it be known. The proceedings took at least six months and then it was a year before the findings were made final. I got physical custody of Kathleen and Danny, and Charlie had visitation rights.

In the midst of the upheaval in her family life, Patti Page signed with a new record label, Epic, a division of Columbia. She released a couple of singles, including "You're Gonna Hurt Me" with "Mama, Take Me Home" on the flip side.

She continued to make high-profile appearances, including on Jerry Lewis's star-studded annual telethon. And she was on the charts, with "Hello, We're Lonely," a duet she had recorded with Tom T. Hall, that reached #13 on the Billboard Country chart.

Around the time of my divorce, the record label Candelite put out an album called *The Golden Memories of Patti Page*. I had golden memories, sure, but when you go through a divorce the world doesn't look particularly golden, no matter how hard you work to keep your chin up.

Things were changing in my career, too. I released my first Country-Western album on Epic called *One More Time*. I'd finished my contract with the Hughes hotels in Vegas, and Jack was negotiating new possibilities.

I was willing to try anything that seemed promising. I even invested in a restaurant started by my stylist Bruce Vanderhoff. He called it "Le Restaurant." At least I didn't fall to pieces or turn to one of the wacky New Age things that were so in vogue in Los Angeles. I've got to admit it gave me a chuckle when an astrologer wrote in an article that as a Scorpio, I'd been undergoing great changes for the last two years. Was he consulting the heavens or the newspapers?

Wanting to make a new start all round, during the divorce I started looking for someplace new to live. My attorney, Guy Ward, had a huge ranch near San Diego in a suburb called Rancho Santa Fe. He offered me the house to stay in because his family wasn't there very often. I started taking the kids down there for getaways. Guy had a lot of horses, and his son, Bill Toman, was the trainer. Bill suggested that maybe the kids would like to ride to keep them occupied. They did, and Kathleen and Danny just fell in love with horses. Before I knew it, Bill got them into showing horses, and I became involved, too.

In August 1973, I sold my house in Beverly Hills to Robert Wagner and Natalie Wood. Bob Wagner loved my house. Before the sale was final, he would come over and ask to just sit in the den and take in the place. It was a cute and classy thing to do, and I'm glad he bought my place.

We moved to Rancho Santa Fe on Labor Day of 1973, renting until I could find us a place of our own. Naturally, I hated leaving the friends I had in the L.A. area, but some that I missed the most were more Charlie's friends than mine, like Millie Castle; her daughter, Geneva, and her son Nicky.

The move didn't change things for Page-Rael Enterprises; we still had our office in Beverly Hills. But I wasn't being offered the kind of work I had been offered before. My career was winding down even though television was still pretty good to me. And I'd soon learn how true it was that when one door closes, another opens up. Life was going to be different, but in many ways, it was going to be better. I was about to meet some of the most genuine and sincere people I'd ever met in my life. And together, we would go through heartache and unexpected life changes that would prepare me for the golden years.

SEVENTEEN | # Life as a Single, Singing Mom

Being responsible for two young human beings who didn't ask to be caught up in the middle of divorce or a show business career, I had to make life as normal and happy for Kathleen and Danny as possible. In the past, I'd hated being on the road without the kids, but I hated being away from them even more after the divorce when we were living in Rancho Santa Fe. I cut my touring down to about thirty weeks a year—and certainly never worked Christmas, Easter, or the kids' birthdays—and I phoned the kids every night when I was on the road. Marie Costello lived with us, which made the kids happy. We thought of her more as family than as "the help."

I was a traveling saleslady of song, and I had to make the "calls." I had to believe that it was the *quality* of the time I spent with my children that was the most important thing. I knew that even if they could have joined me on the road all the time, it wouldn't really have solved the problem because with the late hours I kept as an entertainer, I was usually going to sleep right about when the kids were waking up. Still, even if you're doing the best you can as a parent, you often second-guess the job you're doing.

Rancho Santa Fe was beautiful, but I missed the Malibu weekends with the kids. I still have a tiny little oil I painted there of Danny surfing. Our beautiful house was down the road from Pepperdine University, right on the water, and he was out in the surf every day. I loved to watch my little blond angel riding that surfboard. In the divorce negotiations, I'd offered Charlie the beach house, but he wouldn't take it. Maybe he didn't want the memories. We'd spent time there when the kids were in school. It had been a place to take the kids on weekends, and all their friends enjoyed it. Most of the kids' friends spent the time after school at our house anyway. While they enjoyed the ocean, I would paint.

But that was all gone now, and I was reinventing my life.

The odd thing was, my audiences were reinventing me, too. I was still doing clubs and hotels, but now I was doing just as many fairs and rodeos, and many people now considered me a Country-Western singer. I didn't give too much thought to how I was being classified, though. I just did what I'd always done—I kept singing. On the road with me were Jack; my pianist-conductor, Rocky Cole; my drummer, Kenny Hume; and my stylist, Edgar Fisher. It was a far cry from the days of big band singing.

I could safely say that except for during my headstrong pre-teens, people were listening to my opinion for the first time. I started listening to my body a little more, too. I began taking some time for myself and learned to play tennis, which had long been a favorite of Jack's and Rocky's.

I couldn't play tennis regularly and keep smoking cigarettes, though. Even more to the point, one day I realized that I couldn't go out of the house unless I had a pack of cigarettes with me. The kids hadn't stopped getting on me about it, and they were right to do so. I was addicted to smoking, three packs a day at this point. The 70s were the beginning of everybody going to therapy, and people were finally beginning to read the Surgeon General's notes on cigarette packages. Everybody knew that they were going to eventually ban smoking in public places. I thought, *If that happens, then what will I do?*

I had tried quitting a zillion times before, but I'd only get through one day then be climbing the walls. This time, I got lucky. I heard about a hypnotist in Orange County, and I spoke with him on the phone and liked what I heard, so I drove up there from Rancho Santa Fe. To my surprise, he'd suggested I smoke all the way up, but I didn't. In the waiting room of this hypnotist's office was a little casket filled with packages of cigarettes. He had all his patients throw their cigarettes in there. I don't know what it was about that cigarette casket, but it did something to me. It made me think. I'd begun smoking in high school in an attempt to hang out with the "cool kids" and to impress a boy who handed me a cigarette and flipped open his silver Zippo to light it up. When I coughed as the smoke hit my lungs he asked if it was my first time, but I lied so he would think I was "with it." I didn't dare light up at home; Mom would have killed me. But as I got used to smoking, I learned that if I lit up and inhaled, my fears would drift away, which helped before a performance. It wasn't until much later that I realized smoking might possibly kill me, like it had my friend Nat "King" Cole.

Whatever happened during my one session with the hypnotist, I never had a single cigarette after that. Oh, I thought about it, but when I did, I would pray to God to lift the addiction from me, and He did. My kids were thrilled, and so was I. I took other people to see the hypnotist, I was so impressed by him.

I even went back to him about my weight struggles, but he turned me down.

"Patti," he said, "this is not going to work. You have to have your mind really set on it for me to help you." I guess I never did get my mind set on it. When I was honest with myself, I decided, *I like to eat. Why act like I don't?* I wasn't a twenty-something ingénue trying to wow the boys anymore. I was a single mom in my forties and it was silly to try to look like a runway model. Besides, the hypnotist was right: Cigarettes we can do without while food we can't.

Charlie surprised me after the divorce. I knew he was bitter, but I had no idea of the extent to which he would allow his bitterness to affect the kids after the split.

Though he had full visitation rights, he wouldn't come to pick them up like he was supposed to every weekend. I guess the whole situation wore him out. After about the first year, he stopped coming altogether.

In truth, Charlie loved Kathleen; that little girl was his life. When the children were little, I shared time equally with both Danny and Kathleen, but Charlie loved to play with his little girl. I had wanted to adopt three more, but I stopped because Charlie didn't wholeheartedly agree with me on adoption. I now think that was a mistake, just as putting up with Charlie's personality flaws was a mistake. I'm sorry I stopped adopting.

People who had worked for me at home had told me about disturbing incidents like Charlie burning Danny's arm one time to prove a point. When Danny was being potty-trained, one of Charlie's methods to stop him from wetting his pants was to put Danny's hand in the toilet every time he did. I'd taken these things up with Charlie, but to hear his side, the allegations were never true. At the divorce trial, when they testified, it had dawned on me why Charlie had wanted to get rid of some of the people who worked for us.

After the divorce, Charlie just didn't seem to want to be involved as the kids grew up, and he never helped me with Danny. His attitude would cause deep problems for my son, I later discovered. A boy needs a father, in the home or not.

Sometimes the kids would go see him. Usually it was just Kathleen who visited, and she would take a friend with her. At times, Charlie would actually ask for Kathleen and not Danny to come visit, which devastated my boy, but Kathleen loved it. She adored her father. She was the special one to him.

Danny and Kathleen have both told me that when they visited Charlie, he would bring out all of the court papers from our divorce. He'd have them read them, and he'd say, "See what your mother said about me?" I guess it was his way of getting back at me, by trying to break their attachment with me. I'm not sure how much of what he told them they believed. And I felt they were happy living with me.

Rancho Santa Fe, where Patti moved with her two children after her divorce, was an attractive and well-appointed community near San Diego, California. It was—and still remains—one of the most affluent places in the United States. With homes set well back from the street and landscaped so that they were hidden from passers-by, it attracted numerous stars, but had a small-town pace and charm. When Patti moved there, it was not uncommon for residents to see actors such as Victor Mature and Robert Young when they went into town to collect their mail. Rancho Santa Fe had a modest downtown, just one street and two blocks long, with five banks, two restaurants—one being Mille Fleur, recognized as one of the finest in the country—one gas station, and a post office.

The move to Rancho Santa Fe meant that Kathleen and Danny would attend one of the best public schools in San Diego County, renowned for being able to attract the best teachers and for providing an education the equivalent of a private school's.

Rancho Santa Fe was a beautiful place. And the kids were able to take riding lessons at least twice a week, which helped take their minds off Charlie and me not being together. They thrived there and were genuinely happy. I loved our new neighborhood, too.

The way Rancho was laid out, everyone had to drive; there were no buses from the school. By this time, Marie was both nanny and housekeeper, so if I was out of town, she would drive the kids to school and pick them up in the afternoon. There was no Parent Teachers Association, but there was a large parents group involved in the school. Everyone willingly helped however they could, doing lunch duty or whatever needed to be done. I was at the school whenever I could be. I really wanted to have the life of a mom. When I was not off doing concerts, life in our new city seemed to be getting back to some form of normal. In some ways, I felt as comfortable as I had in small towns in Oklahoma. I could sit in my rocking chair at home and enjoy the scenery. It made me feel like a country girl again. I felt liberated.

New Year's Eve of 1973, the gentleman I was renting my house from invited me to a little party he was hosting with his wife. At that time, I was dating my conductor, Rocky Cole, so he came with me. It can be a bit strange walking into a room full of people you've never met, when they know your name and all kinds of other details about your life. I'm happy to say, everyone at that party settled down to being themselves quickly, and then it didn't feel strange at all. There were about ten people there, including a lovely couple named Jerry and Katie Filiciotto. Jerry was a tall, lanky, funny Italian-American gentleman—a take-charge aerospace executive who ran his own company. Katie was a tall, pretty blonde from North Carolina with close-cropped hair and a honeyed Southern accent. Later, when Katie and I became friends and were spending a lot of time together, people would sometimes think we were sisters. I never saw the resemblance that much, but then I wasn't tall like Katie. At one point that night, Katie mentioned that Jerry was a fan of my singing—and as it turned out, I would soon be a big fan of theirs.

Katie and I hit it off immediately; I knew I'd found a great friend. Sure enough, as 1974 got rolling, we became friendly enough that she would often call and ask if I would join them for dinner. Jerry and Katie's kids were a good bit older than mine. Kathleen was only ten, and the Filiciotto's children were Sam, eighteen, May, fifteen, and Connie, thirteen.

It didn't take long for Katie to discover how much I loved playing bridge. When I found out she and Jerry had played for years as a couple, I made plans for Rocky and me to get together with them. That first night of bridge, Katie and I teamed up against Jerry and Rocky. Rocky was a great musician but not a good card player. Katie and I were great together—so much so that we finally became members of a bridge organization and played qualifying tournaments to get master points. Bridge is an intriguing game; you can play all your life and feel like you've never fully learned it.

It's sort of like dealing with the opposite sex, I suppose.

I was happy enough dating Rocky Cole, but within a few months of being in Rancho Santa Fe, it was obvious I wasn't as close to him as I had become to my friends Jerry and Katie. You'd think I would have been, after all those years together on the road.

This was a problem because Rocky seemed to assume our dating would eventually lead to marriage. He mentioned it a couple of times, but I would always deflect the idea and say there was plenty of time to think about things like that. With everything that had been going on in my life, getting married again—to anyone—was the last thing I wanted to think about.

After I moved to Rancho, I tried to go to church more often, and Rocky may have had something to do with that. Since he was Catholic, I would go to the Catholic church with him. I wasn't going to become a Catholic, but it was nice to feel like I was doing more to honor my faith.

One of the things I regret from those days is not taking my children to church more often. In retrospect, I feel the kids might have had more structure in their lives if we attended services together regularly.

Starting in 1972, Wing Records had been reissuing previously released Patti Page albums. In 1972, Pickwick had brought out one called *Tennessee Waltz; The Golden Memories of Patti Page* came out on Candelite in 1973; and *The Patti Page Collection* was released on Ahed in 1976. At this stage in her career, Page had thirteen gold records to her credit and had sold a total of 70 million records.

By the mid-1970s, I was facing a sad situation in my career—it was hard to get an album released. I was making about eight singles and two albums a year. My albums had been coming out on various independent labels and not the majors. Record companies were focused on Rock groups, not a girl singer in her forties who had been in show business almost thirty years. I was becoming pretty sensitive about people seeing me at public appearances and asking how long I'd been back in show business. I always told them, "I never left!"

By now I'd had some experiences with recording executives that had left me feeling a little jaded, to be honest. Record companies had a tendency to record me and then not really know quite what to do with the tracks. Maybe it was because my songs crossed over boundaries between, say, Country and Easy Listening or Pop, so it wasn't always clear-cut how to market them. And let's face it, the major labels tend to concentrate on artists who are about thirty years of age or younger. Whatever the reason, I found that my tracks were getting parked on record companies' shelves, where they were gathering dust. What I tried to do was get the recording execs to come along to one of my shows. Sometimes, they'd walk away going, "I didn't know she could sing like this." That's what it took to get heard above all the other sounds vying for the executives' attention.

I knew I wouldn't solve anything by stewing about all of that. Although I would rather have been making hit singles and albums, I understood that sometimes the parade moves on and that looking for permanency in the music business is like trying to herd buffalos into a Volkswagen Beetle. Yet, as I celebrated my thirtieth year as a recording artist, I didn't feel that I was ready to pack away my microphone. I wanted to keep trying and maybe have just one more hit record.

When I started out, taxes were a lot higher than they were in the loose and fast days of the 1960s and 70s music industry. Money had never been what drove me as a singer, but still, I couldn't help but muse on how different my bank balance might have looked had I started out in 1967 instead of 1947! If I made one more hit record, it would give my children a secure, comfortable future, I thought, and then I could retire from the business.

Once when I called my mother, who was well up in years, she told me that Country star Roy Clark lived in Tulsa, so why couldn't I come home, like him? She'd seen me appear with Roy in a 1969 episode of *Hee Haw*, a Country cornpone variety show that seemed like it would never stop running in syndication. It was like a Nashville cross between *Laugh-In* and *The Ed Sullivan Show*. Ah, I thought, what would it be like, going home to Tulsa? I always got a real kick out of the hoots, hollers, and applause I'd get in Vegas from audience members who lived in Tulsa. But who was I kidding? I really couldn't see me moving from California or giving up the music industry just yet.

In February 1976, the Academy of Country Music Awards recognized Patti Page's significance to Country music with an invitation to co-host the twelfth annual awards ceremony with her old friend Pat Boone and one of the best guitar pickers Nashville ever saw, Jerry Reed, who would co-star with Burt Reynolds in the #1 hit movie, *Smokey and the Bandit*. Also appearing on the show were Anson Williams from the hit TV show *Happy Days*, Broadway star Carol Channing, and Roots star LeVar Burton, among others. It was a time when Country music was emerging as a major force in the music industry, with a rapidly increasing audience across the nation. There were a record 4,000 people in the audience at the Shrine Auditorium in Los Angeles that night, and viewers at home turned on their TV sets for a live broadcast on ABC.

Mickey Gilley—who had been voted "Most Promising Male Vocalist" by the Academy in 1974—swept the awards, winning for Entertainer of the Year, Best Male Vocalist, and for Single, Album, and Song of the Year. (He would become even more popular after he appeared in the 1980 movie, *Urban Cowboy*.) The Academy's Pioneer Award went to music producer Owen Bradley, who had helped put Nashville on the map as a national music force. The Best Female Vocalist that year was Loretta Lynn's sister, Crystal Gayle.

I wasn't up for any awards, but it was a boost being asked to co-host the Academy of Country Music Awards in 1976. Being selected to host the big national awards show made me feel kind of like they were saying, "You're somebody important to us, and we're glad to have you." And I was very glad to be there.

When I'd moved to Rancho Santa Fe, Jack had called KSON, the big Country station in the area and asked them why they weren't playing my records.

"She's not Country," the station manager told him.

After he got over his stunned silence, Jack said, "Well, what do you think 'Tennessee Waltz' is!"

I thought of that when I learned I was going to co-host the CMAs, and I had to laugh.

In July of 1977, during an engagement at the Fairmont Hotel in San Francisco, Patti Page was honored with a celebration of her thirtieth year in show business, in the Venetian Room. Mayor George Moscone issued a decree declaring it "Patti Page Day" in the City by the Bay.

When she had played at the Fairmont Hotel the first time, in 1975, a critic told her that the prospect of seeing the singer responsible for "How Much is that Doggie in the Window?" was as appealing to her as cutting her own finger off. Then, when the critic listened to Page's full body of musical work, she had been thrilled by it. She went on to write what Page feels is one of the best reviews she has ever received. It is perhaps both a blessing and a curse for a singer such as Patti Page to have such memorable big hits, as it means the full scope of their talents are not always fully recognized, even by critics. But back at the Fairmont in 1977, the same reviewer reported that everything she'd praised in 1975 was even better now.

A month later, Page was in Cape Cod, Massachusetts, appearing at the Cape Cod Melody Tent with Jim Nabors, the star of TV's *Gomer Pyle*, whose variety series was to start in 1978 on CBS. Just as Page surprised recording executives and critics with the range of her work, Jim Nabors' singing voice often amazed audiences, who mostly knew him as the hillbilly Marine. By 1977, he had recorded seventeen albums, and four of them had gone gold.

Though "Old Cape Cod" is Patti Page's own personal favorite out of all her songs, this was the first time she had performed at the Cape. In fact, she had never laid eyes on Cape Cod when she recorded the song in 1957, and wouldn't see it until eleven years later, in 1968. On her opening night at the Cape Cod Melody Tent in 1977, the local Chamber of Commerce presented her with a bouquet of flowers and a sterling silver memorial medallion.

That summer, Patti received a welcome compliment from the star Barbra Streisand, who told a reporter that she had enjoyed Page's recording of her song "Evergreen."

Streisand noted, too, that when she was just starting out on Broadway, one of the songs she would use at auditions was Page's "Allegheny Moon." At the time of writing this book, Streisand had sold around 70 million records during her career, eclipsed by Page's 100 million in sales.

Barbra Streisand was always a much different performer to me. Even before I had children, I kept a low profile and rarely spoke up about anything. Barbra Streisand, on the other hand, has never failed to make her views known to the public. I've sometimes wondered whether my social reticence cost me anything in my career. If I hadn't missed all the parties and kept my mouth shut and ducked publicity, perhaps I would have been better off?

That was only hypothetical, anyway. That was never the route I was going to take because, frankly, it just wasn't my personality to broadcast my opinions. And the fact of the matter was, as much as I had been trying since my divorce to cut back on touring, I should have spent even more time at home because of my kids.

Nobody makes a manual on how to be an effective parent. Rancho Santa Fe offered a wonderful lifestyle for me and the kids, but the happy bubble wouldn't last. Rancho's public school only went up to the eighth grade, so Kathleen and Danny had to transfer to nearby Torrey Pines High School in the Del Mar area past Carmel Valley. Life in high school would be a lot harder to negotiate. For Danny, I suppose it must have seemed overwhelming because for him everything was about to fall apart.

EIGHTEEN

Success Isn't So Sweet with Kids in Trouble

When Danny was probably around ten or eleven, a couple of years after Charlie and I had split, I got worried because his grades were slipping. I got up the courage to call Charlie to ask if he would talk to Danny about it or take him on a father and son trip or something.

"You wanted custody of him," he said coldly. "You got him." That was my first conversation with him after the divorce and would end up to be my last one.

Whatever the reasons were, Danny developed a drug problem at a very early age, probably around the time he turned twelve. I had no idea what he was doing—to what extent he was getting stoned—because I was simply uneducated about the signs. I couldn't even admit that he had started doing anything wrong—not my baby! Even though it no doubt started out as a way of having what they thought was a good time, Danny and some of his friends got deeper and deeper into drugs, and Danny probably got in deepest of all. I'm sure that hanging out at the beach was part of it. That was the thing to do at Torrey Pines—skip school, go to the beach, get high. Despite all my years among musicians, I'd rarely seen marijuana and certainly no other drugs, so I didn't realize what was going on.

And I was off making a living. Though I was no longer with Mercury or Columbia, I was still recording and I was often away from home performing live, simply supporting the lifestyle we were used to. I was as busy as I'd always been, and that was a problem—only I didn't realize the trouble the kids were getting into while I was focused on my career. Both of them were skipping school a lot while I was on the road.

It was easy for me to believe that everything was wonderful because of where we lived. I had bought the beautiful home in Rancho Santa Fe we had initially rented, and I found the lifestyle very relaxing. I could walk back roads for exercise or sit and plink at my piano (I never learned to play properly), and it wasn't hard to be happy. With two kids, two dogs, and a big old cat, I thought we were doing all right. Turning fifty was interesting, in theory; I didn't feel much different, but sometimes I felt I should be coming onstage in a wheelchair. People would make remarks like, "You look great, where've you been?" And I would wonder what they thought I looked like the last time they saw me. The young fans had grown up, and I suppose they thought I'd look much older. I wasn't contemplating retirement, though. My attitude was that as long as I could sing, I'd keep doing it.

Jerry and Katie had become great friends of mine; Katie was my best friend. They were busy with their own three kids, getting them started in life, so I tried not to bother them much with my worries as it became more and more clear that my children were having troubles.

In 1978, Kathleen got pregnant. She was still in high school, just sixteen. She and her boyfriend, Kenny Ginn, declared to me and to his parents that they were going to marry and then they ran away together. Phone calls flew back and forth between me and Kenny's family as we tried to find our kids. I think Kathleen wanted to be found. Once we'd tracked them down, I talked to both Kathleen and Kenny on the phone and told them what they were planning was just something that they shouldn't do.

Kathleen and Kenny resolved the situation on their own and ended their relationship. We never really talked about it again. Unfortunately, going through all that didn't head off further problems for Kathleen. She would skip school and get in trouble, and I'd be called in to see the counselor. She hadn't turned in homework, she'd missed class. I'd ground her for a while, the usual parental punishment, but it didn't work.

Kathleen got a new boyfriend named Larry Smith. I came back from a tour not long before Kathleen's eighteenth birthday and found out Larry had been staying at our house, and I flipped out. They'd been seeing each other for five months, but he was about five years older than Kathleen and should have known better than to stay with her while I was gone. They wanted to get married, but I was against it because I had big misgivings about Larry. As Kathleen was almost an adult, Marie hadn't felt that it was her place to say anything when Larry came to stay while I was away. I was so angry I kicked him out of my house. Kathleen chose to leave with him. I tried to get her to stay, but by that point she wasn't about to listen to me. She was determined, and I let her go.

The tough love thing didn't work. Nothing was going to stop them from getting married, and in the spring of 1979, Kathleen and Larry began planning their wedding. The parents of the bride traditionally pay for the wedding. Charlie didn't have any money to pay for anything, and Kathleen knew I didn't approve of the marriage, so she took it upon herself to make the arrangements all on her own. I offered to buy her a veil and to have her friends who were coming from Beverly Hills to be in the wedding to stay at my house. I went to the wedding at the Lutheran church near our home and so did Charlie as well as a few of our friends from Beverly Hills. The girls Kathleen had known in her school years and her local friends came, too. Kathleen turned eighteen on October 21, 1980 and she got married to Larry the next day.

They lived locally, near Larry's mother, in a dingy and rundown place. Larry's family was very poor, but that wasn't the main reason I objected to their marrying—after all, I'd come from poverty myself. My objection was because Larry had graduated high school with a severe literacy problem. I'm not exaggerating how bad his situation was—he had trouble writing his own name, and I had to get him a checkbook and show him how to write a check. Wanting the best for Kathleen, I'd opposed the wedding because I was worried what kind of a future it would give her.

Larry and I did not get along because he knew that I had not given my okay to the wedding. He never really liked me, but I grew to like him more and more as time passed. I thought he was a nice guy who just needed help but didn't know how to get it. I became sympathetic toward him, and I eventually gained his confidence enough to talk him into learning to read.

Nine months after she married Larry, Kathleen gave birth to a little girl, Sherri Lynn, on July 23, 1981. Naturally, I was elected babysitter a lot, and that was fine with me! Though I had objected to the marriage at first, I felt that once it was done—and especially once there was a child in the equation—it was my job to support Larry and Kathleen's union. I loved little Sherri and devoted myself to her the way I would if I was raising her. I was as proud of Sherri as I'd been when I brought Kathleen home. And when I'd take Sherri shopping with me, people would ask if she was my daughter, which for a fifty-two-year-old woman was a flattering thing.

Meanwhile, Danny's drug problem was growing, and he went in and out of rehabilitation centers. As my best friend, Katie Filiciotto, was very concerned about what was happening. She asked Jerry to try and take Danny under his wing and talk to him, but Jerry didn't get very far. Kathleen always openly resented being given advice, but Danny seemed much more receptive. He appeared to pay attention to Jerry. But as we soon learned, he simply pretended to listen. As we moved into the 1980s, it was a recurring pattern for Danny to enter and then leave rehab. Finally, Danny had been in so many facilities that my insurance wouldn't keep paying for it. Invariably, he'd call me from rehab and say, "Mother, help me out, please." No matter how many times he'd broken my heart, I would believe that this time he would change. I was always there aiding and abetting him.

I was just so dumb. As it later turned out, until I put my foot down, he wouldn't straighten out.

Amidst serious problems on the home front, Patti Page managed to keep performing, and to many listeners, her voice actually seemed to be improving with the years. This could perhaps be attributed to the fact she had stopped smoking. Page played local engagements, such as with the San Diego Symphony at San Diego State University and in Rancho Bernardo, for the Symphony on the Green series. She appeared on TV shows in Los Angeles such as *The Mike Douglas Show.* Patti also ranged further from home, playing numerous dates on the East Coast and touring Australia.

In 1980, Patti Page received the prestigious Pioneer Award from the Country Music Association for being the first artist to develop multiple-voice recording techniques and for being the first artist to make Country music popular with the general public by crossing over to the Pop charts with "Tennessee Waltz."

It was a wonderful honor to receive the CMA's Pioneer Award. I was beginning to realize that I might receive more accolades in the future, but that now I was getting older, they would be of the "things I already did" variety. When you hit the point in life where you've lived more years than you probably have left to live, thoughts of diminishing returns and mortality can't help but creep in. I was only 52, but in show business, there's always a nagging fear that one day, your lovely ride will come to an end. Working was therapy for me, and I was very grateful that I could still do it.

On June 27, 1981, my mother died in a Tulsa hospital. She'd fallen two weeks before and never quite recovered from it. She was almost ninety-two, and had been living in Tulsa for most of the last four decades. She'd recently become a bit of a celebrity in her own right, being featured in a regional telephone company advertising campaign featuring relatives of stars "reaching out to touch someone." She'd joked to me on the phone about becoming a star at age ninety-one. Mom had ninety-five grandchildren and great-grandchildren, as well as one great-great-grandchild when she passed.

My mother was really something else. She never spent a lot of time telling any of us she loved us, but we could always tell from the way she devoted herself to her children. I had learned a lot from her about service and family. Thankfully, due to my career, I'd been able to make sure she was very comfortable in her later life. I felt we'd done very well as daughter and mother, and I would miss her dearly.

To cope with the death of my mother and my concerns for my children, I tried to involve myself in planning for the future. I invested in a clothing business in Los Angeles run by Jack's second wife, Ann Gordon, called Le ReFinery, recycling designer gowns first worn in films or on television. Some of the gowns from couture houses like Balmain and Chloe were worth thousands, so the opportunity to buy them at a quarter of the original price made Le ReFinery a popular shop. Occasionally I'd get a laugh when Ann would tell me stories about the clients, like about one wealthy woman who would call over and over to make sure that no one knew they were her dresses that were being sold. That kind of vanity and insecurity was rife in the entertainment industry, and it was one of the things I was glad I'd managed to avoid all those years by hardly ever going to the "A" parties.

In 1981, I performed at Disneyland and Disney World, did television in New York and on PBS, and played at the elegant Greenbriar resort in West Virginia. While I was headlining at Disneyland in the new Rolling River Revue in Frontierland, Jack got me a new record deal with Plantation Records in Nashville. The owner of the label, Shelby Singleton, had been an A & R man at Mercury who in the past had told me that if he ever had his own record company, he wanted me on it. I was glad to see that his dream to start his own label had become reality and happy that I would be on it. Shelby had been involved in a lot of Country projects when he was with Mercury, but his own label wasn't limited to Country. Everybody was going to Nashville to record; they were recording as many Pop songs in Nashville as they were Country. Additionally, Nashville had a great symphony orchestra, which I'd sung with in the mid-1970s. So, Plantation was just fine with me.

The music business, like film and TV, generally has an emphasis on youth. At the time I was promoting my first Plantation single, "No Aces," people in charge of radio and TV stations were much younger than I was, didn't know my name, and probably didn't really want to know it. So, I was thrilled when it came in at #39 on the charts. I guess I still had something left in me, after all. To get to know the Country fans better, I made my first appearance at the annual Fan Fair in Nashville, which I'd been hearing about for years. Fan Fair is a multi-day musical festival where fans from all over the world come to Nashville to meet the stars and watch them perform. After one visit, I was sold. It was amazing to be so well-received by such friendly people.

I never knew how the kids would be when I got back from touring. Jack tried to offer advice on the best way to get them through their troubles, but I wasn't receptive. He always phrased it with "You should do this" or "You should do that," but what I think I really needed at the time was a shoulder to lean on and for Charlie to do his bit as a father. Jack took a much harder line than I did. He advised me to be more strict, especially with Danny. I thought Jack didn't know the children's situation because he wasn't living with it, and he didn't have any more understanding of psychology than I did. But if I'd listened a bit more carefully to him, I might have seen that Jack was right at least part of the time. Because I was so caught up in worrying about how to help the kids, I didn't see that until much later.

When Danny wasn't in rehab, he would be living at home. Each time Danny fell back into his bad habit it got worse, until finally I lost him altogether. He was just out on the street at age fifteen. I didn't know where he was sometimes. Then the next thing I knew he was in jail for drug use. As heartbreaking as that was, at least I knew where to find him. It wasn't the last time Danny would go to jail, though it would never be for any criminal activity like dealing, only for drugs found on him. I was at least thankful that he wasn't arrested for assault or something worse. But it was a source of great pain that neither of my kids finished high school.

My way of coping with all this sadness was singing. I could sing my heart out and it was like telling someone my troubles. It saved me. I could get out there and sing and emote and I was doing my job at the same time.

America was not yet a tabloid society in the 1980s. If you had personal or family problems and you weren't the star of the moment, chances were good the public would never hear about them. And if you'd always avoided the party circuit like I had, and weren't living in greater Los Angeles anymore, well, you could keep your life even more private. Therefore, hardly anyone outside my community and friends knew about what my children were going through.

In 1982, it seemed like I hadn't been so busy in years. I did a concert at the

Municipal Auditorium in Kansas City with Bob Hope, an orchestra, and an Irish band called The Rovers, and the place filled up and everyone had a good time. Ronald Reagan was president. People were buoyant, thinking maybe it really was a new morning in America for us all. I hoped it was, anyway. When Bob had been onstage a while he called me back on. (I was still second on the bill to him; that would never change.) I began singing "Help Me Make It Through the Night" and that's when he cut in.

"Patti," he said. "Do you know the difference between chicken hash and sex?"

"No," I answered, feeling like the teenager on the stage in Tulsa years before.

"Let's have lunch tomorrow," he quipped, and the crowd roared. Oh, for the simpler times.

In October 1983, Patti Page was inducted into the Oklahoma Hall of Fame, along with William W. Caudill, Kenneth H. Cooper, Howard C. Kauffmann, Clarence Page (no relation to Patti), James Ralph Scales, Harold C. Stuart, and Robert T. Thomas.

Page played to Country fans when she appeared at the National Music Publishers' Association awards in Nashville that year. For a time it seemed likely that she would have her own television show on The Nashville Network, but negotiations stalled.

In 1984, Page shared billing with Mickey Gilley at Harrah's Marina in Atlantic City, New Jersey, and appeared in San Francisco, Lake Tahoe, and Reno. She also played state fairs around the country. While she recorded new tracks on Plantation, much of Page's earlier music was being reissued on labels such as Everest, Good Music, Harland, Hindsight, and Memory Lane.

In March of 1985, Patti entertained a crowd of 3,000 people at a concert in Washington, D.C. with the U.S. Air Force Band. Larry King mentioned the concert in a

USA Today column and revealed that Patti's recording of "Old Cape Cod" was still one of his all-time favorite discs.

The nice thing I found when I played live was that audiences wanted me to sing my old hits as well as Country songs I'd recorded more recently. I found it reassuring that people like me who'd been big in the 50s and 60s—Tony Bennett, Rosie Clooney, Vic Damone, and Andy Williams—were still packing in the audiences. I didn't mind that most of my albums these days were the ones being re-released by the less well-known labels. I still got to record new tracks on Plantation, and at least I wasn't getting lost in the shuffle like I had at times on major labels.

In 1986, I hit a milestone I would never have imagined that day I left Tulsa to join the Jimmy Joy Band: I was forty years into my professional career. It was longer if you counted the years I spent singing on the radio in my hometown, but to most people I was considered a professional when my recording career got started, in Chicago in 1947. As I closed out the 1980s, I would be honored to receive further public recognition for my music, but my kids would continue to battle their demons, and to my horror, I would lose my best friend. And something else entirely unexpected would shake up my family in a dramatic way.

NINETEEN

Old Friends and New and Unexpected Consequences

The celebration of Patti Page's forty years as a performer went on all year long in 1986. Bob Bowling, who ran the Patti Page Appreciation Society, archived the letters of appreciation the star received during the year from old friends such as Bob Hope, Glen Campbell, and Teresa Brewer. One letter stands out from the collection—that of President Ronald Reagan, on White House stationery. In his inimitable style, the president summed up Patti's career as "a splendid example of the American dream come true." By this point in her career, Patti had sung for a total of five U.S. presidents, including Reagan.

Five presidents, imagine that. With President Truman, I'd had a bit of interaction but had none with Eisenhower. I did a fundraiser for Jack Kennedy in the Boston area and met him briefly; his brother, Bobby, was there. I was sent by CBS to sing for Lyndon Johnson after he became president in a big Washington, D.C. gala. The most enjoyable time I'd ever had singing for a president, however, was when Ronald Reagan was elected and my friend Frank Sinatra was in charge of the five balls the night of the Inauguration. You might not associate Frank Sinatra with an operation like that, but he did a great job getting the entertainment for all of them; the events were presented in the style of the big bands. I performed three numbers at a ball in the Mayflower Hotel in the ambience of the big band era. President and Mrs. Reagan were there, making an appearance as they did at all the balls.

To this day, though, I haven't got to sing in the White House, which would be a magnificent honor.

Country music remained a key part of Patti Page's career. In 1986, she recorded a duet with George Jones called "You Never Looked That Good When You Were Mine" that went on his *Rose Colored Glasses* album. Epic released it as a single that September to coincide with the biggest celebratory event of her fortieth anniversary in show business when she played to a sellout crowd at the Brady Theater in Tulsa. The town's mayor, Dick Crawford, read a proclamation making Friday, September 19, 1986, Patti Page Day in her hometown, and then Oklahoma Governor George Nigh proclaimed it her day all across the state. It was an astonishing moment for a local woman who, as a little girl, had run barefoot through the Oklahoma cotton fields and by the Katy railroad.

The event was filmed for an ABC TV series called *Fame, Fortune and Romance*. Page might have been expected to simply sing a medley of her hits, but instead she chose the Country tune "For the Good Times," the Duke Ellington classics "Solitude" and "Sophisticated Lady," and Barbra Streisand's hit "The Way He Makes Me Feel" from her movie *Yentl*. A favorite moment for many in the audience was when she brought her granddaughter, Sherri, onstage to help sing "How Much is That Doggie in the Window?" In a role reversal from the early years when girl singers were always the warm-up act for the men, Patti's opening act was Frankie Laine, her old friend from the Mercury Records days.

Male opera singers are well-known for ripening as they age, and that's also what seemed to be happening with Patti Page. Her years of experience also meant that she had remarkable versatility. She could play a set with just Rocky Cole on piano and Kenneth Hume on drums, or she could perform with the entire Grand Rapids Symphony Orchestra, as she did that September. In some respects it was a musical reunion, in that she and the conductor, Richard Hayman, had been acquaintances since the 1950s, when they were both signed to Mercury Records.

At this time, Page had recorded a total of eighty albums and over 150 singles. Her recording of "Tennessee Waltz" was still the #2 biggest-selling song of all time, behind Bing Crosby's "White Christmas." Every year from 1948 to 1982, she'd had at least one song in *Billboard's* Top 100. Page's fan club president, Bob Bowling, calculated that at this point, she had been on the Billboard Top 100 charts for 954 weeks of her career. Her records had been in the top 100 for 18.35 years and in the Top 40 for 16.2 years.

I rang in the New Year in Des Moines, Iowa, singing in a Pops Gala with the Des Moines Symphony at the Civic Center. I was tickled that the conductor was a woman, Dianne Pope. And you know what? I was glad I was a woman, too.

Back home, I thanked God that my kids' lives seemed to be back on track. Kathleen and Larry were living nearby in Escondido with my granddaughter, Sherri, who was five, who I saw as often as I could. I'd bought Kathleen and Larry a trailer home so they could keep a roof over their heads, and Larry had a job working for Jerry Filiciotto at his aerospace company nearby. Since my son-in-law still had trouble with literacy, Jerry would make sure Larry took oral examinations when any tests were called for in connection with the job, which was a great help. Kathleen was pregnant again, and this time it was a boy. Baby Jayson was born on January 28, 1987. I was appearing at the Fairmont in San Francisco and came home as soon as I could to see my beautiful new grandson. Everything was hunky-dory for Kathleen and Larry and their growing family— or at least, I was under the impression that they were.

Danny was attempting to be a musician and artist—like mom, like son— and was living in San Diego. Although Danny was not completely over his drug problems, I was hopeful that he would eventually pull out of it, just as I thought Kathleen had made it through her struggles.

With no kids at home anymore, in 1985, I had sold my original Rancho house and bought a smaller home on a three-acre lot not far away. It had a circular drive and a small grove of lemon trees and suited me just fine. I'd taken up needlepoint since I'd quit smoking, and when I wasn't doing that I'd have bridge parties in the sunny family room of my house. I'd also done a little fishing and had a six-foot marlin hanging over the fireplace, caught on my first trip to Cabo San Lucas in Baja, Mexico. As a single mom, I felt like my ship was finally making its way out of the choppy seas of the last few years.

Life never seems to be without pain, though. In 1987, my best friend, Katie Filiciotto, was diagnosed with leukemia. Jerry and her children were utterly devastated, as was I.

Katie and Jerry had met when he attended engineering school at North Carolina State. At first Katie rebuffed his advances but was finally won over by the easy charm and persistence of a very funny Italian-American. My friend was a joy to be around and flippantly unconcerned about what people thought of her. Once when entering a polling place with her husband, she'd drawled, "So Jah-rome, how'm I supposed to vote again?"

"Jerome" had retired from an aerospace career with the intention of owning and running a favorite local hardware store, but Katie had talked him out of it because he knew nothing about such a business. Instead, Jerry talked to some people and ended up buying his own small aerospace company. Eventually, he was able to put a lot of people to work, including my son-in-law. But without Katie there to support and guide him, I wonder if he would have done as well.

When Jayson was only a few months old he had to go into the hospital due to some problems with his esophagus. Katie had gone into rapid decline from her leukemia and knew she only had a short time left, but she was the type of person who always put her friends and loved ones before herself. I was sitting in the hospital room with little Jayson one day when, to my surprise, Jerry walked into the room. Katie had sent Jerry to the hospital to check on me, to make sure I wasn't too upset over what was going on with my grandson's health.

Jerry had a dream to retire to a beautiful farm in New Hampshire that he'd bought for Katie and himself. He spent a lot of money rebuilding the 7,000-square-foot house. I'd seen pictures, and it looked spectacular. Thankfully, Katie was able to spend Christmas there with her family in 1987, though they had to fly her to New Hampshire on a hospital plane.

In 1987, Patti Page fitted visits to her friend Katie Filiciotto's bedside into another hectic year of touring. She played in Fort Lauderdale, San Francisco, Phoenix, Honolulu, Atlanta, and Buffalo in the first three months of the year. In April, she performed at the fiftieth birthday celebration of Hershey Park Arena, in Harrisburg, Pennsylvania. She imprinted her hands in cement in the Starlight Arcade in the park, along with Mary Hart from TV's *Entertainment Tonight* and ninety-one-year–old George Burns. The comedian no doubt would've approved of Page's busy schedule. He told a reporter that day: "Don't retire. What do you do when you retire? You sit around, like these guys at the club, and play with your cuticles. Do you ever play with your cuticles? Playing with your cuticles is pretty boring."

After that, Page was in Laughlin, Nevada then North Dakota, then Costa Mesa, California. The rest of the year took her to Detroit, Calgary, and Montreal.

Early 1988 was as scattered for me, travel-wise, as the previous year, with a big swing through Florida in February. March and April were also busy, but then I curbed my travel because I was losing my best friend.

Katie passed away in May of 1988, almost exactly a year after she'd been diagnosed with her illness. There was a beautiful service for friends, family, Jerry, and the three kids. It was one of the saddest days of my life.

It's strange sometimes when you're a performer: You can have great tragedy in your life one morning yet need to perform with a smile on your face that night. And no matter what I had going on at home or in my personal life, I had to keep performing and making a living, especially as a single mother. When my kids had troubles and struggles, I was the only one they could look to for help.

As usual, I went back on the road to sing away my worries and grief.

On July 12, 1988, Patti Page played in New York for the first time in nineteen years, for two weeks at a club called The Ballroom, on W. 28th Street. When a reporter asked about her choice of songs for the shows, she explained she wasn't going to restrict herself to Country tunes but would sing Ellington songs, a Streisand song—in short, anything she liked.

"And what style would you call that?" he asked.

"Comfortable!" Page replied.

A month later, Patti Page played the Hollywood Bowl as part of the *Great American Concert* series. The reviewer for the *Los Angeles Times* said: "Remarkably, both the song and the singer sounded refreshingly pleasant. Page's voice—always a smooth and easy sound—has lost nothing in the intervening years since its greatest popularity."

I appreciated the *Los Angeles Times* reviewer's kind words, but why did he think that a singer's voice should decline over the years? After all, I was only sixty—not dead! When I walked among the 16,000-strong audience singing my hits at the end of the show, it made for one of my favorite summer performances of my entire career.

Whenever I wasn't away touring or recording, I stayed close to home, in Rancho Santa Fe. Jerry Filiciotto and I spent a good deal of time together. He'd become the best friend that Katie had been to me before her passing. In turn, I believe Jerry found solace in having me to talk with. I knew it wasn't easy for him getting over the loss he felt after a long marriage to a woman he dearly loved.

In my professional life, the highlight of 1989 for me was on July 22. That was the night I joined fellow Oklahomans Roger Miller and Reba McIntire performing in the opening ceremony of the U.S. Olympic Festival for a crowd of over 76,000 people—an Olympic Festival attendance record—at Owen Field, on the campus of the University of Oklahoma. Sports heroes like Mickey Mantle and Barry Switzer were in attendance. Florence Griffith Joyner ran the torch into the stadium, and the Olympic flame was lit by Oklahoman John Smith, a wrestler who'd won an Olympic gold medal. At the end of the evening, my old friend Bob Hope took the stage with President Ronald Reagan, who had arrived at the stadium in Marine One, the presidential helicopter. When the president walked into the stadium, a massive roar went up. It was the night when I was the most proud I'd ever been of being both an Oklahoman and an American.

After that grand high came a deep low in August. Rocky Cole and I stopped dating and ended our professional relationship after thirty-five years. I had lost my best musical friend. We'd been through a lot of road adventures with each other, and he'd been a great guy to know. We'd written a couple of Country songs together, though they hadn't gone anywhere. We'd even opened a business, the Total Photo finishing lab in Solana Beach. I was sorry to see him go. He still hadn't given up thinking we were going to get married, but I had tried to make him understand that I never saw our dating moving toward permanency. I simply felt we enjoyed each other's company.

Rocky felt hurt because I'd begun seeing less of him socially ever since Katie passed away. But I couldn't tell him the reason why. You see, Katie had told me a couple of things in her hospital room one day that changed everything.

"Patti," she said, "Jerry's always been in love with you. You know that, don't you?"

I didn't know what to say. "Really, Katie? Do you really think so?"

Katie just smiled at me and patted my hand. "Promise me you'll take care of him when I'm gone," she said.

"Don't talk like that," I admonished. "You could get better. We shouldn't be having this conversation."

She smiled at me sadly. "Just promise me, okay, Patti?"

I agreed I would. I wasn't sure what she meant, since Jerry could take care of himself pretty well, but I kind of felt Katie was passing a baton.

How could I tell anyone about a promise that intimate? And how could I tell Rocky that a long and warm friendship with Jerry had somehow changed into something very different, only two years after Katie, my best friend, was gone? It had started innocently enough with my making sure that Jerry wasn't alone and sad over the loss of Katie. The more time we spent together, the more enjoyable it became. We'd never known each other in anything approaching a romantic way, only as friends. It just goes to show that you never know what kind of path God will put you on. I enjoyed Jerry's company more than anyone I knew, and Rocky couldn't live with that.

After Rocky left, I spent even more time with Jerry than in the previous fifteen years we'd known each other. Jerry had sold his company and had plenty of free time, and I didn't have any plans for New Year's, so I went to New York City with him, to see his mom. She was a feisty Italian lady whom everyone called Nana. When we were introduced, she called me "Betty," and she kept that up for many years. She had never been to school, had done everything on her own, and was full of life.

Jerry and I were sitting on her living room floor on New Year's Eve just talking when suddenly he got a little smile on his face.

"Hey, Patti," he said quietly. Knowing Jerry, I figured some kind of joke was coming.

"What, Jerry?"

"You think you'd marry me?" he asked.

I could tell he was nervous. The question had been so unexpected I didn't have time to be nervous myself. "Why, yes, Jerry," I said. "I would."

He didn't have a ring or anything; maybe it was just something that popped into his head, spur of the moment, but I knew he meant it, and so did I. And that's how it worked out; I'd met Jerry at a New Year's Eve party and now, in one of those bizarre twists in life, after so many years as a friend he was about to become my husband.

TWENTY

A New Husband, New Media, and a Big Split

I had a five-city tour of Florida to do in January 1990, and Jerry had things to do back in California. So, although we visited a jeweler back home to pick a ring, he wasn't able to give it to me personally—I got the ring shipped to me in Florida via FedEx. It had a lovely oval diamond, distinct from the round one Katie had worn.

On May 12, 1990, Jerry and I were married in a formal ceremony at Solana Beach Presbyterian Church. I was sixty-two, and Jerry was sixty. I'd been single for almost twenty years, and Jerry and I had known each other seventeen years.

It was a very happy occasion but tinged with sadness. I had wanted Kathleen to be my matron of honor and Danny to walk me down the aisle. But Danny's drug problems had again taken the upper hand in his life, and Kathleen, too, had slipped into drug addiction. I had two kids with drug problems, and neither one was there on the day of my wedding. It broke my heart, but I did all I could to keep a smile on my face. Jerry helped me do that.

Jerry's daughters, May and Connie, thought it was too soon for Jerry to be getting married. They knew how much Katie and I had loved each other, but they didn't know the story of how Katie told me to take care of Jerry for her. Jerry and I knew that we couldn't please everyone, and that for us it was right to join our lives in marriage. We both felt that we were stronger as a couple than alone.

Jerry and I were both members of the Solano Beach Presbyterian Church, and he and Katie had been members there for years before that. There were about 200 friends and family members in attendance but no showbiz contingent. Jack Rael gave me away. It was a last-minute thing because my brother, Charlie, was supposed to walk me down the aisle. The night before the ceremony, Charlie got sick and had to be taken to the hospital. He was at the ceremony but couldn't walk me down the aisle so, as a fill-in, I asked Jack to do it. Jack tried to make it funny as he came down the aisle, faking a trip like old vaudeville people would do, but I squeezed his arm hard enough to get him to stop.

My youngest sister, Peggy, was my matron of honor. Five of our granddaughters were bridesmaids and our grandson, Jayson, was the ring bearer. He was two, the youngest of our combined grandkids, and he and one of Jerry's little granddaughters lie down on the floor and went to sleep just as the minister was marrying us. That was a nice comical touch at our very formal ceremony, and the minister added to it.

"Jerry," he said, "you stay off the stage when Patti is on it, okay?"

Jerry laughed and agreed.

"Patti," he told me, "I would suggest you stay out of the kitchen when Jerry's there."

I agreed—who wanted to mess with an Italian in the kitchen? There were laughs all around.

The next week, I had a concert to do in nearby Oceanside and then, 10 days after our marriage, Jerry accompanied me on an extended tour of cities in Japan. Sayonara, honeymoon!

In 1991, I was busy singing all through summer and early fall, but the winter eased up, which was fine with me. Jerry and I spent Thanksgiving of 1991 in Old Cape Cod, to see Jerry's sister, Mary, who was getting over an operation. It starts getting cold in the Northeast at that time of year. We brought Nana up from New York to see her daughter and, after getting my mother-in-law back home, we returned to California and sunnier weather. That didn't last long, though, because we spent December at the farm in New Hampshire. Jerry's kids and grandkids and my grandkids stayed over Christmas and New Year's. It was quite a gathering. There's something special about a white Christmas in a beautiful house in New England, and I enjoyed that holiday season.

Baby Boomers were becoming nostalgic for the jukebox era, when Patti Page reached the height of her success. She signed up to host *Jukebox Saturday Night II*, a two-hour special featuring music of the 1940s and 1950s, which aired on public television. Joining Page on the show were friends from her New York TV show days such as Teresa Brewer, The McGuire Sisters, Julius La Rosa, and Margaret Whiting. Page sang "All the Way," "Where Or When," and "Tennessee Waltz." Compact discs were just becoming popular, giving new life to decades-old recordings. In a sense, CDs provided what jukeboxes had provided back then—the opportunity to choose music rather than simply accept what was being played on the radio. Patti Page's first CD came out in the summer of 1992. Titled *Tennessee Waltz*, it featured twelve hits from her Plantation Records days. That year she also re-recorded "How Much isThat Doggie in the Window?" with the Cincinnati Pops Orchestra for their children's album, *Young at Heart.*

Patti's work also began cropping up on another medium becoming popular at that time—VHS video. A video titled *Sentimental Journey* hosted by Pearl Bailey featured Page singing "Tennessee Waltz"; and *The Magic of Bing Crosby: Part One* featured a duet of Page and Bing Crosby singing "True Love," with Dean Martin coming in on the song toward the end to make it a trio.

Page herself tapped into the newly booming VHS market by releasing *The Patti Page Video Songbook*, a forty-five-minute video of eighteen of her hits performed on her television shows. It featured songs such as "Tennessee Waltz," her theme, "This is My Song, and "How Much is That Doggie in the Window?"

It always amazes me how people never forget the old music, particularly "Doggie in the Window." Time after time in my appearances—it even happened the week we were shooting the *Jukebox* show—people come up to me and explain how that it is one of their all-time favorite songs. I suppose the fact that it was at its most popular in 1953 means that a lot of young kids who are now grown up hold a particular fondness for it. Occasionally, I'll hear from someone who owned one of the Bonnie Books that had Patti Page and doggie statuette dolls or a Playcraft record like "Arfie Goes to the City with Patti Page as Pattibell." Pattibell was a takeoff on Tinker Bell from *Peter Pan*, which was a major character in the minds of young kids of the 50s who saw the TV special starring Mary Martin as Peter. Instead of a fairy with wings, I was depicted on the cover of the record as an angel in an evening gown with a magic wand.

In April 1992, Patti Page returned to Claremore, Oklahoma, as she was being honored with another "Patti Page Day." It was part of the fifth annual Lynn Riggs Award Friday, which commemorates Oklahomans who have shown commitment and dedication to the arts in the state. Claremore Mayor Tom Pool and Oklahoma Governor David Walters made it "Patti Page Day" in the city and state, respectively.

It was always special going home to Oklahoma. Five of my sisters were there for the Patti Page Day in 1992: Ruby, Peggy, Virginia, Hazel, and Louise. Half a dozen other relatives were there, too. It was great to see them because we didn't get much of a chance to be together. Another relative that my sisters and I wished was there that day was my great-nephew, Tim Akers. At twenty-two years old, he seemed to be my biggest fan in the world. He owned copies of all my records and had ideas about starting a Patti Page Museum in Claremore. Generally, if I had a question about any of my records and Bob Bowling, my fan club president, couldn't answer it, Tim could. It thrilled me to know that someone in the younger generation of my family was getting enjoyment from my songs.

The next month, I played the wonderful resort town of Branson, Missouri for the first time, doing a few days at the Roy Clark Theater. Roy was as jovial and relaxed as he'd been when I'd first met him on *Hee Haw* all those years ago. Jerry and I liked Branson quite a bit, but we were perplexed to discover that it seemed that just about every food offered was fried. Fried chicken, fried catfish, you name it. Jerry wondered out loud if they fried the milk.

I'd been offered my own theater in Branson in the 60s and again in the 70s, but that would have meant being there for half a year or so at a time, which was something I hadn't been willing to do. My friend, Andy Williams, made it work, but I'd never been as good a businessperson as Andy and looked toward the future enough. By the time I would have taken an offer to have my own theater, no one was offering.

Jerry and I spent the summer of 1992 at the farm in New Hampshire making new memories together as a married couple, and Jerry even convinced me to camp out in a tent. My discomfort with certain camping conditions away from the house convinced Jerry to build a large guest house that became known as the Cabana. He was always being thoughtful like that. But then, I wasn't too crazy about using bushes for a bathroom with a roll of toilet paper suspended from a tree on a coat hanger.

The contribution Patti Page had made to Country music over the course of her career was undeniable. And so it was that on October 1, she was inducted into the Walkway of Stars at the Country Music Hall of Fame and Museum, in Nashville. She was in good company that day: Billy Ray Cyrus, The Four Guys, Connie Smith, Marty Stuart, Steve Wariner, and Trisha Yearwood were also inducted. The emcees of the event were Emmylou Harris and Bill Ivey, the executive director of the museum.

At the museum, each inductee has an area set aside for them, in which their memorabilia is displayed. For her section of the museum, Patti donated a Platinum Record Plaque, one of her gowns, and several smaller pieces of memorabilia.

Country people are the best, and Country music feeds my soul, so to be inducted into the Country Music Hall of Fame was like one of my dreams coming true. That night I met Garth Brooks and his wife, Sandy, who were from Oklahoma, and made sure to get autographs for my kids and grandkids. It was a real pleasure to appear with Garth on the popular *Crook & Chase* TV show together, talking about the induction and our careers. All in all, Jerry and

I had a superb time in Nashville as the guests of Plantation Records owner, Shelby Singleton. I loved being in Nashville again. It is an unselfish city; the stars there don't have the jealousies or the egos that you find in show business elsewhere.

I continued my typical touring schedule, playing concerts all around the country, including Harrah's in Vegas. Jerry often traveled with me, and as he did, he began familiarizing himself with all the aspects of the business that I usually let Jack take care of. I was happy to hear his opinion, but I began to realize that he and Jack weren't exactly seeing eye to eye. It wasn't long before I realized they just didn't get along. It was clear to me that Jack was worried about someone new coming in and usurping his position.

It was a different kind of clash than Jack had with Charlie because those two both knew show business yet neither were geniuses about business in a larger sense. Jerry didn't know show business, but he knew business. Jack's attitude to Jerry was probably even worse than it had been toward Charlie because Jerry wasn't in show business. To Jack, that meant Jerry didn't know a thing about anything. Jack wasn't doing bad with my bookings, particularly considering that I was now in my sixties, but I'd gained enough control of my life and my act that I was beginning to sense there were important business details I'd missed over the years.

Like all husbands and wives do, Jerry and I talked about our pasts. After hearing me talk about my divorce from Charlie and then reading the court transcripts, Jerry felt that Jack had pushed harder in court than my lawyer. I couldn't argue with that because Jack and Charlie had clashed from the beginning, and Jack had felt threatened. But more and more I was realizing how important it had always been to Jack to have control over me.

On the home front, Jerry and I had many discussions about my kids both before and after we got married, and I don't know what I would have done without him as Kathleen's troubles were rapidly escalating. Then, one day she just walked out, leaving Larry with the kids. It seemed she didn't want to be a part of their lives anymore.

In the past, I had made the trip to their trailer in Escondido almost every day whenever I was in town. Now I felt like I had to do more. I hadn't been successful in figuring out how to help my kids keep out of trouble. I thought I could at least try to do a better job with my grandkids. Jerry and I wanted to take Jayson into our care, and we agonized over what was best for Sherri, who was now of school age. Sherri loved horseback riding, and we discovered an accredited, well-known boarding school in Scottsdale, Arizona that emphasized riding. We put Sherri in that school and it did her a world of good. And with our help, Larry did okay with Jayson.

Danny's drug problems worsened. We always expected bad news might come at any moment. We were thankful that at least he was still alive. That was the sad state things had gotten to in those days: The most we could hope for was for Danny to stay alive. To Jerry's credit, all these troubles never seemed to faze him a bit, and his support never wavered.

December of 1992 was very big for the Filiciotto family because it marked the one hundredth birthday of Jerry's mom, Nana Concetta. In preparation for the celebration, Jerry and I took a little trip to Italy to find his mother's birth certificate. It gave us a chance for the honeymoon we didn't have time for two years earlier.

I never knew what to expect from Nana. Once I was doing a big show for PBS at the Marriott in downtown New York City. We were going to stay with Nana in Westchester County afterward, and Jerry tried to make sure she understood that.

"Patti's coming in the limo," he told her as he left the house, trying to explain that he and I would arrive separately. "So, don't be afraid when she shows up."

"Oh, nonch you worry," Nana said, as if he was silly to think there would be a problem.

He wasn't at the house when I arrived and stepped in the back door. "Nana?" I called out.

"Who is it!?" I could hear the apprehension in her voice.

"It's Patti!"

She stepped into the kitchen and shook her head at me. "Who you!?" she challenged.

"Patti!" I said. "Jerry's wife."

"Ah," she said, I suppose now recognizing me. "Betty."

For some reason, she couldn't say Patti.

People flew in from all over the country for her hundredth birthday party at the Hilton in White Plains, New York. Jerry had been planning it for a year. The room was decked out like a festive wedding with Italian tricolors everywhere. Even the glasses were painted with the Italian colors. Everyone was impressed.

I sang a couple of songs for the crowd, but the treat of the evening was when Nana's favorite singer; my old friend, Julius LaRosa; sang for her. She'd seen Julie sing on *The Arthur Godfrey Show* in the 50s and was a big fan, so we recruited him for the party. When he was finished singing to her in Italian, she took him in her arms and kissed him and Julius just cried. What he didn't know was that later she asked Jerry who he was; she didn't recognize him because she was overwhelmed by having all those friends, children, and grandchildren there celebrating her life. He was extremely gracious, and every time we've seen him since, he's wearing and showing off the watch we gave him that night as a thank you for making Nana's night extra-special.

In 1993, Nana came to live with us. She was a delight to have around but I never knew what would come from her next. The way she saw things, it was her kids and then the rest of the world. The three of us would have breakfast together and Nana's standard morning meal was a banana, an English muffin, and coffee. One morning we only had one banana. Nana cut it in half, keeping half for herself and pushing the other half toward Jerry. He pushed it back to her, and she pushed it back to him. This went on a few times.

"What about Patti?" he finally asked.

"She no wanch," Nana said. "I know. She no wanch."

"Well, I do," I protested, half-kidding.

She looked me up and down, and then pronounced, "No, Patti, you don't need!"

Nana used to call Jerry an Italian name for a wise guy and use other phrases I didn't understand. "Talk in English!" I'd protest, and every time I got the same reply.

"No worry," she'd say.

It was okay because Jerry assured me that if Nana didn't like me, I'd know about it, and I believed him. Thankfully, she accepted my family, as well. She loved all her grandkids, but she took a special liking to Kathleen's son, Jayson, and showered him with gifts and cash.

Career-wise, it was a relatively easy year, and in November, Jack Rael moved to nearby Rancho Mirage.

In July 1994, I was in the paper for the first time in a while. It was the front page of the Sunday Arts and Leisure section of the *New York Times*. There was a publicity picture of me from way back when, wearing a lovely feminine gown, side by side with a picture of the rapper Snoop Dog with the headline "How Pop Music Lost the Melody." "It's a long way from that little doggie in the window to Snoop Doggy Dog," wrote Stephen Holden. He contrasted a 1953 Saturday morning radio show, *Make Believe Ballroom*, that was popular when my song had been #1, to a Saturday morning in 1994, with sounds of a roaring car and booming speakers blasting out the obscenity-laced stories of sex and crime on Snoop Dog's 3-million-selling album *Doggystyle*.

It was a long way, all right. How innocent and naïve the world had been throughout the years I'd been selling hit records and how degraded popular music had become in contrast.

The naiveté of those early years had spilled over into the business side of my career. In addition to splitting my earnings down the middle with Jack, we had several joint companies. Our main one was Page-Rael, and we also had Argap Productions for movies, Pattack Productions for television, and Egap Music Corporation and Lear Music for music publishing. Egap was Page spelled backward and Lear was Rael spelled backward. I wasn't the only person Jack managed. Over the years he'd done business with The Everly Brothers, the comedian Soupy Sales, and Carmen McRae, among others. But by most people's accounts, Jack and I had the longest and most successful manager/artist relationship in the entertainment industry. We'd traveled millions of miles together. He'd seen me through two marriages and into another one, and I'd been to his kids' bar and bat mitzvahs. We knew each other like family, or so I thought.

The odd thing is, unlike the way people in families talk to each other about where they're going in life, Jack and I rarely discussed the direction of my career because I didn't question Jack that much. I thought he knew everything. I had faith in him and what he did, so I thought, *Why question it?* I didn't worry about my long-term prospects because I thought I had people taking care of it for me. As the years went by, though, especially after I married Jerry, I found that some things weren't being done as I had expected, and that's when I began to get more involved.

When Jerry had begun to ask questions of Jack about his new wife's side of the Page-Rael business, he hadn't exactly encountered open arms. Jack would tell Jerry that he couldn't tell him what he was doing with the money. Jack's reasoning was that he knew show business and Jerry didn't—which was fine, but Jerry had run his own high-end company making airplane parts that had to be perfect to the micrometer. He knew more than a little bit about doing big business and finance.

Jerry grew concerned when he heard Jack discuss how he'd been shrewd and not paid certain people our companies had business dealings with, for this or that reason. Jerry began to fear that if Jack hadn't done things ethically or properly, some of those people might someday come after me in court. After all, I was the one making most of the money—the various companies Jack and I owned together weren't big moneymakers.

I never asked for 25 percent of music publishing when I recorded people's songs. I could have, but I didn't put my name on anything because I wasn't a writer and I didn't believe in anything like that. Jack didn't share those sentiments. I don't know if the music publishing brought him any wealth, but he believed in having ownership.

Around this time, Jerry started a maple syrup company in New Hampshire. It wasn't doing as well as he wanted, so I said to Jerry, "If it would help, I wouldn't mind you using my name." Jack put up a little stink about that, which I found strange. I'd never questioned Jack on investments he made for himself and his second wife, Ann, so why would he be concerned about me using my name to help my husband? He didn't tell Jerry that he wanted half of the maple syrup business, but that's what he intimated.

After Jerry began looking into some of Jack's business practices, he told me, "Something here isn't right." Even though Jerry was my husband, it took me a long time to go along with his doubts about Jack. When he finally convinced me there were serious problems, we decided we had to take action. I wanted to make sure that all of our business arrangements were legal, and that not only the future of my kids, grandkids, and me was being looked after but the future of Jack and his heirs, too. I told Jack and suggested we get together with the accountant, financial advisor, and lawyers to make sure everything was in order. It was the first time I had ever done anything like that. Jack just didn't understand why I wanted to look over everything.

"Everything is all right," he told me with a dismissive air. "You haven't wanted to see these things before. It's been open to review any time you want."

Jerry had told me I'd just been getting lip service all these years, and suddenly it was very apparent to me.

"This is all Jerry's doing," Jack added.

"No, it isn't," I said firmly. "It's mine, Jack."

With that I brought up a specific problem: We'd had a couple of incidents where secretaries had access to funds and money had disappeared. The first time, $20,000 went missing, then $30,000 vanished another time when we had a different secretary.

"How could you let those things happen?" I questioned. "Why didn't you catch them?"

Jack didn't like that. He put on a big show. "I send everything over to Sid," he said, referring to our accountant, Sid Pazoff. "He handles those things. Every month he has a profit and loss statement. It's all on the up-and-up."

For the moment, I went along with him, but I wasn't happy. I should have called Sid right there but I always hesitate when it comes to confrontations. What I learned later was that poor Sid, who worked out of his own office, not in Jack's, was simply copying down the numbers that Jack gave him. Jack wasn't watching the store and was not aware of the secretary shenanigans, and that money was missing. We never got the money back. Jack wanted to sue the bank. Then he wanted to sue Sid. I put my foot down.

"No way," I said. "That man has been at our side since the beginning and no way you're going to take him to court."

"Well, somebody was to blame," Jack came back—only he'd never consider that that someone could be him.

I couldn't fault Jack completely because I had not been staying on top of my own business, and I'd trusted him completely. For instance, whenever a contract was to be written for a record company, Jack told them what he wanted, which was supposedly what I wanted, but he never ran it by me. I should have asked. To this day I don't know how many signing bonuses (a lump sum payment made at the signing of an agreement) he might have gotten from different people in the business or what happened to them.

Finally, the arguments escalated and the evidence mounted up to such a degree that I told Jack I wanted to dissolve our decades-old partnership. He wouldn't accept the idea unless he could get the better half of everything. I was willing to give him half of whatever I had in the business and the two music publishing companies, but Jack would just increase his demands. Finally, I said, "Okay, Jack, you get nothing. Let's just go to court."

Jerry stayed out of it. He was by my side but didn't want to appear that he'd engineered my decision, which indeed he had not. I filed the action in September 1996 and went to court in Vista, in San Diego County, seeking to dissolve all our companies. I offered Jack a lot of money to dissolve the performing arm of our enterprises, where the royalties came in. He wouldn't be reasonable; he also wanted half of my pension, which would include all the royalties in perpetuity, and half of my Social Security, too! It confirmed my suspicions from years before— Jack thought he was Patti Page.

The conflict snowballed, and I began to think Jack had gone a little crazy, given some of the things he wanted. Jack had a lot of videotapes of my shows, which had been given to him by a myriad of publishers and television networks, such as NBC. I wanted copies of them because there were shows that could be remarketed. We could work the profits out fairly. But Jack was simply unreasonable; he refused to give them to me.

Jack also tried to claim that he had been an "author" of certain things I'd created during my career. Ultimately, that wouldn't hold up in court because of copyright laws, but at least now it was finally becoming clear to me why, over the years, Jack had put his name on things he didn't do.

When a television program about the upcoming fiftieth anniversary of my show business career was in production for PBS, the producer wanted to use video excerpts from my TV show in the program. Jack told the owner of Research Video, where a lot of the material was stored, that he was the sole owner of the video rights. They were copies of *The Oldsmobile Show; The Patti Page Show; The Big Record*, my Perry Como fill-in; *Scott Music Hall*; and the Patti Page filmed shows. Well, needless to say, we had a battle over those.

Another item of contention was who should take ownership of a cordless microphone worth several thousand dollars that belonged to one of our companies. Jack wasn't a singer. Since it was obvious he and I weren't going to reconcile, I couldn't see why he'd even care about it, but he did.

It seems like we had hundreds of witnesses at the trial. Jay Cooper, the lawyer for The Society of Singers, testified on my behalf that Jack's deal with me was, let's just say, very strange. Jack brought some folks in from New York, people who used to work for me, just to testify that he was there every time I did a record. There was no contention that he wasn't there; but that didn't mean he owned me and my name as well. Nevertheless, he actually claimed that he had the rights to the name Patti Page. It was horrendous, just ridiculous. I was heartbroken because I really liked Jack, I really did. And what was tragic was that I had started out trying to make sure that his interests and those of his children were covered in the future, as well as mine.

Throughout the proceedings, Jack wouldn't stop with his demands, and after every session I'd say to the lawyers and to Jerry, look I'll do this, I'll do that, let's just end this.

"Don't you dare!" they would all say. "You've given in and given in and given in. You can't give in anymore unless you want to throw everything down the drain."

Our dissolution could have been as simple as our accountant telling us that we had to make different distribution arrangements for whatever Jack had in the business and whatever I had and to make sure that our children got what was supposed to go to them whenever we passed away. Yet Jack didn't want anything changed with how it was set up. So, as we went through the checks and financial records, something that I was not prepared for, there were just too many things that were wrong. I was disillusioned, and became even more so when Jack wanted half of my pension that I was going to get from the American Federation of Television and Radio Artists (AFTRA). AFTRA is the union I joined as a recording artist and made contributions toward my pension with the dues I paid throughout my career. Jack wasn't even a member of AFTRA, but he wanted half of my pension!

By the time we finished litigating the first dissolution, a year had passed. We went into arbitration to dissolve the other companies we had and distribute the assets. My career hadn't stopped during the court battle. Jack had booked me a lot of engagements before the fight began, so that meant there was still money coming in. This posed a problem because that money had to be considered when the dissolution became final. I was willing to give Jack half of what he had booked, but he turned that down. He turned everything down that I offered, every time, never flinching. Finally, the arbiter, Judge Flynn, told Jack, "Mister, you're going to take what I say you're going to get."

Then Judge Flynn, a really nice gentleman, died of a heart attack. Another arbiter, Judge Miller was assigned, and he, too, ruled that Jack would accept what I offered him. I was told what to offer Jack, and I did what the judge said.

Finally, early in November 1996, Jerry and I got a letter from our attorney that instructed us to grab a chair and sit down before reading any further because he had shocking news. Jack and his attorney had signed the settlement agreement without making any further changes. The microphone and videotapes were on their way to my attorney's office. I had to pay for future use of songs I chose to sing from the Egap and Lear catalogs, but I got all the royalties from songs I'd recorded. I got to keep my name. (Why Jack thought he could ever claim it, I have no idea.) We had to pay our own attorneys' costs, but basically, I got what was mine and what was fair. The first judge had ruled that way, and the second one did the same.

The dissolution of our relationship hurt me an awful lot. I had offered Jack the world because I was that faithful to our relationship. I had given him the credit that I thought he deserved. When I accepted the Pioneer Award from the Country Music Association I had said that part of it belonged to Jack, and I really meant it. It was very disheartening to realize that Jack really didn't have the same feeling for me that I had for him. I adored him for his talent. It was all a rude awakening for me, and the time that we spent in court was awful.

One line in a press release that came out shortly after the court's decision concisely summed up the basis of Page and Rael's forty-eight-year management contract: "The judge determined the agreement, fashioned in the form of an indefinite partnership agreement, to be unconscionable."

Page may have been rocked by the acrimonious split but she was far from beaten. As was clear from the press release, she intended to face 1997 with her usual vigor: She was planning her upcoming Carnegie Hall concert, had been selected for induction to the new Oklahoma Music Hall of Fame, and was soon to debut on the Home Shopping Network promoting her and her husband Jerry's line of New England Maple Syrup products. The last line read: "As Miss Patti Page hits a golden career milestone you might say this legend has done it all…but in 1997 she is ready to do it all over again."

When the dissolution was finished, I began to learn that a great many people didn't like Jack. He was a sharpie in their minds; they'd always felt that way. No one had ever suggested that I get somebody else. No one wanted to go that far.

On balance, I was glad they'd never said anything to me because had I found out all these things about Jack earlier, I would have been a nervous wreck. My musicians and stylists, who had been with me for so many years, were all on my side. They knew the story. And I never received any flack from any of them for parting company with Jack.

In reflection, I believe Jack began changing when the big money started coming in, after "Tennessee Waltz." He wasn't used to that. His family was not wealthy, and he was getting recognition that he would never have gotten as a saxophone player. He knew that he had stumbled onto something really worthwhile, with longevity. I should have seen the end coming over the years, but hindsight is easy. When he went to buy his first car as Patti Page's manager, he bought a Rolls Royce. I bought a Cadillac. Money and prestige meant a lot more to Jack than to me.

When our split was final, I was very spent. I couldn't believe all the things that I had heard, the facts that came out, and how he had misused my trust. I couldn't believe someone that close to me would do those things.

TWENTY-ONE

Why My Grandkids Stopped Calling Me Grammy

W hile the legal battle was raging there were all sorts of other things going on—some good, some bad. Tragically, Ann Gordon-Rael passed away while the court proceedings were taking place. Kenneth Hume, my drummer of thirty years, also died in 1995. Rocky Cole had been very ill, too. I worried about him.

Jerry and I spent Christmas at the farm in New Hampshire. The place was so beautiful at Christmas, with a twenty-foot tree under the thirty-foot ceiling in the main room. The house was filled with perhaps the happiest sound in the world: the conversation and laughter of all our kids and grandkids. Jerry's mom was now 103; Nana had received a call from the president and appeared with *Today* show weatherman, Willard Scott, on television. I hope that I live as long a life as her, and my own mother, of course, who lived to almost age ninety-two.

Country was still big in my music. In November, I'd appeared on the *Grand Ole Opry* in Nashville, and I began 1996 with an appearance on *The Statler Brothers Show* on The Nashville Network. I was back on the road before long, helping with a February 1996 event to benefit the Young Arts Foundation and

Christian Youth Theater in El Cajon, California, near our home.

Jerry was handling my management, and doing well at it, especially for someone who had gotten into show business by default. I thought it was amazing—and a little amusing—that after five decades I was finally having the kind of relationship with my manager that people had speculated I'd had with Jack Rael. But it can be trying to both live and work with someone twenty-four hours a day, seven days a week, so while in the midst of the Rael dissolution, Jerry and I began to think about finding new management for me. My conductor, Joe Mele, suggested I meet with Michael Glynn, out of Boston, who had managed both Connie Francis and Don Rickles and was instrumental in hiring Joe as Don's conductor. Joe said Michael was a nice guy and would do a good job, so in 1995 I had him come to Atlantic City, where I was working, and we had a meeting. In May of 1996, I made a deal with Michael, and he became my new manager. It was good timing getting Michael on board because 1997 marked my fiftieth year as a recording artist, and that meant a whole new round of opportunities to get out and perform to audiences across the country, including the honor of singing at Carnegie Hall.

Michael encouraged me to step in and have more input in picking out songs and to have the last word about what I sang. It was helpful to have that kind of advice and support after dealing for so long with Jack, who was always there telling me what to do. It felt good, making my own decisions.

One of the honors in my fiftieth anniversary year that really touched my heart came that April when I was inducted into the Oklahoma Music Hall of Fame in Muskogee. Receiving this honor in the city where I first sang on the radio, in a trio with my sisters, made it all the more special to me. Governor Frank Keating led the ceremony, and I was in good company that night, with fellow Country artist Merle Haggard, master Jazz violinist Claude Williams, and the late folk musician Woody Guthrie also being inducted. Jimmy LaFaye sang some of Woody's songs in his honor; Woody's daughter, Nora, had picked Jimmy for the occasion. Claude Williams made us all smile by performing the first song he'd ever learned to play and then donated his violin to the museum. I sang "the Waltz" and shared with the crowd how proud I was to be the first woman to be inducted and that my hope was to bring some credit to a state I'd always loved so much. And naturally, Merle Haggard brought the house down with "Okie from Muskogee."

For once in my career, I didn't feel such a great pressure to make new records because *Reader's Digest* had put together a three-album boxed set of my songs called *Greatest Hits—Finest Performances*. I was glad to see the boxed set released as some of the songs hadn't been available to the public since 1948. It featured fifty-eight tracks from Mercury, one from Columbia, and one from Plantation.

Mercury Records commissioned Colin Escott to assemble a four-CD boxed set called *A Golden Celebration* to commemorate my fiftieth anniversary. It was a labor of love for them and was a fabulous package that had one CD of early hits, one with later hits, one with Country cuts, and one with Blues, Jazz, and Standards. It came with a booklet looking back at my career, and Colin got a lot of useful facts for it from the Patti Page Appreciation Society Archives, which Bob Bowling had been assembling for decades. I remain ever grateful to Bob for his support over the years, and I greatly appreciated Colin's efforts, too. What wonderful years I'd had with Mercury. In hindsight, it seemed amazing that back in 1947 I was their first and only female artist. The Mercury boxed set meant that I could share my memories all in one place. Having that set on the market made me feel like an author having a collection of her works published. The release of the boxed set was to coincide with my Carnegie Hall concert, which only heightened my sense of anticipation and excitement.

Mercury's *A Golden Celebration* boxed set was well-received, garnering reviews such as this, from the magazine *Stereo Review,* "Patti Page was once denounced by

Rock historians as the personification of 'establishment' culture, but this retrospective marking her seventieth birthday and the fiftieth anniversary of her first record makes it abundantly clear that 'The Singing Rage' was a true godmother of contemporary Pop. In retrospect, it seems impossible to imagine how Page could have been anything other than the biggest-selling female singer of all time."

Although my show at Carnegie Hall was to last only two hours or so, the preparations would take several months and a lot of effort for a whole team of people. But then, the special moments in life never do come easy, do they?

I decided that because a night like this comes along rarely in a career, the show should be recorded, then maybe we could get a deal for a CD release. We set to work hiring the best recording crew in New York—after all, a venue as famed for its acoustics as Carnegie Hall deserves the very best. They would be based in a forty-foot mobile studio parked at the back of the hall for the night.

It was crucial to get my set list just right. It made me happy, picking all my own numbers for my Carnegie debut. For the most part, Jack Rael had selected my program in the past—which was okay because I had trusted his judgment and simply loved singing. Now, though, it felt liberating to do it all on my own. I had recorded over 1,000 in my career, and sung many others in past shows, so I had a lot to choose from.

Even though the evening was commemorating my fiftieth anniversary in show business, I didn't feel the need to present my whole musical life. And I wanted to do more than simply pick out the musical high points of my career. I wanted to tailor the show to fans who had been with me since the very beginning but also to newer listeners, too. Whether we filled Carnegie Hall or had only a small audience, I wanted to give them something they'd never forget. So, I picked some of my older songs, some newer ones, and some very current tunes in the hopes that my concert would appeal to a wide audience.

Peter Nero and the Philly Pops were providing the musical accompaniment, and there would be a section during the show in which they would perform on their own. I was glad to have such talented musicians with me because at the time, 90 percent of the acts that played Carnegie Hall were classical in nature. I planned to do something that hadn't really been done at Carnegie before: I wanted to combine the elegance of a classical music performance and the warmth of a supper club. This wasn't such an easy balancing act, though, as we would be playing to over 2,800 seats.

The main hall, five levels deep, was built in 1890, and is one of those rare New York buildings that are all bricks and mortar. There's no steel frame. Maybe that's part of the reason the acoustics are so fabulous. Classical musicians love to play there against the gorgeous wooden walls. I read that the violinist Isaac Stern described the hall as an instrument in itself that takes what the performer does and makes it larger than life. The auditorium has a curvilinear design, which in real-people terms means it was designed to focus the sound at the stage area to benefit the audience. The sound in the hall is often described as warm and lively. That was perfect for me! What woman doesn't like to think of herself as warm and lively?

Tickets for the performance ranged from $15 to $60. I thought about my beginnings in Tulsa. When I'd appeared at the Bengalair Club, there was no cover charge. I did three forty-five-minute sets, five nights a week, for the grand salary of $50 a week. Of course, back then a cold Coca-Cola cost three cents. When I'd first appeared in Las Vegas, the price of admission was a drink with no minimum!

In the days immediately leading up to the show I busily rehearsed, while Jerry took care of organizing all the accomodations for our family. With five children and eleven grandchildren, from both his side and mine, that's a lot of people. Danny couldn't be there, which was heartbreaking; every day I prayed that my son would find a way through the drug problem that dogged his life. Kathleen had made it to New York to be with us, which was a source of great joy to me.

I received some uplifting letters of support from friends who unfortunately couldn't make it to the show, such as this one that came in from Beverly Hills:

Dear Patti,

The "Apple" is sweeter this evening because of your presence. How marvelous to congratulate you on 50 years singing the music we both adore.

Barbara joins me in wishing love, warmth, and everything good for you...enjoy the grandeur of the Hall, my friend.

He signed it "Francis Albert."

It saddened me that Frank Sinatra couldn't make it to the concert. I thought of how we'd both gotten big boosts to our careers at the same New York theater, the Paramount, and how many years it had been since we'd played Vegas at the same time and seen each other socially. Good times and great music. What a classy letter from a classy man.

Other letters made me smile. Bob Hope closed with: "Do I wish I could be in the audience at Carnegie Hall to lead the applause." I wished it, too. Ginny Mancini wrote a sweet letter on behalf of the Society of Singers.

And believe it or not, they still had Western Union telegrams in those days. I got one from my old Las Vegas friends Steve Lawrence and Eydie Gorme:

DEAR PATTI,

50 YEARS. SEEMS LIKE YESTERDAY...AND YOU KNOW HOW YESTERDAY WAS. CONGRATULATIONS ON THIS GOLDEN CELEBRATION. WE LOVE YOU.

STEVE AND EYDIE

I certainly did know how yesterday was, and I loved all those show business friends over the years. They understood the struggles, the view from the top, and the uncertainty you always have, wondering how long it will last. And that when you've been doing it for fifty years, it's just kind of baffling when it keeps on going.

Patti Page's fiftieth anniversary in show business was commemorated beyond the music industry. Governor Don Sundquist of Tennessee marked the occasion, writing that she was "a national treasure." His fellow Tennessean, Vice President Al Gore, sent a long and gracious letter reflecting on her achievements as a performer. But it was President Clinton who perhaps best summed up her extraordinary talents and the impact of her career, writing: "Fans the world over have delighted in the smooth elegance of your voice, your effortless delivery, and the depth of feeling you bring to each song."

The morning of the concert dawned, and I still hadn't heard if the *New York Times* would be covering the show. Part of me hoped that they would send someone along, but another part of me didn't even want to know; it would only make me nervous if I knew the reviewers were there.

Jerry and I got to the hall a couple of hours in advance. When we arrived, Michael Glynn and Jim Murtha, my booking agent, told me to follow them because they wanted to show me something.

"What is it you want me to see?" I asked. I looked at Jerry, who pushed his glasses up his nose and shook his head and looked mystified. Neither one of us knew what to think.

"We need to go outside," Jim said.

"Outside? What in the world for?" Reporters waiting? I didn't think so!

"You'll like it," Michael said. "Come take a look."

I chuckled and followed.

"Maybe he knows about a secret exit if they mob the stage," Jerry joked.

"Don't I wish!" I laughed.

Actually, it was almost as good. At the front of the building, in a poster box, it read "Patti Page: A Golden Celebration." That much I knew. What I didn't know I soon learned from the words pasted across the poster in capital letters: SOLD OUT.

No one could have wiped the smile off my face.

But wouldn't you know it, there was a catch. I couldn't expect an event such as this to go off without *some* major problem. In the middle of the sound check, Michael came to Jerry and me and explained that the horn section was drowning out the strings. To balance the orchestra's sound for the audience and get the concert recorded properly, a certain electrical circuit would have to be switched on to connect the recording truck with the hall's sound system. Why was that a problem? Because of the union, a certain person had to do it; and due to rules, it had a cost.

"How much?" I asked.

Michael gulped. "An extra $10,000."

I looked at Jerry and sighed.

"Flip the switch," Jerry said.

$10,000 to flip a switch. Even after all these years, I still scratch my head at the crazy, outrageous things that go on all the time behind the scenes.

Before I knew it, the auditorium was full, the members of the orchestra had taken their places, and it was showtime.

To set a classical mood, we opened with a four-minute overture from the orchestra. Then, with footage of my TV shows playing on a big screen at the back of the stage, I sang "Person That Used to Be Me," which led into a more upbeat "Brand New Me."

The lyrics of my next number, "With My Eyes Wide Open, I'm Dreaming," were so meaningful to me on a night like this, particularly the part, "Do I deserve such a break? Pinch me to prove I'm awake."

I moved on to "It's a Wonderful World"—"It's a wonderful world, I'm just walking on air. It's a wonderful world, I've got more than my share"— and "Can You Feel The Love Tonight?" from Disney's hit movie *The Lion King*. My grandkids loved that movie, and when they asked me to do the song, I couldn't refuse. I was feeling a lot of love that night, especially with them there in the audience.

I thanked the audience for sharing this special evening. "It is an awesome one for me, to realize that I am standing on this stage after so many years of dreaming about it," I said. "And there are so many people that I have to thank for this evening—there have been many beautiful years along the way—and some of those examples are here with me tonight. My husband, our children, our eleven grandchildren...."

The audience interrupted me with applause. Maybe my words weren't coming out exactly right, but they knew what I meant. The good years with family mean everything, don't they? The real spotlight is the one we all have on us when we give and share with the people we love. I looked to my right as the spotlight swung around and revealed my family in their box seats, and I got a lump in my throat.

I sang what I called a sunshine medley, with that great Bill Withers song "Ain't No Sunshine" leading into "You Are My Sunshine"— a happy song made famous by Jimmy Davis, who wrote it with Charles Mitchell in 1940, and later recorded by Stevie Wonder. I was old enough to remember how that song had helped Jimmy Davis get elected governor of Louisiana.

Next, I wanted to be a bit more intimate with the audience, which meant it was time for a love medley, starting with "Wee Small Hours," then a little bigger with "Nearness of You" and "When I Fall in Love." I have never moved around much onstage, but I truly do mean the lyrics I'm singing so I often express my feelings by sweeping a hand outward, and as I began the love medley, it was up toward the balcony where Jerry was sitting. If you're blessed with real love, it's so much easier to sing about it.

I got a standing ovation after that one. It amazed me, really, and it touched me.

We then played "All the Way," but our version was not the slow ballad that Francis Albert made famous. It swung—lots of horns, a fast pace, a rousing tempo. I could almost scat the lyrics, what a blast! Afterwards, I explained, "No one could sing that song like Frank, so we changed the tempo so no one would think I was trying to." I laughed, and the fans laughed with me.

The crowd really came alive as I broke into "Old Cape Cod." I couldn't help wondering how many people have fallen in love, gotten married, and had children with that romantic tune helping them along. Does that make me a bit of a matchmaker?

There was the other side of love, though. I knew that from my own life, so the lyrics to "Release Me" were easy to interpret. It, and the next two songs, took me back to my Country roots. Since the wistful "Release Me" was a bit on the down side, I followed it with the upbeat songs "Go On Home" and "Less Than the Song." I smiled as I repeated the line "All your dreams are real" in "Less Than the Song." Because I'd started out as literally a barefoot country girl, I meant it when I sang the line, "As a young girl I wanted to be free." Don't believe anyone who tells you that you can't have a dream.

After that was a love song associated with New York, the beautiful "Unchained Melody." Many in the audience would have remembered my recording of the song, but over the opening bars, I explained that I had first heard the song in 1953, sung by the great Al Hibbler. The mention of his recording of the song got a round of applause. Then I talked about Bill Medley and Bobby Hatfield's wonderful version in 1963, and how much I'd loved it in the movie *Ghost* in 1990. And I acknowledged the latest hit version, by Lee Ann Rimes, right then in 1997. Some songs just never die, and that was one of them. The audience loved it as much as I did.

Peter Nero made a brief appearance on stage at the end of the first half and we closed with "The Way He Makes Me Feel" and "Sunday in New York," two very pleasant tunes, with just Peter on the piano and me singing.

After fifteen minutes for intermission, back we went. In the second half of a concert, I'm settled in and happy. Intermission flies by, with just enough time to relax and talk over any necessary adjustments before the concert resumes.

Only tonight, I wasn't onstage when the music started. I was at the back of the auditorium. The orchestra began, with the lights low, and the spotlight came up on me, walking down the aisle in a different gown, shaking hands and saying hello to many old friends as I sang "The More I See You." I loved seeing so many familiar faces. It was like singing in my own giant, happy living room. Oh, it might sound corny, but it's a ton of fun and everyone always loves it—perhaps me most of all.

Once back onstage, I began with a personal favorite, "Allegheny Moon." If you've ever been in the Alleghenies on the East Coast of the United States and seen one of those big full moons, the song may have special meaning for you. I take pride—and comfort—in the fact that it went to #2 in the midst of the Rock 'n' Roll revolution led by my friend Elvis because it goes to show that no matter how much tastes and values change, romantic songs will always hold a special and enduring place in music.

For many years, I'd been demonstrating onstage how the special overdubbing effects of my early career were done, by singing "Tumblin' Tumbleweed," gradually layering in the three different parts. Still, I got just a little bit nervous as I launched into it on the stage at Carnegie Hall. It's one thing to hear the famous Sons of the Pioneers version—not so easy to do all those parts alone. But then, I wasn't alone. I was singing with Patti Page and Patti Page, which can be a lot of fun!

Larry McKenna did a great job on the sax solo on a swinging version of

"Foggy Day" next, and I thanked him sincerely for it.

The following song, "I Stayed Too Long at the Fair," felt personal. Gee, I wondered, are they thinking I've stayed too long in my career by this point? "I wanted the music to last forever...have I stayed too long at the fair?" As my voice swelled on the big parts and floated over the subtle guitar riffs, I felt immersed in the music and lyrics, thankful for the chance to share my joy in singing.

When you're really going strong at your chosen work, time slips away. As we launched into "Detour," I really didn't feel much different than I had when I'd performed it back in the 1950s. What forty years? Are you kidding me? The musicians rocked, and the audience cheered and whistled.

Then I thanked my marvelous backup singers, who I call the Page Four, and I explained to the audience: "The pretty girl on the right came to rehearsal this past week and said, 'I have regards for you from my mom and dad.' She said, 'They were with the first group that you sang with in Chicago, The Honey Dreamers.' I laughed and added, "So, I'm glad that the legend is living on."

Isn't that amazing? In my fiftieth year concert, one of my backup singers was the daughter of two of my original backup singers. It was a special kind of moment.

I also thanked the two men who had been my right and left hand for many years—my talented drummer, Chuck Hughes, and my conductor and arranger, Joe Mele. Naturally, I gave my sincere thanks to the fabulous Peter Nero and The Philly Pops, and the audience was equally appreciative.

After that, I couldn't keep the crowd waiting any longer. Whenever you go to a show, you always want to hear the performer's best-known hits, so I did what I affectionately call a *Reader's Digest* medley of: "Doggie in the Window," "You Belong to Me," "Changing Partners," "I Went to Your Wedding" "Would I Love You," "Hush, Hush, Sweet Charlotte," "Mockin' Bird Hill," and "Cross Over the Bridge."

It was a bit of a fluke really that we put the dog bark on the recording of

"How Much Is That Doggie in the Window?" but everyone has been having fun with it ever since. That night, the whole orchestra joined in. It was as if a whole pack of pooches had snuck in to Carnegie Hall! I couldn't help but laugh as I sang.

As I began "Changing Partners," some people in the back cheered. It was wonderful to think that the song must have a special romantic significance for them.

I've recorded a lot of songs about romantic longing. That was true of "I Went to Your Wedding" and "Would I Love You" and then "Hush, Hush, Sweet Charlotte."

"I'll bet you thought Bette Davis did that," I joked with the audience as I finished.

The medley lasted about seven-and-a-half minutes, and I was relieved that my voice was still holding out when we got to "Cross Over the Bridge." What a feeling of exhilaration I had as the medley came to a close.

After all the preparation, the two hours of the show seemed to flash by. The audience had really got into it and showed their appreciation—more than I could ever have hoped for—and that made it all the more enjoyable. I was having fun onstage and I could feel the excitement throughout the hall even though I was now coming to the end of the show. As I began my last number, "Tennessee Waltz," I heard a hoot and holler. People get such joy and comfort out of that song. I guess it's like an old friend who puts an arm around your shoulder and says, "It's okay, I understand." You're glad to see that friend arrive. I never get tired of singing "Tennessee Waltz."

As the orchestra reached its crescendo at the end, I saw someone standing at the foot of the stage with a huge bouquet of roses for me, and I gasped a little. I did it! Carnegie Hall! The fans were on their feet and I was on a cloud, waving my thanks to them as I found my way offstage to find a place to put those roses.

And then I really got a surprise. As I stepped back onstage, there was a gentleman standing there in a white tuxedo, holding a microphone.

"Hello, Patti," he said. "You don't know me but my name is Ron Hawking, and I come in peace." I laughed. "We'd like you to sit down over here if you would." He produced a folding chair. "Your husband, Jerry, and Michael, your manager, have asked me to come out and sing a very special song to you."

No one told me about this! Ron, one of Michael's clients, was a fabulous singer/impressionist from Chicago and had a tribute show to my old friend, Frank Sinatra, called "His Way."

I took a seat, and the opening bars of a song from the Broadway play *Jekyll and Hyde* rang out through the auditorium. The lyrics had been changed to suit the occasion. Ron sang, "This is your moment, this is your day, this is your moment, when I know you're on your way." He had a beautiful voice.

"This is your day, you've passed the test. For all you've worked for, you've passed the test." The audience exploded into applause. There was a heartfelt smile on my face and tears in my eyes.

"And when you look back, you will recall, this was your moment, your greatest moment, the greatest moment of them all."

Ron dropped on one knee and kissed my hand, and I felt like a queen.

Then I learned that I wasn't the only one who could use videotape projected on the screen behind the stage: Friends from across the country had recorded well wishes for me for everyone to see.

Carol Channing joked, "Patti, I must say, fifty years in show business to me, it means you're still a baby!"

Then came Jeff Foxworthy and Country stars Trace Adkins, Tracey Lawrence, George Strait, and Brooks & Dunn.

I felt overwhelmed as more messages followed, from actress Crystal Bernard, the legendary Dick Clark, "Mr. Television" Milton Berle, Country star Tanya Tucker, and then a couple of great friends, Shirley Jones and her wacky husband Marty Ingels, who was wearing a T-shirt with a picture of my face printed on it. It gave me a smile when Shirley said, "I couldn't have let this night go without sending my love to you personally, on this deeply deserved fiftieth tribute. You know, we're like old wine—we get better with age."

My eleven grandkids came onstage to hand me a collective fifty gorgeous roses for Grandma. Peter Nero handed me one more, a white one. I could barely hold them all.

"I thank each and every one of you for making it happen," I told the audience. My heart was bursting with joy. "I'll just sing a song to all of you."

The grandkids stayed onstage as the orchestra and the backups joined me in "This is My Song."

"Every note is a part of the love in my heart for you," I sang, and you know I meant every syllable. I introduced each grandchild as I completed the song. "I sing my song for no one but you." And I meant it for every single "you" in that audience.

"They don't want to leave!" I laughed to one of my granddaughters during the applause at the end. I'd spent fifty years getting to this moment, and you know what? I didn't want to leave, either.

After the concert we had a reception for about 200 people. I don't really recall much of what went on because my feet felt like they weren't really touching the ground.

In the weeks after the concert, the media had a renewed interest in my career—it's nice to make a comeback even though you've never been away! One story from the time was a piece in *The Globe* that pictured me with Jerry with the caption "Love's better the third time around,"—a sentiment I agreed with wholeheartedly.

It was a year of big anniversaries, and August marked forty years since the release of "Old Cape Cod." I took part in the celebrations, performing again at the Cape Cod Melody Tent in Hyannis. There was a rule that the audience wasn't allowed to take photos, but at the end of my concert, I was almost blinded by all the flashes going off. I was laughing the whole time.

At the time of Patti Page's fiftieth anniversary concert at Carnegie Hall in 1997, she was a recording industry phenomenon, having sold 100 million records. "Tennessee Waltz" accounted for 10 million of those sales, making it the best-selling record of any woman in the history of the music industry.

By this point in her career, Patti had also reached another astonishing milestone: Eighty-four of her singles had made it on to *Billboard* magazine's Top 40 chart, the first being "Confess" in 1948.

Throughout the course of the Carnegie Hall concert, she received five standing ovations from the audience. "All is calm, bright and reasonable in the music of Patti Page," Jon Pareles, music reviewer at the *New York Times*, wrote after the show. "The concert was a testimonial to a bygone Pop era...."

Jerry's mom was a real one-in-a-million—feisty and headstrong, outspoken, and pretty funny, too. Jerry liked to spoil his mom—as much as she'd let him, that is. He would have me take her to the beauty shop regularly for some pampering, so she could look and feel nice all the time. But she didn't want to go.

She'd tell me, "Talk to him, Patti (she had finally stopped calling me Betty). Tell him I don't want to go."

"Nana," I'd say, "he won't listen to me."

She'd come back with, "He'll listen to you!"

Finally, she resigned herself to going to the beauty shop and eventually loved it so much and became such good friends with the ladies that worked there, she began making bread for them, as well as pasta, sausage, and lasagna. I suppose it was to make up for the times she'd cussed them out when she hadn't been so amenable about going.

"The poor things have to eat," she'd say. "Don't tell Jerry."

Nana lived with us until it got to the point that she couldn't get around by herself. Since neither Jerry nor I could lift her, we made the difficult decision to find her a place in a nursing home. She protested, saying that if we could just move her once in the morning, she could stay there all day. We knew that wouldn't work, so we found a great place for her where she could be looked after and get all the care she needed.

She couldn't understand why she had to be there with "all these old people." Translated, that meant the next-oldest resident in the place was actually fifteen years younger than her. Still, Nana did make friends there. Whenever she liked a woman, Nana would refer to her as a "nice girl," and pretty soon she was referring to several of the ladies at the home as "nice girls."

Yet in all the time I had known her, she had never referred to me as a "nice girl." I admired Nana and loved her, but I have to admit, that did hurt a little. And when we would go and visit Nana, she had a way of subtly making Jerry feel bad about making the decision that she needed to go into a nursing home.

Nana had a mini-stroke in August of 1997. She didn't have much suffering, but she had some physical impairment and couldn't do some of the things she'd been able to do beforehand. She told us this wasn't the way she was going to live. Many times in the past she had remarked to people that she wanted God to take her so that she wouldn't see her youngest child, Jerry, die before her.

The day before she passed, we went to visit Nana at the home. She took Jerry aside and, to his surprise, said, "They're very nice at this place." She paused a moment, leaned closer to Jerry, and said, "And Patti's a nice girl."

Nana passed away peacefully that night, before she turned 105, and the family held a beautiful ceremony for her. I learned a lot about aging gracefully from Nana.

Jerry had lost his mother, and some of my old gang was gone. As always, I turned to singing to get past it all. I didn't really want to tour at that point, but I needed to. I think going on the road with me helped Jerry feel better, too.

There was a PBS concert in December called *Cincinnati Pops Holiday: Big Band New Year's Eve*, and it featured Doc Severinsen from *The Tonight Show*, along with ballroom dance champions, Tim and Barbara Haller. It was a blast bringing in the New Year at the home of the Pops, the Victorian-era Music Hall, with a classy crowd. And it's always a great pleasure to perform for the audience of the Public Broadcasting Service, which to my mind is a national treasure.

And then we were back in California. I put on a concert at Peter Marshall's Basin Street West in Rancho Mirage—a wonderful re-creation of a famous New York supper club—and was the guest of honor at the Pacific Pioneer Broadcasters luncheon saluting my career. I was even back on the radio again, on *Music of Your Life*, which was syndicated on more than 100 stations across the country.

But by 1998, Jerry and I felt that my career wasn't moving as well as we'd hoped, so we parted company amicably with Michael. I hired another manager who had a good reputation in the entertainment business, but he fell way short of our expectations. We needed to quickly make a change, and I had the bright idea of contacting a gentleman who had worked with The Oak Ridge Boys and been in the business a long time. At one point in my association with Jack, this man had said that if he handled my career, it would be different. I called him, and it turned out he was not in the business anymore, but he agreed to handle my bookings.

So much for my bright idea. As Jerry later said, the guy turned out to be a "feather merchant." I paid him a monthly retainer of $2,500 for six months and got zero bookings. Jerry got on the phone and got me more bookings than any of Michael's replacements had done. Then one day, we sat down and talked and we both agreed that I'd been better off with Michael and that he was the best manager I'd had.

Looking back, I realized that I had made the decision to part company with Michael when my mind was focused on my concerns about Kathleen and Danny, whose lives were still in turmoil. I had thought Michael and I weren't being helpful to each other, but now I realized how mistaken I was. So I called him and asked if we could start our association again. We drew up the papers and he's been my manager ever since.

In March of 1998, I was pleased to attend and perform at the annual "Tennessee Waltz" in Nashville, at which a different artist sings "the Waltz" each year. That year the elegant gala, which raises money for the Tennessee State Museum Foundation, was hosted by Governor and Mrs. Don Sundquist.

I am always happy to take part in a fundraiser for a good cause, and I was thrilled when I got a letter from Ray Charles, the composer and conductor of The Ray Charles Singers, inviting me to perform that October at The Society of Singers 7th "Ella" Lifetime Achievement Award gala in honor of my friend, Rosemary Clooney. Joe Mele accompanied me as I sang one of Rosie's hits, "A Foggy Day." Other singers doing Rosie's songs that night included Linda Rondstadt, Joe Williams, John Raitt, and Barry Manilow. The Society of Singers is a great organization that raises funds for scholarships and to help the many singers out there who are going through tough times, struggling to cover their health and other expenses.

Ah, Rosie, what a wonderful evening it was, and what a host of memories cascaded down on me. It seemed like only yesterday that I had first recorded in Los Angeles and gone to visit Rosie. She had moved there and had been continually asking me to come see her on one of my trips. That was when I was shuttling back and forth from New York to LA all the time so I could be with Charlie. When I moved to Los Angeles and lived on Canon Drive, Rosie and I became tight friends again, and our kids went to the same school. I also remembered meeting her brother, Nick, who was a lovely man.

But the night brought back some unhappier memories, too: There was an earlier period when Rosie and I had a regrettable falling out and barely spoke to each other. It all started one night when we both went to the opening of Nat "King" Cole at the Coconut Grove. Charlie and I were at Louella Parson's table; Louella had taken a liking to me, and she adored Charlie. Nat and Maria Cole were there, and I adored Nat. I used to tease him that if I hadn't met Charlie, I could have fallen for him.

Into this mutual admiration society came Rosie, who stopped by to say hello to our table. But when Rosie saw me, she seemed to act like we barely knew each other.

"Hello, Patti," she said nonchalantly. Rosie was more comfortable with seeking publicity than I was, so I imagine her focus was really on Louella that night. Knowing what the business side of entertainment was like, I certainly didn't begrudge her that.

"Oh hi, Rosie," I said, in the usual friendly way we had.

"You know that I'm a mother now," she said.

In the past, we'd talked about our motherhood aspirations. I was thrilled for her. She looked radiant and glowing.

I replied, "You look like it, Rosie!"

I was trying to pay her a compliment, but it didn't turn out that way. Before I knew it, Rosie was on her way to the ladies' room, tears rolling down her cheeks.

Maria Cole and I followed her into the restroom and Maria said, "Rosie, stop it! You know Patti. She would never hurt you."

Rosie wouldn't listen. I later learned that she was having problems with her husband, Jose Ferrer, and when I said that, it set something off, stirred up the emotions of a woman who had recently given birth. Not having been through that, I had little idea. She probably felt I was saying she looked heavy and unattractive. Rosie, like me, constantly battled weight, which perhaps explains her sensitivity over my comment. I felt dreadful that my words had been taken the wrong way. It took a long time before we got over that misunderstanding, and I was thrilled when we patched up our relationship.

As her friend for so many years, I was proud of Rosie that night in 1998 when she received her "Ella" award. She looked fabulous. I was sorry about our upset all those years ago. Rosie passed away in June 2002 and I still miss her today.

It was a year of performing at galas. In June, I flew to Tulsa to sing with the Sinfonia in a benefit show for the Tulsa Community College Foundation. During the show, I told the audience about the album coming out later that year of my Carnegie Hall concert, and as I did I wondered how it would do. After all, we'd paid for the recording ourselves, Jerry and I, and it wasn't being issued on a major label.

I suppose after some of the things that had happened in my life, I should have simply trusted God that things would work out for the best. We licensed the album to Hugh Fordin, a record producer and distributor who had done very well issuing albums of Broadway productions. One of his singers—Broadway musical star, Barbara Cook—had won a Grammy for her recording of Irving Berlin songs. He was convinced I could win a Grammy.

"You're gonna win it," he said.

"Well, that would be fantastic," I replied. What else can you say to a comment like that?

When the Carnegie Hall album came out, it got some good airplay and had moderate sales, but that was all. Hugh was undeterred. He kept saying, "We're going to put this up for a Grammy and you're going to win it."

I wanted to believe him but I couldn't, not wholeheartedly. And then, just as Hugh had predicted, the album was nominated for a Grammy for Best Traditional Pop Vocal Performance. That was fantastic news, but I was up against daunting competition: Shirley Bassey for *The Birthday Concert*, Michael Feinstein for *Michael and George: Feinstein Sings Gershwin*, Jack Jones for *Jack Jones Paints A Tribute to Tony Bennett*, and Maureen McGovern for *The Pleasure of His Company.*"

The first Grammy Awards were held in 1958. I was still making hits then, but I never got a nomination. Rock 'n' Roll had taken over as the most popular genre, and I wasn't doing that type of music. Over the years, the categories expanded, but the Grammys and I had never seemed to be on the same wavelength. I felt like I was in good company, though: Amazing as it sounds, Elvis never got a Grammy, despite all his hits.

Each year there are so many people nominated in so many categories, they have to hold a ceremony in the afternoon prior to the big awards ceremony broadcast on television. Jerry, Michael, and I were sitting three rows from the stage that afternoon, behind the Mercury Nashville people. As many events as I had been to in my life, I couldn't help but be nervous as the nominees names in my category were read off, and then in one of those slower than life moments, I heard:

Patti Page: Live At Carnegie Hal—The 50th Anniversary Concert!

I looked at Jerry, then at Michael, then back at the stage and called out: "I did it!" And with that I got up and went to get my statuette. If I could have run, I would have.

I managed to regain some composure onstage. "When my first grandchild was born," I told the crowd, "I always said she could call me Grammy because I'll never get one! Now I'll have to tell her to call me Grandma!"

It had taken a lot of hard work and years to achieve it and that only made me even more elated to have The Recording Academy honor me so highly on my first nomination. After our ceremony was over, Maureen McGovern came up to me and congratulated me on my win. It reminded me of the old days, when singers enjoyed and respected each other's talents. In music, that's the way it always should be.

There was a big party after the awards that night at the Biltmore Hotel in downtown L.A., but we only spent a short time there. When you're seventy-one years old, parties aren't as appealing as they are when you're twenty-one.

Winning the award was lovely, but it didn't exactly get me a music video slot on MTV. That's what I told my great-nephew, Eric Celeste, when he wrote an article about me for the *Star-News* back in Claremore. I laughed when I read the article; in it, he said he'd mentioned my name to one of his cohorts, who'd wondered out loud why Eric's great-aunt had been named after a street in town!

With the ups, you have to anticipate the downs. Winning my Grammy was thrilling, but on the home front, Kathleen's life remained troubled. It was putting at risk two of the kids who would now be calling me Grandma. When all the dust was settled, they would begin to wonder out loud if I was their mother.

TWENTY-TWO

The Toughest Fight I Ever Fought

B etween the Carnegie Hall concert in May 1997 and the coming of autumn, there were major changes in my life that had nothing to do with my music.

Danny hadn't attended my Carnegie Hall concert because he was still caught up in drugs. One thing I was thankful for was that while in prison on a drug conviction, he got his General Equivalency Degree, or G.E.D. Jerry thought Danny was a pathological liar, but I didn't agree. My perception of a pathological liar was that they never change, but I'd seen Danny change, though not enough.

I had never stopped being concerned about my daughter Kathleen and would try to help her. But much as I tried for a different result, she and I had been drifting apart since she was in high school. She had gotten a divorce from Larry, remarried, moved up to Susanville in northern California, and had a couple more children—a little girl, Sarah, and a baby, Page. It was in Susanville that Kathleen's life just went off the deep end.

One time when I was working in Reno, which was about an hour and a half's drive southwest of Susanville, Jerry and I drove up to see Kathleen.

I looked at where she was living and just died within myself. We had lunch at a hamburger joint with Kathleen and her in-laws, who I could tell were the ones who were really taking care of her kids. After I got home, I got four phone calls from Kathleen; her husband was mistreating her. Supposedly, he was beating her up and all kinds of abuse.

Page was just weeks old. I told Kathleen I wanted to get her and Page and Sarah out of that environment and into an apartment, out of harm's way. I had friends go and get Kathleen and the kids out of their place and take her to a hotel until we could come and get her. Jerry got a U-Haul truck and went up and got all of her stuff. Kathleen's husband had already gone to jail by then. With the help of Jerry's daughter, May, we brought Kathleen and her kids down to southern California and set her up in an apartment in Escondido.

I had all sorts of things in storage that I'd taken from my former house in Rancho Santa Fe—furniture, silver, things I didn't need anymore. I got them out of storage and gave them to Kathleen to furnish the apartment. I would go visit her and I would notice things were different each time— a piece of the furniture I had given her would be gone, for instance. Initially, she had been very grateful about escaping Susanville. Now she had changed completely and was being unkind to me. I knew something was terribly wrong. Finally, I arrived one day and found all of her furniture gone. I knew she'd sold it to get drugs. As I talked it over with experts, I realized she had a drug problem perhaps worse that heroin. She was on methamphetamines.

I couldn't let my granddaughters continue to live in that environment, so I found a family lawyer to advise us on how we could gain custody of them ourselves. She recommended that Jerry and I just physically go and take Sarah and Page without going to court first. The reasoning was that if we went to court we could be tied up in legal wrangles with the kids still in danger. This way, we could get the children in a safe environment first.

She suggested we not tell Kathleen anything other than we were taking the girls to stay with us for a night. That's what we did. It was deception, but it worked.

Jerry and I realized that we would have to raise the children until—and if—Kathleen got straightened out. It wasn't an easy prospect for two people in their seventies, but it had to be done. It took almost two years before the court officially ruled that I was Sarah and Page's guardian, but we got custody. If Kathleen wanted anything to do with her girls again she would have to submit to drug tests administered by the State of California.

Kathleen wasn't in much shape to do anything but comply. She would call every Christmas and we would always monitor the calls until the girls became old enough to reason for themselves. In the beginning, when Kathleen would say something like "Your grandmother won't let me see you" we'd just take the phone from them. We'd never put Kathleen or her husband down to the kids. From the moment they came to us and went to bed and said their prayers, we made sure it was always "God bless Mommy and Daddy."

One night, little Page looked up and me and said, "You're my mommy."

"I'm your grandmother," I said quietly. And I'm glad I did.

The way that I was raised gave me values that have carried me through a long life and some troubles I wouldn't wish upon anyone. I believe in those values. Sarah and Page say their prayers nightly, just as I did. I believe they're better for it, and that whether they choose to be artists, or singers, or anything else at all, they'll have a foundation for success that will help them have happier lives.

At first, I wouldn't discuss the circumstances because they were just too painful. Eventually, I realized there were far too many people in mine and Jerry's shoes, raising grandchildren. Finally, I was willing to talk about it on television with Bill O'Reilly on the Fox News Channel.

A couple of years earlier Jerry and I had downsized from the big house to something more manageable. To accommodate our new family, we moved into a beautiful house on a cul de sac overlooking a golf course in Solano Beach, where we live today.

My heart stayed broken over Danny. I had completely lost touch with him, hadn't seen him in months. He had tried to call but I wouldn't take his calls because I knew he just wanted money for drugs, like every other time in the past. It seemed like nothing would get him straightened out—not counseling, not jail, not anything. Luckily, there are still miracles.

Jerry and I were Christmas shopping near San Diego and as we were driving into a store parking lot, I saw this good-looking kid with a book in his hand, just sitting on the curb. My mouth dropped open.

"Jerry!" I said. "That looks like Danny."

There he was, wearing a nice cardigan, clean-shaven, with his unmistakable blond hair—but he looked spaced out.

"It is, Jerry," I repeated. "It is Danny!"

Jerry pulled into a parking spot away from Danny because Jerry knew it was him, too. I just broke down crying, and became hysterical—and Danny saw us.

"We're not going in there," Jerry declared. "We're going home." And he backed out of the space and we drove away.

I understood; all our efforts to help Danny had proven futile. What else could we do? It was the Christmas season, and there was the son I loved, in sight but out of reach.

Thank God we'd seen each other because that was the turning point for Danny. He called again, only this time it was to apologize for us seeing him in his stoned state. I still wouldn't talk to him. It's probably good I didn't because Danny later told me that was the point when he realized he had to do something. He got sober, and he's remained so ever since.

From then on, I chose to take more time for family matters. Between the two of us, Jerry and I had five kids, ten granddaughters, and one grandson. And friends to play bridge with. I became more social than I'd ever been.

Patti Page continued to work, though she scaled back her touring schedule to about forty shows a year, with symphony orchestras or at casinos in Atlantic City or Nevada. She continued using the technique she had debuted at Carnegie Hall of opening her show with clips from *The Patti Page Show* from 1956 and then coming onstage in a spotlight singing the song "Person That Use To Be Me." Patti also performed in shows to raise funds for public television.

Two years after winning her Grammy, Page recorded the album *Brand New Tennessee Waltz* with guest appearances by Suzy Bogguss, Emmylou Harris, Alison Krauss, Kathy Mattea, and Trisha Yearwood. It was released on the record label she now ran with Jerry, C.A.F. Records—standing for Clara Ann Fowler. To celebrate the release of the album, she did a concert at the Ryman Auditorium in Nashville.

Patti's fans from the 1950s had grown up now and were beginning to bring their grandchildren to watch her shows, so Page also recorded a new children's album, called *Child of Mine*.

She and her husband Jerry began spending half of the year at their farm in New Hampshire, which is just over 200 acres in size. The couple's nineteenth-century pale blue, two-story Victorian farmhouse there was featured on the hit TV show *Lifestyles of the Rich and Famous* in 2000 and in the show's magazine. On the farm they produce maple sugar, maple candy, pancake mixes, and maple cream spread.

When I reached the three-quarter of a century mark, I realized how it important it was to keep active, keep my mind working. Jerry and I heard that if you did crossword puzzles, you wouldn't get Alzheimer's, so we would drop what we were doing, get together at lunch, and do crossword puzzles. Whatever was going on in our lives, we were never bored. At my concerts, Jerry ran the table selling CDs, and I found myself autographing them as well as our maple syrup and pancake products.

I'd never imagined that in my mid-seventies I would be doing forty concerts a year, playing with a nine-piece band in midsize cities. I put my longevity as a performer down to my faith in God and my belief that He has always placed me exactly where He wants me to be. He's taught me there's a place for each of us. Whether you're a celebrity or a singer or someone keeping the wheels of the world turning, you can do things no one else can, and we all need to take stock of that within ourselves.

I also believe that thinking of others is primary to a happy life. When Jerry and I selected a church to attend, we based our decision on our granddaughters so that they could experience the joy of a relationship with the Lord. I was baptized when I was thirteen, and I don't think I will ever feel the same way again. The beautiful feeling that I gained as a follower of Christ has matured over the years and nurtured me. It has kept me grounded. Not a little grounded, a lot grounded. It is the driving force of my marriage to Jerry, and each night before we go to sleep, we pray. We share a marvelous faith that can keep any couple very much together.

In October 2004, Patti Page was inducted into yet another hall of fame—the Casino Legends Hall of Fame, in Las Vegas, along with Debbie Reynolds, Ben Vereen, Sheena Easton, Tempest Storm, and Jack Jones, who had been up against her at the Grammies. On November 6th, two days shy of her seventy-seventh birthday, she received the Puccini Foundation Baccarat Award at Lincoln Center in New York for achievements in the arts. And the Olympic Committee presented Page with an award for all she had done to support Olympic athletes over the years.

On July 4, 2005, I was invited to Petco Park to sing the National Anthem to a sold-out crowd at a San Diego Padres game. You can bet your boots that this time I didn't forget the words! Prior to the game, I took part in the "Dog Days of Summer" event where hundreds of fans brought their pooches to the park for a doggie parade and then sat with their dogs in a special section during the game. You can imagine which of my songs I sang for the group during that parade.

In September, I went to play at Branson, Missouri again—this time for six weeks. It came about via a booking agent in Palm Springs who had asked me several times over the years to appear in shows he put on in Palm Springs. I kept turning him down because he wanted a half-year commitment, which meant I'd have to stay in Palm Springs. I'd never wanted to be away from home that long in case Kathleen or Danny needed me. When the same booker offered me six weeks in Branson, I said okay. That was longer than I'd ever played any place. Even at the height of my career in Las Vegas, I only did four-week engagements at any one time.

The Follies Theater in Branson was new, and frankly the crowds weren't that big, but I didn't care—the old Maurice Chevalier lesson, you know? We were told that every new theater there took a while to catch on. Andy

Williams came to see the show, and he said I shouldn't feel bad about not having a full house because it took years for his own theater to catch on. By then, you couldn't get a seat to Andy's show, or in any established theater in Branson, for that matter. Still, I was a little disappointed, as well as a little jealous of Petula Clark because she had a nice job opening for Andy. Nevertheless, I found Branson to be a wonderful place to work. For people in the business, it's like we're all together as a family.

I loved doing my show at the Follies because there was an added twist to it: Everyone who played the Follies—which originated in Palm Springs—were supposed to be at least sixty years old! The show recalled the golden age of variety shows with golden years performers. Well, okay, I didn't check to see if the dogs in *Bob Moore and His Amazing Mongrels* were all sixty in doggie years, but everyone else was at least a sexagenarian—myself, comedian John Byner, and "The Beautiful Women of the Branson Follies" (who were sexy sexagenarians). Some of the dancers on that stage didn't look like senior citizens. If you didn't know their ages, you'd have thought they were Vegas showgirls. As the promotional material said, "Over 60 Never Looked So Good." We even had an eighty-seven-year-old tap dancer! When the run was done, the cast and crew put together a wonderful scrapbook for me that I still treasure today.

In November, I focused my efforts closer to home. Jerry and I put on a fundraiser for our church, Faith Community Church by the Sea. I performed at the benefit gala at the Escondido Center of Performing Arts with the Escondido Faith Emmanuel Choir and the Heritage Kids, a choir made up of homeschooled children. We raised $100,000 toward a new church building that evening, something we were both very proud of.

Though she no longer played in Las Vegas, Patti Page did make the rounds in Laughlin, Reno, Lake Tahoe, and at Whiskey Pete's in Primm, Nevada, and still drew large crowds. At the Cerritos Center for the Performing Arts in January 2006 she had a full house. She performed with The Mills Brothers at the Robinson Theatre in Waltham, Massachusetts; was Grand Marshal of the Pacific Palisades, California 4th of July Americanism Parade in 2006; and rode on the Oklahoma Centennial Commission's float in the Rose Bowl parade in 2007.

Her fan club was still operating and releasing a newsletter, *The Rage.* Patti was particularly fond of an interview that appeared in it around Christmas of 2005—with her son, Danny. In it, he said there were no drawbacks to being the child of a famous person, and that Patti was "ALWAYS" there when he needed her. Mother and son had reconciled to the point that he had asked her to bequeath him her awards and memorabilia, of which he was proud.

I felt deep gratitude and love for the people who were keeping my fan club going. It heartened me that my singing still spoke to them, that it still endured. The more years I kept singing, the more I understood the pull that the simple, touching songs like "Tennessee Waltz" have on people. And that songs like that can mean so much. In June of 2006, I attended a Vince Gill concert in Escondido, near my home. I was in the audience when Vince introduced me to the audience and asked me to come onstage and sing "Tennessee Waltz" with him. He told a story of how his mom had taught him to dance the waltz to that song, and he said that made it very special for him that I was onstage with him, singing the song live. I launched into it, backed by his fabulous band, and kept waiting for Vince to come in, but he never did. Finally, as I finished, I looked back and saw tears streaming down his face. He later explained that it brought back such a flood of memories, he'd been too choked up to be able to sing a word.

Back when I started becoming successful, only five years after World War II, it was a simpler time and music was simpler, too. I remember that a couple of reviewers criticized my records for being too placid and restrained. But I believe that my songs filled a need. Simpler is easier to understand than complex, and songs that comfort ultimately last longer than those that stir darker emotions.

As I was writing this book, a fellow Oklahoman, Garth Brooks, passed Elvis Presley in all-time record sales. I could hardly believe it, but in a way I could because people of all types love the simple heartfelt emotions in his music. It endures.

Leading the busy life that I had, traveling all over the world and performing in front of thousands of people, was so different than what I imagined for myself when I was growing up. The reason I had wanted to be an artist was that when I painted, I could smooth over the anger I felt about being constantly reminded that I was born and lived on the so-called "wrong side of the tracks." I planned to grow up painting portraits of the simple beauty I saw in my everyday life. My career would've been completely different if I had taken that path, but still, perhaps I accomplished my aim—not by painting but by singing.

With each song, I'm telling a story and acting. For me, singing has always been a substitute for the psychiatrist's couch. I can tell it all in song: pathos, gladness, unhappiness, love, joy.

TWENTY-THREE

Still Singing After All These Years

Danny and I get along fine now. He's been sober for more than ten years, has his own family, and works for a plumbing company in Escondido. I love him as much today as I did that day in 1964 when I took home that precious baby boy from a hospital in Arkansas. I don't see Kathleen or keep in touch with her enough, usually only when I have the children call her on her birthday or Christmas.

Kathleen divorced her abusive husband and is married now to Kenny Ginn, the boy she wanted so badly to marry when she was sixteen. I can't help but wonder how it might have worked out if I'd let her marry him then. Kathleen had another child about the same time Sarah and Page came to live with us. I didn't know she was pregnant when I started the process. Jakob is now ten years old and, regrettably, doesn't see his sisters. Kathleen and Kenny live in Tucson, next door to Sherri Lynn, Kathleen's oldest daughter, and my oldest granddaughter. Sometimes Kathleen babysits for Sherri, who has a little boy named Daniel, who is a year-and-a-half old. After Daniel was born, Sherri drove out with the kids and spent some time with us in Solano Beach. I say "kids" because Sherri married a single father, and as a result also has a stepson, Bobby, who is now six.

I'm not sure how things will be between me and Kathleen in the rest of the years I have left, but no matter how things work out between us, the little girl whom I have loved all these years, through great times and bad, will never be out of my mind, and that's a blessing for me.

Jerry and I took a wonderful trip to Italy in the summer of 2007, marred only by the fact that Jerry lost his hearing aids somewhere before we got on the plane which made communication a bit challenging. After the trip, I told him that he now knew more Italian sign language than any man on Earth. We got a good laugh about that, and we laugh a lot, which is why our relationship has endured.

As I wrote this book, I made a new album for Curb Records in Nashville on which I did a lovely duet with Vince Gill, another Oklahoman, titled "Home Sweet Oklahoma." He sang his part in that beautiful high lilting tenor that he calls his "woman voice." I did another track on the album as a commemoration to the heroes and victims of the 9/11 tragedy. It's a song called "Little Did She Know She Kissed a Hero."

Although I generally think that my greatest entertainment thrills could be behind me, I'm continually surprised. As I was finishing this book, I appeared at the Oklahoma Centennial celebration, which featured more stars than I could count. What is it about the Sooner State that produces so many entertainers?

It was at the Ford Center in Oklahoma City, for a crowd of about 10,000 people and another 50,000 people watching on huge video screens in a nearby stadium. Native Americans paraded down the aisle in full dress costumes, acrobats dropped from the ceiling, and the entertainers included Garth Brooks, Reba McIntire, Toby Keith, Carrie Underwood, Vince Gill, and myself. Shirley Jones appeared in a tribute to the musical *Oklahoma* since Shirley had starred in the movie. There were five Miss Americas there, all of whom had been Miss Oklahoma. I sang "Tennessee Waltz," and "Route 66" (the famous highway runs through Oklahoma). The theme song for the show was written by Vince and the famous songwriter Jimmy Webb, another Oklahoman.

It was one of the most impressive shows I'd ever seen, and made me very proud to be an Oklahoma girl. I'd performed at Oklahoma's fifty-year celebration and then again at its 100th. I really cherished the fact that I'd had such grand opportunities, five decades apart.

So here I am, eighty-one years old, raising two granddaughters who are going into high school, doing thirty or so concerts a year, still recording new material, and pitching maple syrup products from our farm. It's not a bad life. I've had some back surgery and move around a little slower onstage than I used to, but God's blessed me with the wonderful ability to keep singing.

Oh, there are still some things I'd like to achieve or accolades I thought I might have received, but ultimately they don't matter. What is most important to me is something I see all the time—the faces in the audience, whether it's in a small club, a performing arts center, or even at church. When I look at the audience and see faces light up—the same way my granddaughters do when I tell them goodnight or my husband does when we share some laughs—that's enough love to keep me going for a long, long time. I feel blessed to be able to share music with millions of people around the world and my greatest wish is that, even if for a few minutes at a time, life might seem a little better, a little happier, a little fuller.

My mother lived into her nineties. I wonder—has anyone ever recorded an album at 100 years old? It's something to consider.

Your voice dries up if you don't use it. Hopefully, by the grace of God, I will always be singing.

Patti's latest CDs now in release...

Tennessee Waltz
Crazy Ole Moon

Sing You Back

Money Marbles and Chalk

Home Sweet Oklahoma

You Don't Know Me

Mockin' Bird Hill

Little Did She Know

Except for Monday

You Needed Me

Family Love

If I Had Only Known

(How Much Is) That Dog-
gie In The Window

With My Eyes Wide Open
It's A Wonderful World
Can You Feel The Love Tonight
Old Cape Cod
Release Me (And Let Me Love
Again)
Go On Home
Unchained Melody
Allegheny Moon
Detour
Tennessee Waltz

In 1952, I recorded an innocent and simple tune about a 'doggie' in a pet shop window. At the time, 'Doggie in the Window' seemed like a sweet and harmless message, but times have changed. Now, the doggies in pet store windows mostly come from puppy mills, so I've changed my tune—literally. I recorded a new version of "Doggie" with the same familiar melody, but with totally new lyrics as part of a national campaign of the Humane Society of the United States.

I hope that when people now hear the old familiar "Doggie" melody, they'll think about homeless animals and animal shelters instead of pet stores and puppy mills. **Visit: HSUS.org**

"Do You See That Doggie in the Shelter"

Do you see that doggie in the shelter
the one with the take me home eyes
If you give him your love and attention
he will be your best friend for life

In each town and city across the nation,
there's so many dogs with no home
Hungry with no one to protect them
lost is this world all alone *repeat chorus*

Collies and beagles by the roadside
puppies and dogs in the street
Once they are rescued by a shelter
they'll finally get something to eat

Doggies and kitties who are homeless
with sad eyes and tails hanging down
Let's do what we can to show them kindness
and let them know that they've been found